THE SOURCEBOOK OF
ARCHITECTURAL & INTERIOR ART 16

GUILD Sourcebooks

Madison, Wisconsin
USA

THE SOURCEBOOK OF ARCHITECTURAL & INTERIOR ART 16

Publisher

GUILD Sourcebooks
An imprint of Ashford.com, Inc.
931 E. Main Street
Madison, Wisconsin 53703
TEL 608-257-2590 • TEL 877-284-8453
FAX 608-257-2690

Administration / Art Division

Toni Sikes, Co-President
Gordon Mayer, Co-President
Michael Monroe, Artistic Advisor
Katie Kazan, Chief Editorial Officer
Joyce Link, Director of Artist Services
Paula Cosby, Artist Services Associate
Rebecca Rex, Administrative Assistant

Production / Design / Editorial

Nikki Muenchow, Editorial Manager
Cheryl Smallwood-Roberts, Production Manager
Bob Johnston, Production Artist
Susan Troller • Tricia Nolan • Martha Phillips, Writers

Artist Coordinators

Michelle Spude, Artist Marketing Manager
Carol Chapin • Stacie Chappell • Carla Dillman
Laura Marth • Jennifer Stofflet • Anna Trull

Cover Art / Top

Arthur Stern,
The St. John Millennium Cross Window,
leaded blown glass,
PeaceHealth Medical Center, Longview, WA,
24' x 24'.
Photo by Blake Praytor.
See pages 96-97 and 414-415.

Cover Art / Bottom

Leslie C. Birleson,
Traveling Light, large-scale
installation, Sacramento
International Airport,
180'L x 12'H.
Photo by Glen Korengold.
See pages 207 and 377.

John Medwedeff,
Smysor Plaza Fountain, 1999,
forged and fabricated bronze,
Murphysboro, IL,
10' x 6' x 6'.
Photo by Jeff Bruce.
See pages 217 and 402.

Elizabeth MacDonald,
ceramic tile fireplace,
private residence,
Sherman, CT,
16' x 5.5' x 7".
See pages 42-43,
248 and 399.

Steve Fontanini,
forged bronze railing,
Roney residence,
Teton County, WY.
Photo by Florence McCall.
See pages 25 and 385.

Visit *The GUILD Sourcebook Online* at GUILDtrade.com.

"GUILD Sourcebooks" is an imprint of Ashford.com, the Internet's leading retailer
of personal and home décor accessories, including fine art and fine craft.

The Custom-Built Environment

com·mis·sion, *noun,* from the Latin *commissio,* "to entrust." The grant of authority to carry out a particular task or duty — or, in relating to art, an agreement with an artist to create work that does not yet exist.

In this book, when we speak of a commission, we mean an arrangement with a specific artist to create a specific work of art, singular to the parameters and ideas agreed upon by the artist and the client. Art commissions are infinite in their variety. They can be as small as a glass doorknob and as large as a house. They can be as simple as a ceramic serving dish and as intricate as a tapestry for the wall.

When you include art in your building or design project, your job doesn't necessarily become easier. Art is one more thing to think about, to coordinate, to discuss with your client. But think for a moment about the term so often used by artists who undertake commissioned projects — the term "design solution."

That's right. Beyond being just plain beautiful, site-specific art can indeed be a solution. In the hands of the right artist, it can provide a focal point for an amorphous space, hide structural elements or knit clashing components into an exhilarating whole.

And how can you find the right artist? That's why this book exists. The projects shown on these pages illustrate the quality and variety of work available to you and your clients. Every artist included is seeking art commissions; their contact information is included at the back of the book.

So call, e-mail or knock on his or her door. Entrust an artist to create something "that does not yet exist." By doing so, you'll cast a vote for adventure, for beauty and for the extra effort that brings a memorable result.

TABLE OF CONTENTS

Articles

The Commission Process 12
Our featured essay is a step-by-step guide on how to commission artwork — from choosing the right artist for a project to using the right terms on a contract.

Commission Stories
GUILD advertisers share their most memorable projects.

Resources

How to Use THE SOURCEBOOK OF ARCHITECTURAL & INTERIOR ART 11
An overview of the book's features and possibilities.

Artist Information 372
Details on the artwork and artists of THE SOURCEBOOK OF ARCHITECTURAL & INTERIOR ART, including the artists' contact information.

Index of Advertisers by Location 426

Index of Artists and Companies 433

TABLE OF CONTENTS

Featured Artists

ARTISTS BY SECTION

ARTISTS BY SECTION

ARTISTS BY SECTION

ARTISTS BY SECTION

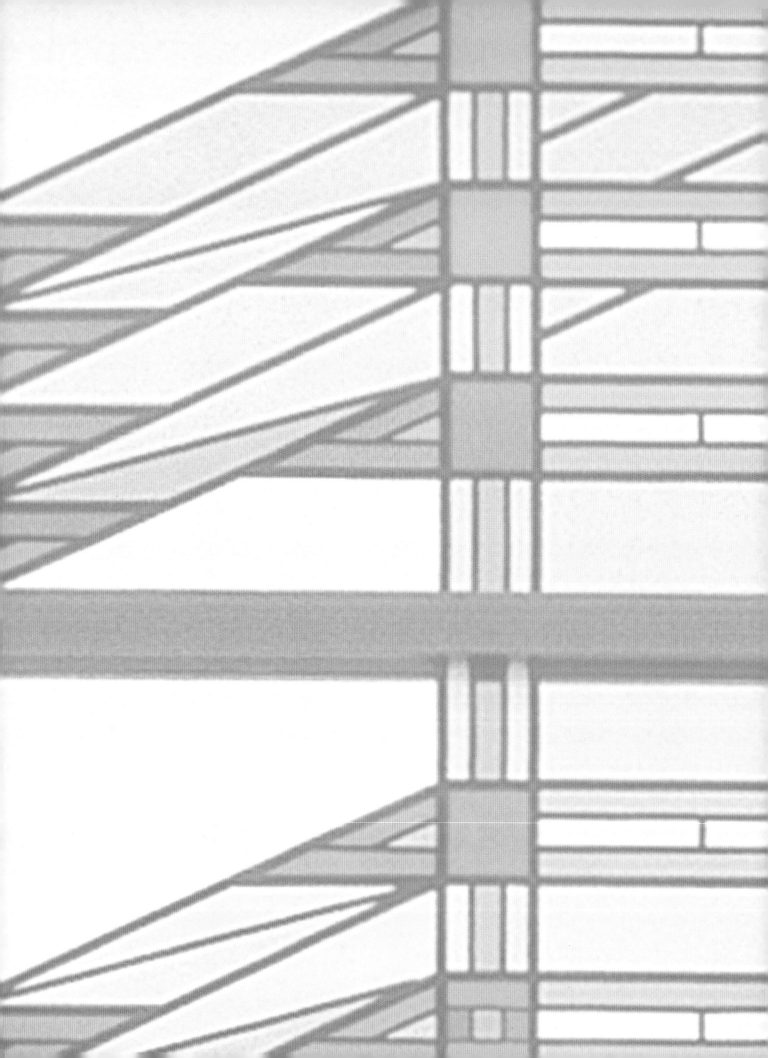

How to Use

THE SOURCEBOOK OF ARCHITECTURAL & INTERIOR ART 16

THE SOURCEBOOK OF ARCHITECTURAL & INTERIOR ART 16 is designed specifically for individuals and trade professionals seeking artists to create large- or small-scale commissioned artwork. For the sixteenth edition of the sourcebook, further information about the artists is located in the Artist Information area at the back of the book. These listings are organized in alphabetical order by the heading on each artist's page (either by personal or company name), and contain the information needed to contact the artist about your project, making the sourcebook a unique direct-call resource.

Product Search

If you already know what type of work your project calls for, a search by section will help you quickly find results. Artists in the sourcebook are arranged into 17 different sections, covering work as varied as large-scale glass in the Architectural Glass section to art quilts and tapestries in Art for the Wall: Fiber. Check the Table of Contents in the front of the book to find a list of sections.

When paging through a particular section, keep in mind that the photos presented on each of the artists' pages are representative of the work that they do, not the full extent of their capabilities. If you like an artist's style but are interested in having him or her take on a different type of project than the ones pictured, contact the artist and see if it's a good fit. Likewise, you can broaden your searches to several different sections to find an even wider variety of choices. If you are searching for freestanding sculpture, for example, you might want to try not only the Representational or Non-Representational Sculpture sections, but the Public Art section as well.

Artist Search

If you know the name of the artist you want to work with, you can easily search using the Artist Information section or the Index of Artists and Companies, both found in the back of the sourcebook. In the Artist Information section, you will find details about the artist and his or her work, including materials and techniques, examples of the artist's commissions and collections, and publications the artist has been featured in (including previous sourcebooks). Both the Artist Information section and the Index of Artists and Companies include page number references, so you can easily locate the artist's full-color page in the book.

Want to know more about an artist's work? Don't hesitate to call for more information.

Location Search

Looking for an artist in your area or another particular region? The Index of Advertisers by Location is an invaluable tool for such searches. Located in the back of the book, this index can help you find artists from all across the United States, Canada and abroad.

Inspirational Browsing

Even if you don't have a project in mind, THE SOURCEBOOK OF ARCHITECTURAL & INTERIOR ART 16 can prove a valuable tool. It can be taken to client meetings to show a world of possibilities, browsed through for future inspiration and used to see what sort of projects the artists you've collaborated with in the past have been working on recently.

The Commission Process

The nearly 300 artists featured in THE SOURCEBOOK OF ARCHITECTURAL & INTERIOR ART 16 represent a remarkable spectrum of artistic talent and vision. Whether you're looking for a large-scale public sculpture or a residential accessory, this book can put you directly in touch with highly qualified artists throughout North America. Any one of these artists can be commissioned to create a unique work of art — but with so many exceptional artists to choose from, finding the right one for your specific project can be a challenge. Once the artist has been selected, careful planning and communication can help ensure a great outcome.

Having watched art commissions unfold since the first GUILD sourcebook was published in 1986, we can suggest steps to ensure successful partnerships between artists and trade professionals. We especially want to reassure those who have been reluctant to try such a collaboration because of questions about how the process works.

This article is a how-to guide for the commissioning process. We suggest strategies to help the selection and hiring processes go smoothly. We also discuss the advantages of including the artist in the design team, and doing so early in the process. And finally, we have a lot to tell you about the full spectrum of services now offered through GUILDtrade.com. That's right: we've expanded services to trade professionals; turn to page 17 to learn more.

Finding the Artist

By far the most important step in a successful commission is choosing the right artist for your particular design, project and budget. This choice is the decision from which all others will flow, so it's worth investing time and energy in the selection process and seasoning the search with both wild artistic hopes and hard-nosed realism. The right choices at this early stage will make things go more smoothly later on.

Some clients will be very interested in helping to select the artist, and will want to work closely with him or her once the choice is made. Others will want only minimal involvement, leaving most of the decision-making to the design team. Whoever is making the decisions, there are several ways to find the right artist. Obviously, we recommend browsing through THE SOURCEBOOK OF ARCHITECTURAL & INTERIOR ART 16. Every artist featured on these pages is actively seeking commission projects; that's why they're included. Many of these artists already have strong track records of working with designers, architects and art consultants. You will gain from their professionalism and experience.

The Trade Sales Consultants at GUILDtrade.com are another unique resource for trade professionals seeking artists for specific projects. Our consultants are trained to discuss your project with you, determine your art requirements and suggest artists who can fulfill your particular design needs. If the project is a large one, you may go through a request-for-proposal (RFP) process that can draw responses from all over the continent. Our Trade Sales Consultants can assist you by posting your RFP on our "Post a Project" feature (see page 17). With this feature, we can electronically broadcast your RFP to our list of almost 1,500 artists and invite them to respond to your call. A GUILDtrade.com staff member can be a great ally both when seeking an artist and when steering your way through a commission project.

Narrowing the Field

Once your "A-list" is narrowed down to two or three names, it's time to schedule meetings, either face-to-face (for local artists) or by phone. During these discussions, try to determine the artist's interest in your project, and pay attention to your own comfort level with the artist. Try to find out if the chemistry is right — whether you have the basis to build a working relationship. It's also the time to confirm that the artist has the necessary skills to undertake your project. Be thorough and specific when asking questions. Is the artist excited about the project? What does he or she see as the most important issues or considerations? Will your needs be a major or minor concern? Evaluate the artist's style, approach and personality.

If it feels like you might have trouble working together, take heed. But if all goes well and it feels like a good fit, ask for a list of references. These are important calls; don't neglect to make them! Ask about the artist's work habits, communication style and — of course — about the success of the artwork. You should also ask whether the project was delivered on time and within budget. If you like what you hear, you'll be one important step closer to hiring your artist.

Expect Professionalism

If this is an expensive or complicated project, you may want to request preliminary designs at this time. Since most artists charge a design fee whether or not they're ultimately hired for the project, start by asking for sketches from your top candidate. If you're unhappy with the designs submitted, you can go to your second choice. If, on the other hand, the design is what you'd hoped for, it's time to finalize your working agreement with this artist.

As you discuss contract details, be resolved that silence is not golden and ignorance is not bliss! Be frank. Discuss the budget and timetable, and tell the artist what you expect. Now is the time for possible misunderstandings to be brought up and resolved — not later, after the work is half done and deadlines loom.

Working With an Art Consultant

As your project gains definition, you'll need to pay attention to the technical aspects of the project, including building codes, lighting specifications, and details related to zoning and installation. Most designers find that the artist's knowledge and understanding of materials, code, safety and engineering is complete and reassuring.

However, complex projects may warrant hiring an art consultant to help with these details, as well as the initial selection of art and artists. Make sure the consultant is sophisticated and experienced enough to provide real guidance with your project. This means the ability to help negotiate the technical details of a very specific contract, including issues like installation, insurance, storage, transportation and possible engineering costs.

The Contract: Putting It In Writing

It is a truism in any kind of business that it is much cheaper to get the lawyers involved at the beginning of a process rather than after something goes wrong. A signed contract or letter of agreement commits the artist to completing his or her work on time and to specifications. It also assures the artist that he or she will get paid the right amount at the right time. That just about eliminates the biggest conflicts that can arise.

Contracts should be specific to the job. Customarily, artists are responsible for design, production, shipping and installation. If someone else is to be responsible for installation, be sure you specify who will coordinate and pay for it — if not the artist, it's usually the client. With a large project, it's helpful to identify the tasks that, if delayed for any reason, would set back completion of the project. These should be discussed up front to assure that both parties agree on requirements and expectations.

Most trade professionals recognize that adequate compensation for the artists is in their best interest, as it assures the type and level of service needed to fulfill their expectations. The more skill you need and the more complex the project, the more you should budget for the artist's work and services.

Payment Schedule

Payments are usually tied to specific points in the process. These serve as check points, and assure that work is progressing in a satisfactory manner, on time and on budget. Payment is customarily made in three stages, although this certainly depends on the circumstances, scope and complexity of the project.

The first payment is usually made when the contract is signed. It covers the artist's time and creativity in developing a detailed design specific to your needs. You can expect to go through several rounds of trial and error in the design process, but at the end of this stage you will have detailed drawings and, for three-dimensional work, a maquette (model) that everyone agrees upon. The cost of the maquette and the design time are usually factored into the artist's fee.

The second payment is generally set for a point midway through the project, and is for work completed to date. If the materials are expensive, the client may be asked to advance money at this stage to cover costs. If the commission is canceled during this period, the artist keeps the money already paid for work performed.

Final payment is usually due when the work is installed. If the piece is finished on time but the building or project is delayed, the artist is customarily paid on delivery, but still has the obligation to oversee installation.

You will find that most artists keep tabs on the project budget. Be sure that the project scope does not deviate from what was agreed at the outset. If the scope changes, amend the agreement to reflect the changes.

The Artist as Designer

We should say up front that not every artist charges a design fee. Some consider preliminary sketches a part of their marketing effort and figure they will be compensated for their time by the client once the project is approved. But it's more common for an artist to require a design fee of 5% to 10% of the final project budget. In some cases, especially when the artist has considerable experience and a strong reputation in a specialized area, the design fee may be as high as 25% of the project budget; this is most common when an artist is hired to envision specific solutions to complicated architectural problems. Obviously, in this kind of situation the artist is not merely asked to supply a product, but also to contribute a significant part of the design solution; here, the artist's ideas and experience are as important as his or her tangible work.

A few points about design are worth highlighting here:

1. Design Ideas Are the Artist's Property

It should go without saying that it is highly unethical, as well as possibly illegal, to take an artist's designs — even very preliminary or non-site-specific sketches — and use them without the artist's permission. Some artists may include specific language about ownership of ideas, models, sketches, etc., in their contracts or letters of agreement. Even if an artist does not use a written agreement, be sure you are clear at the outset what you are paying for and what rights the artist retains.

2. Respect the Artist's Ideas and Vision

When you hire a doctor, you want a thoughtful, intelligent diagnosis, not just a course of treatment. The same should be true when you hire an artist to work with a design team. Most GUILD artists have become successful through many years of experience, and because of their excellence in both technique and aesthetic imagination. Take advantage of that experience and expertise fully by bringing the artist into the project early, and by asking him or her for ideas.

3. Keep the Artist Informed of Changes

Tell the artist about changes — even seemingly minor details — which may have a significant impact on the project's design. If the artist is working as a member of the design team, it's easier to include him or her in the ongoing dialog about the overall project.

4. Consider a Separate Design Budget for Your Project

There are specific conditions when a design budget is particularly helpful:

• if you want to get lots of ideas from an artist
• if you need site-specific ideas that involve significant research
• if you require a formal presentation with finished drawings, blueprints or maquettes

To evaluate designs from several artists for a specific project, consider a competition with a small design fee for each artist.

It comes down to an issue of professionalism. Artists have the technical skills to do wonderful and amazing things with simple materials. But they also have sophisticated conceptual and design talents. By being willing to pay for these talents, trade professionals add vision and variety to their creative products. In such a partnership, both parties gain, and the ultimate result is a client who is delighted by the outcome of the collaboration.

A Collaborative Atmosphere

With most commission projects, it's best to bring the artist into the process at about the same time you hire a general contractor or are completing the final design.

By involving the artist at this early stage, the space will be designed with the art in mind, and the art will be created to enhance the space. As a result, there will be no unpleasant surprises about size or suitability of artwork to the space. Furthermore, when art is planned for early on and is a line item in the budget, it's far less likely to be cut at the end of the project, when money is running low.

Early inclusion of the artist also helps ensure that the collaborative effort will go smoothly throughout all phases of the project. If the artist is respected as part of the team, his or her work can benefit the project's overall design.

Naturally, the scope of the project will determine the number of players to be involved with the artist. It's important that all individuals understand both their own responsibilities and the responsibilities of their collaborators. How will decisions be made? Who is the artist's primary liaison? Will a single person sign off on designs and recommendations? Are committees necessary?

Seek Two-Way Understanding

Be sure the artist understands the technical requirements of the job, including traffic flow in the space, the intended use of the space, the building structure, maintenance, lighting and environmental concerns. By doing this, you ensure that the artist's knowledge, experience and skills inform the project.

Commission Guidelines

Some Simple Rules

• Contact GUILDtrade.com for assistance in recommending artists or posting your project.

• Bring the artist into the project as early as possible.

• Be as specific as possible about the scope and range of the project, even in early meetings before the artist is selected.

• Be honest and realistic when discussing deadlines, responsibilities and specific project requirements, and expect the same from the artist. Don't avoid discussing the areas where there seem to be questions.

• For larger projects, use specific milestones to assure continuing consensus on project scope and budget. It may also be necessary to make adjustments at these points.

• Choose an artist based on a solid portfolio of previous work and excellent references from other trade professionals. And remember that it's less risky to use an artist you know has worked on projects that are similar in size and scope, who can handle the demands of your kind of job.

• Consider hiring an art consultant if the commission is particularly large or complex. The consultant should help with complicated contract arrangements, and should make certain that communication between artists and support staff (including sub-contractors and engineers) is thoroughly understood.

• Trust your instincts when choosing an artist. Like selecting an advertising agency or an architect, choosing an artist is based partly on chemistry. You need to like the work and respect the artist, and you also need to be able to work with him or her.

Keep the artist apprised of any changes that will affect the work in progress. Did you find a certain material you specified unavailable and replace it with something else? Did the available space become bigger or smaller? These may seem like small changes to you, but they could have a profound impact on an artist's planning and work. If the artist works as a member of the design team, it's easier to include him or her in the loop.

At the same time, the artist should let you know of any special requirements his or her work will place on the space. Is it especially heavy? Does it need to be mounted in a specific way? Must it be protected from theft or vandalism? What kind of lighting is best? You may need to budget funds for these kinds of installation expenses.

Most artists experienced with commissioned projects factor the expense of a continuing design dialog into their fee. There is an unfortunate belief harbored by some trade professionals (and yes, artists too) that a willingness to develop and change a design based on discussions with the client or design team somehow indicates a lack of commitment or creativity. On the contrary. The ability to modify design or execution without compromising artistic quality is a mark of professionalism. We recommend looking for this quality in the artist you choose, and then respecting it by treating the artist as a partner in the decisions made affecting his or her work.

Of course, part of working together is making clear who is responsible for what. Since few designers and architects (and even fewer contractors) are used to working with artists, the relationship is custom made for misunderstanding. Without a firm understanding from the outset — nurtured by constant communication — things can easily fall through the cracks.

Forging a Partnership

The partnership between artists and trade professionals is an old and honorable one. Many venerable blueprints indicate, for example, an architect's detail for a ceiling with the scrawled note: "Finish ceiling in this manner." The assumption, of course, is that the artisan working on the ceiling has both the technical mastery and the aesthetic skill to create a whole expanse of space based on a detail sketched by the architect's pen.

The artists whose work fills these pages — and with whom we work every day at GUILDtrade.com — are capable of interactive relationships like those described here. We're delighted to see increasing numbers of trade professionals include artists on their design teams. After too many years of the arts being separated from architectural and interior design, we're happy to be part of a renewed interest in collaboration.

GUILDtrade.com

A Collection of Services for the Trade Professional

THE SOURCEBOOK OF ARCHITECTURAL AND INTERIOR ART 16 is only one of several tools for trade professionals from GUILDtrade.com. For more than 15 years, GUILD sourcebooks have introduced architects, interior designers and art consultants to top artists. Since 1998, GUILDtrade.com has expanded on the basic functions of our sourcebooks through a series of companion services for trade professionals. These services are found under the umbrella of GUILDtrade.com's "Trade Resource Program."

The GUILD Sourcebook Online

The hallmark of our Trade Resource Program is *The GUILD Sourcebook Online.* Created in response to the growing number of trade professionals who use the Internet to source products and services, the online sourcebook provides busy trade professionals quick and easy access to our comprehensive artist listings. Visit www.guildtrade.com to browse *The GUILD Sourcebook Online.*

Post a Project

The popular "Post a Project" feature is a great complement to GUILD's online sourcebook. This feature allows trade professionals to list upcoming projects that require artwork, and is equally useful for large RFPs or small design accessories. Post a Project listings are broadcast to our entire database of artists; individuals respond to projects that match their abilities and interests. Post a Project is an efficient and effective way to broadcast a general call for artists and ideas.

Contact the Artist

If you've perused the sourcebook and found an artist you'd like to consider for a project, fill out the electronic "Request Commission Information" form linked to that artist's online page. This form gives the artist basic information about your project, enabling him or her to respond with insights, possible solutions or alternative options. These responses are a good way to gauge the initial interest and suitability of particular artists.

Trade Sales Consultants

Perhaps the most valuable service our Trade Resource Program offers is the personal assistance provided by our experienced staff. Our Trade Sales Consultants are available via e-mail or phone to make art recommendations and offer expert advice. Simply give our knowledgeable staff an idea of your art needs and they'll put together a comprehensive portfolio of recommendations, available in electronic or printed versions. Call 1-877-565-2002 during business hours to speak with a consultant.

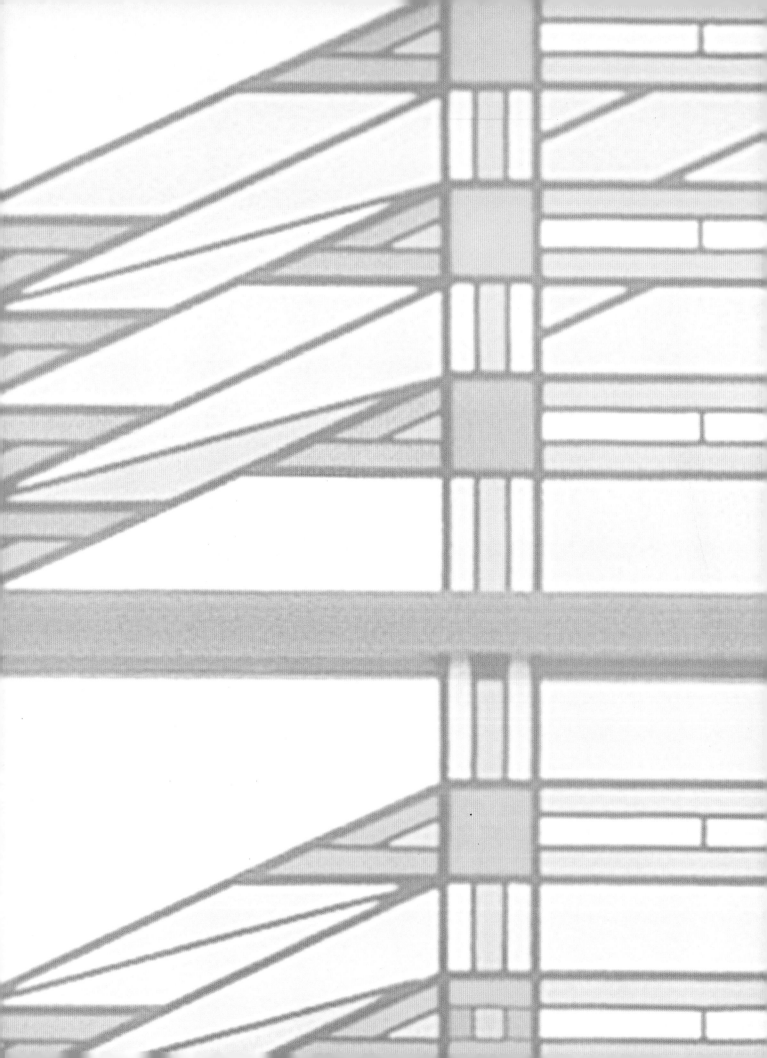

Featured Artists

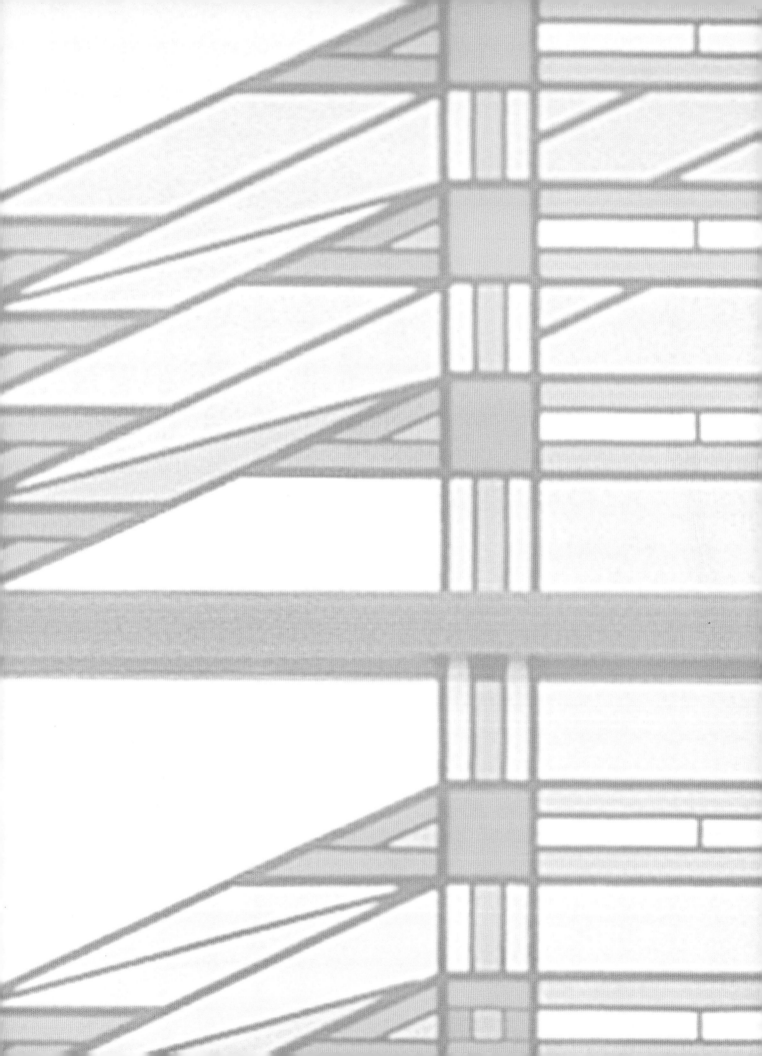

Architectural Metal

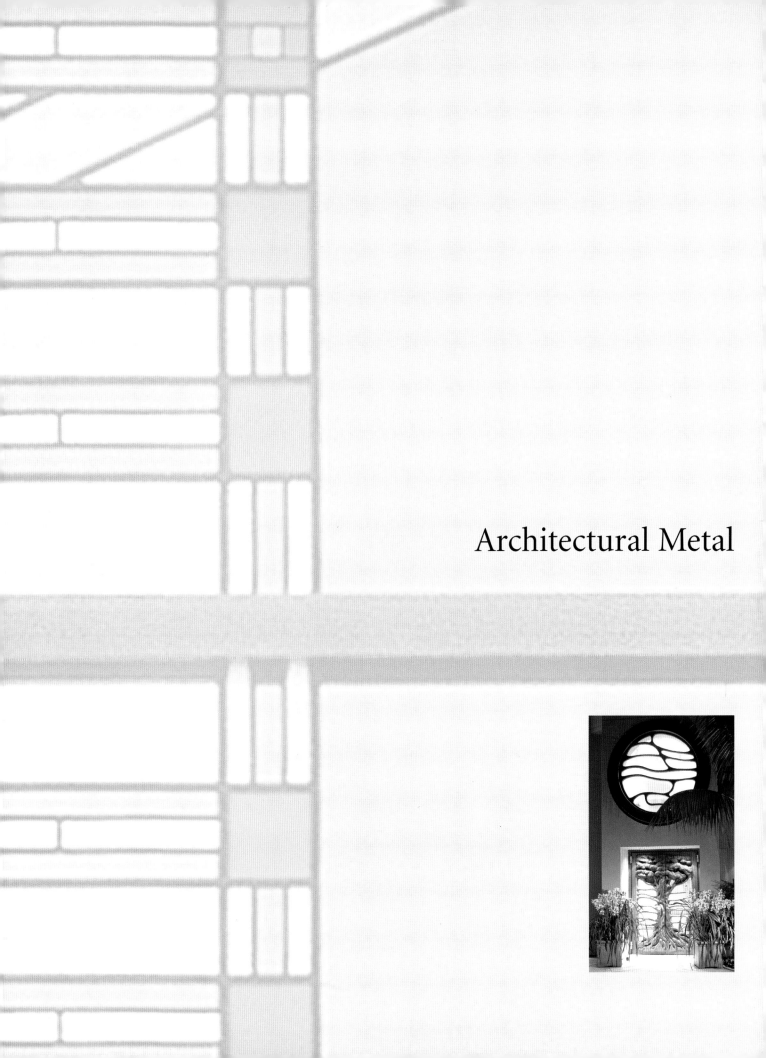

Louis DeMartino

Bronze fountain, private residence, Coronado Island, CA, 16'H

Sculpted bronze doors and window, door: 6' × 8', window: 8'

Bruce Paul Fink

Great Blue-Breasted Nesting Cranes (detail)

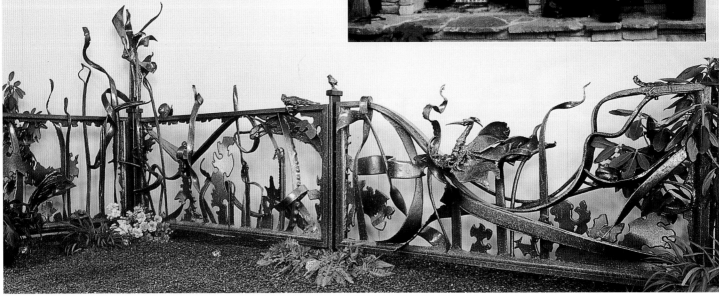

The Gregarious Swamp Village Collective, 16' section of a 65'ʟ cast and fabricated metal backdrop railing, 6'ʜ × 22"ᴅ; inset: *Great Blue-Breasted Nesting Cranes*, cast metal, left side: 40"ʜ × 30"ᴡ × 14"ᴅ, right side: 114"ʜ × 76"ᴡ × 22"ᴅ

Steve Fontanini

Forged bronze railing of winter aspen trees and birds, Roney residence, Teton County, WY

Photos: Florence McCall

chandelier & bar stools

ARTIST
Mollie Massie

TITLE
Globe Chandelier and custom bar stools

YEAR
1998

DESCRIPTION
Cor-ten steel chandelier: 32"H × 38"W
Bar stools: 32.25"H × 17"W × 17"D

SITE
Private residence, Whistler,
British Columbia, Canada

TIMELINE
9 months

"The pure enjoyment of working with both the clients and their interior designer stood out the most for me on this commission. From our first meeting, we "connected" on what was needed, and continued to feed off of each other's ideas throughout the project. My clients were clear about what they wanted from me, but did not limit my creativity. I felt challenged and excited to learn new skills. Working on this job (which included four chandeliers, light sconces, three fireplace screens, bar stools and fireplace tools) was like reading a good book — a wonderful experience leaving you sad when it's over."

favorite commissions

Photos: Rob Melnychuk

Mollie Massie

Globe Chandelier, Cor-ten steel

Custom bar stools, Cor-ten steel

Bear Family, firescreen doors, Cor-ten steel

Photos: Rob Melnychuk

Daryl Rush

Door with handmade grill, stainless steel and bronze, Cunningham/Charman residence, Oakland, CA

Wall sconces, bronze and steel, Cunningham/Charman residence, Oakland, CA

One leaf of a stainless steel gate, Navaho Ridge, Moab, UT, total size: 6'H × 32'L

Photos: Buck Engle

Doug Weigel

Petroglyph Badger, .75" steel, 8'ʜ

Petroglyph game table and chairs; Petroglyph wall circle

Free Spirit Butterflies, 4' × 4' on 5' to 8' rods

Architectural Ceramics,
Mosaics & Wall Reliefs

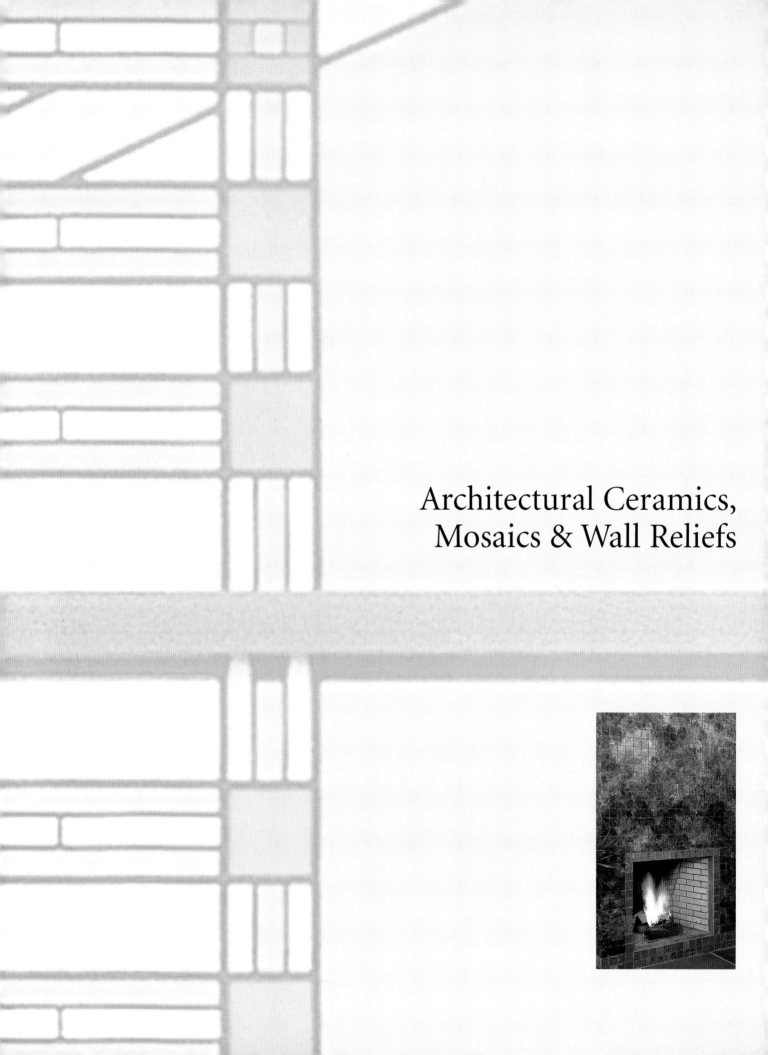

Mary Lou Alberetti

Ornato, 23"H × 19"W × 2"D

Frammento, 25"H × 20"W × 4"D

Uccello, 17"H × 23"W × 2"D

Photos: Bill Quinnell

Eleen Auvil

Journey, 2000, copper, bronze plates, 8'H × 14'w

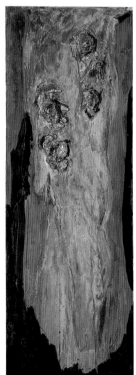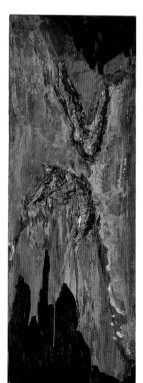

Search, 2000, copper, cast lead, patina, 46.5"H × 92"w

Photos: Rick Pharaoh

Architectural Ceramics

Fountain, 1999, relief mural with handmade tile and luster, 54" × 80"

Christopher Bunn

Clay Architectural Murals LLC

The Music, 3' × 8'

Ballerinas, 2.5' × 4'

French Tapestry, 4' × 4.5'

Italian Palace Facade, 4.5' × 3.5' × 7"

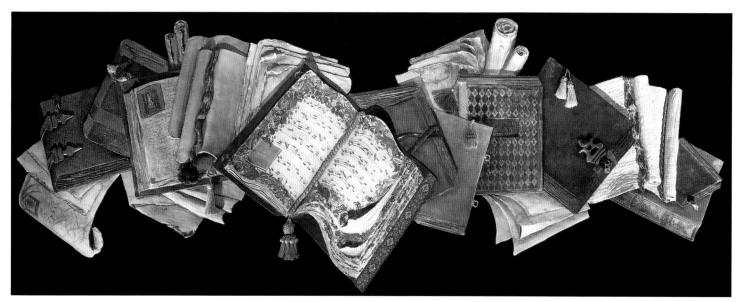

Florentine Books, 3' × 8'

Photos: Joe Hyde

Joan Rothchild Hardin

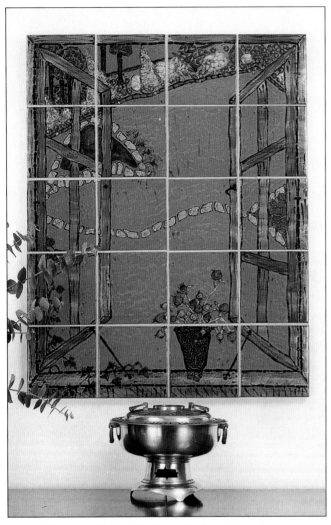

Open Window, 2000, tiled panel, private collection, 30" × 24"

Mocha Vine, tile in wrought iron table, 31" × 14.25" × 7.25"

Tiled windowsill for a New York City loft, 2000

Photos: Erik S. Lieber

Karen Heyl

Gargoyle, limestone, private collection, Augusta, GA, 4.5' × 3'

Heal, Health, Wellness, limestone, Scripps Memorial Hospital Chula Vista, Chula Vista, CA, three panels, each: 4' × 1.5'

Photos: Charles Behlow Photography

Claudia Hollister

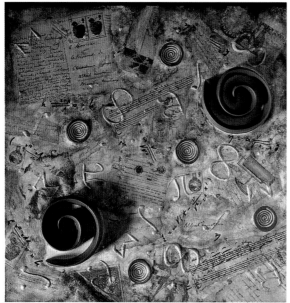

Einstein, 2000, porcelain and photo imaging, paint, private collection, 12" × 12"

Grace Weston

Clockwork, 1998, porcelain, COCA Museum, 10" × 10", total size: 30" × 40"

David Kingsberry

Untitled, 2000, porcelain, Anderson Consulting, Houston, TX, 24" × 24"

Grace Weston

Clockwork, 1998, porcelain and gold leaf, COCA Museum, 30" × 40"

David Kingsberry

Bruce Howdle

Peaceable Kingdom, installed March 2000, Mercy Hospital, Oshkosh, WI, 8'ʜ × 18'ᴡ

Ceramic relief, installed May 2000, City Hall, Menasha, WI, 53'ᴡ × 32'ʜ

Photos: Munroe Studios

Marlene Miller

Requiem, 2000, glazed stoneware, private collection, Snohomish, WA, 25.5" × 10" × 20"

Tyson Joyce

Head, 2000, stoneware with stains, private collection, Germantown Hills, IL, 19" × 15" × 13"

Tyson Joyce

Tribute, 1999, glazed stoneware, Illinois Central College Library/Administration Building, East Peoria, IL, 9.5' × 24'

John Beam

Elizabeth MacDonald

A Diary of Days — Landscapes, 2000, ceramic, each: 11.5"H × 11.5"W × 1.25"D

Bob Rush

Elizabeth MacDonald

Landscape, 1998, ceramic tile, St. Francis Hospital, Hartford, CT, 40" × 40" × 1"

Bob Rush

Franz Mayer of Munich, Inc.

Glass and stone mosaics on four towers and stairways, New Carrollton Train Station parking garage, New Carrollton, MD, artist: Heidi Lippman, architect: Ben Van Dusen, SOM

One of 14 mosaic murals in photo-realistic and other mosaic techniques and materials, MTA Art in Transit, Grand Central Terminal-North Access, New York, NY, artist: Ellen Driscoll

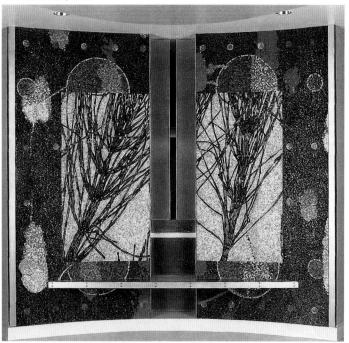

Mosaic mural in glass mosaic tesserae, Swedish Hospital, Seattle, WA, artist: Ann Gardner, architect: NBBJ

The Frankfurt Stairs, hand-chopped and hand-set glass tesserae mosaic, Hessische Landesbank, Frankfurt, Germany, photo-realistic area: 430' sq., blue background mosaic: 650' sq., artist: Stephan Huber, architect: Schweger + Partner

E. Joseph McCarthy

Tropical mural painted on 6" × 6" tiles, *Zenieth*, Celebrity Cruise Lines, 22'w × 8'h

Claire Houston

Tropical mural (detail)

Claire Houston

Abstract painted on 6" × 6" tiles (detail), Savannah Hotel, Barbados

André Banville

Rita Paul

Green Turban (T. De Lampicka), tile installation, C3 Restaurant, Washington Square Hotel, New York, NY

Fred Slavin

Carolyn Payne

Wine cellar floor, grape vines painted on stone-textured floor tile with eight scenes hand painted on Italian quarry, private residence, 9' × 11'

Window effect in hand-painted tiles above jacuzzi area, Napa Valley wine country theme, private residence, 3.5' × 4'

Photos: Mike Chaloupka

Peter Colombo Artistic Mosaics

Photos: Graphic Solutions, Wallington, NJ

Handmade ceramic tile mosaics, two parts in a series of three, 1999-2000, 9th Street Path Station at 6th Avenue, New York, NY, commissioned by the Port Authority of New York and New Jersey, original paintings by Jose Ortega, each panel: 64" × 64"

Angelica Pozo

Cleveland Marshall College of Law Library, Cleveland State University, OH, 8' × 42'

RTA Station, Cleveland Hopkins International Airport, 2000' sq.

Photos: Hanson Photographics

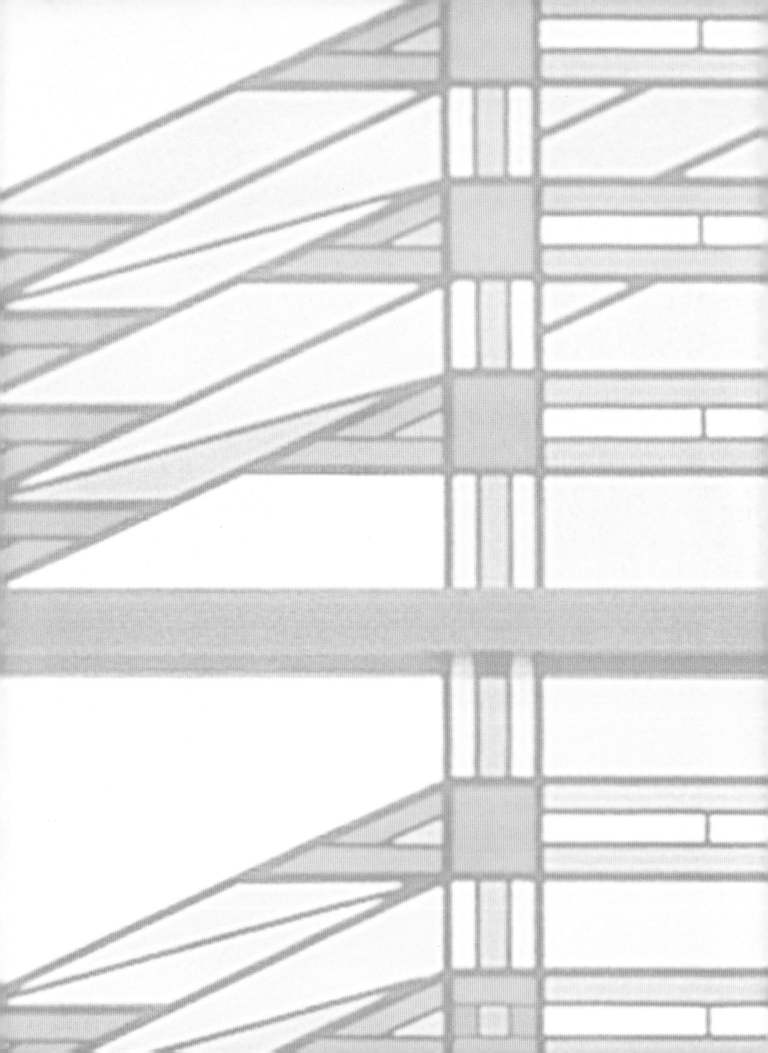

Architectural Glass

Ellen Abbott
Marc Leva

Pate de verre bowls, 6" × 3", 10" × 5"

Kolanowski Studio

Studio entry, Houston, TX

Sandra C.Q. Bergér

Multi-colored screen, 7'H × 8'W × 3"D

Photos: William A. Porter, San Francisco, CA

Architectural Glass Art, Inc.

Three First Union, 2000, Charlotte, NC

Architectural Glass Art, Inc.

Aquamarine Vortex, Orlando International Airport, 2000, Orlando, FL, 100' × 15'

University of Toledo/School of Engineering, Toledo, OH, 1996, 11 columns, each: 10' × 2'

Greg Murphey

University of Toledo/School of Engineering (detail)

Greg Murphey

Kathy Barnard

Stillwater National Bank, before art glass installation

Night view of illuminated carved and etched glass, Stillwater National Bank, Tulsa, OK, 40' × 35'

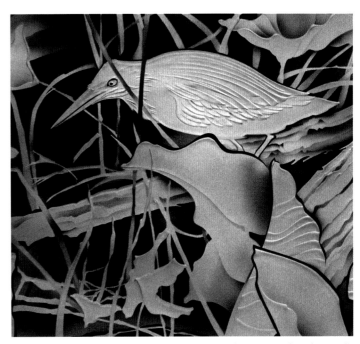

Details depicting indigenous Oklahoma wildlife, Stillwater National Bank, Tulsa, OK

Kathy Bradford

Faces of the Forest (detail), 1997, multi-layer sandcarved wall, Chicago, IL, 21' × 8' × 5"

Kathy Bradford

Bear Ballroom with 10 arched panels of Russian performing circus bears, 1999, sandcarved, Russian Tearoom, New York, NY, each: 5' × 10' × .5"; inset: *Circus Bear* (detail)

Provided by Russian Tearoom

Warren Carther

Sea of Time, 1999, part two of *Chronos Trilogy,* a three-component sculpture, Lincoln House office tower, Hong Kong, 100' × 23' × 6'

Gerry Kopelow

City Glass Specialty, Inc.

Resurrection, Concordia Cemetery Mausoleum, Fort Wayne, IN

General Anthony Wayne, office window at City Glass Specialty, Fort Wayne, IN

Conrad Schmitt Studios, Inc.

Leptat® etched glass, Eucharistic Chapel, St. James Catholic Church, Menomonee Falls, WI

Conservation project, Basilica of the Sacred Heart, University of Notre Dame

Ecumenical *Family Tree* window, LaPorte Hospital family chapel, LaPorte, IN, 26'H

Leptat® etched doors, Annunciation Greek Church, Wauwatosa, WI

Phil Daniel

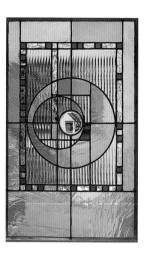

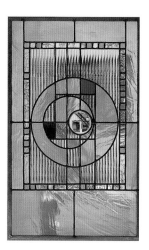

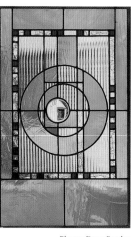

Millennium Series 2000

Architectural Glass

David Wilson Design

Exterior view

Interior view at night from lobby floor

Glass installation (detail), 1999, Sellinger Hall,
Loyola College in Maryland, Baltimore, MD

Photos: Richard Walker

stained glass

ARTIST
Beyer Studio, Inc.

TITLE
Passion

YEAR
2000

DESCRIPTION
Glass blown by hand, various
sizes of lead cane, 15'H × 14'W

SITE
St. Joseph's Church, Aston, PA

TIMELINE
10 weeks to fabricate

"This commission challenged traditional design and function concepts about stained glass and provided an opportunity to indulge in purely emotional, abstract design. Stained glass was used at the focal point of the church, behind the altar, yet was specifically designed to recede into and create a background for the ornate 110-year-old crucifix. The theme of "passion" was chosen to heighten the drama of the crucifix/sculpture and the color palette (cast in a minor key of secondary and tertiary color relationships) that evoke the solemnity of these associated events."

favorite commissions

Jerome R. Durr

Leaded art glass windows, Livingston, TX, 4 of 15

Glassic Art

Leaf Sails, leaded glass doors

Mirrored fireplace with Glassic Art columns, 80" × 110"

Carved pearlescent glass countertop, 72" × 32"

Photos: Sampsell Preston

Glassic Art

Carved and welded glass doors

Carved, painted and kiln-formed glass with shadows

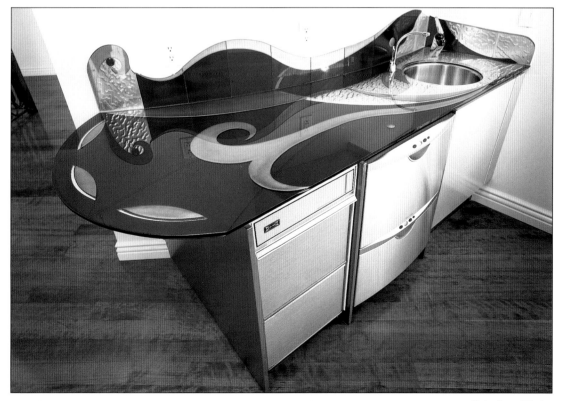

Carved, painted and mirrored countertop and backsplash on round wall, 87" × 42"

Photos: Sampsell Preston

Mark Eric Gulsrud

Epiphany Lutheran Church, Kenmore, WA; inset: baptismal font and window

Photos: Roger Schreiber

Mark Eric Gulsrud

Interior totem, stacked glass and powder-coated steel, Denney Juvenile
Justice Center, Everett, WA

Exterior totem, stacked glass and powder-coated steel, Denney Juvenile
Justice Center, Everett, WA

Carved, cast and patinaed glass and
powder-coated steel

Photos: Roger Schreiber

Henry Halem

Fused glass panels, student center entrance, Ohio University-Ironton Branch Campus, Ironton, OH

Fused glass panels, student center window, Ohio University-Ironton Branch Campus, Ironton, OH, 8.5'DIA

Photos: Henry Halem

Henry Halem

Vitrolite glass murals, lobby, Ferro Corporation world headquarters, Cleveland, OH

Vitrolite wall mural, Ferro Corporation lobby, Cleveland, OH, 4' × 3'

Photos: Albin Dearing

Gordon Huether + Partners

J Wine Tasting Bar, Healdsburg, CA, 1999, patinated steel, glass cullet, glass on edge, 24' × 20'

Entertainment Partners, Burbank, CA, 1998, mouthblown, etched and insulated glass, 35' × 8'

Photos: Michael Bruk

Laurel Herter

Detail of beveled, brilliant cut, jeweled front entryway, private residence

David Soliday

Front entry, carved and sandblasted peach plate glass, The Jazz Corner, Hilton Head, SC

Paul Keyserling

Front entry, clear antique background, light green bevels, private residence

Paul Keyserling

Paul Housberg

Lightfall (detail), 1999, laminated float and colored glass, William J. Nealon Federal Building and U.S. Courthouse, Scranton, PA, General Services Administration (GSA) Art in Architecture Program, 14' × 40'

Michael Thomas

Tom Holdman

Tree of Life, temple in Palmyra, NY, 9' × 9'

Joseph Smith's First Vision, temple in Palmyra, NY, 7' × 5'

Photos: Willie Holdman

Jurs Architectural Glass

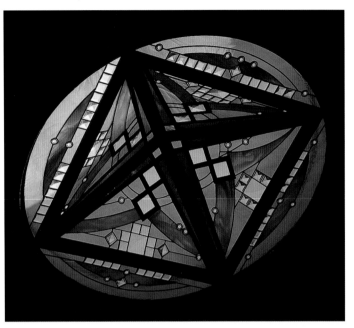

Ocular Skylight, 2000, custom steel frame with three-dimensional pyramid pointing upward, eight individual panels of imported handblown and hand-cut glass

The New Millennium, 2000, hand-cut and polished faceted jewels, pyramids and round lenses, Oakland, CA

Le Chateau, private entry, 2000, custom aluminum frames, triple-glazed hand-cut and polished crystal glass and black, bronze and streaky hand-blown glass, front door: 3' × 8', sidelights: 4' × 8'

Photos: Hugo Steccati

Gary Kazanjian

Crafts 3, Torf residence, total size: 31"H × 285"w

Motion Study, Lauter residence, 58"H × 20"w

Clear Autumn, left door; *McCauley,* right door; each: 67"H × 28"w

Photos: Jeffrey Meyers

Guy Kemper

So Long Bro, Greater Orlando International Airport, 100' × 14'

Guy Kemper

Walt Roycraft

Stephen Knapp

Sculptural light painting (detail), dichroic glass, steel, light,
Worcester Medical Center, Worcester, MA, 17' × 60' × 10"

Kiln-formed art glass wall, Sam Nunn Federal Center, Atlanta, GA,
one of four walls, each: 9' × 7'

Kiln-formed art glass wall, Fox Chase Cancer Institute, Philadelphia, PA, 8' × 24'

Tom Bernard

Duncan Laurie

Aerial topography of lower Manhattan in three sections: buildings, streets, docks and terrain, with two autonomous panels; Milbank, Tweed, Hadley & McCloy, New York, NY; 7' × 9.5' × 1'; architect: Swanke, Hayden, Connell & Partners LLP

Photos: Peter Aaron/ESTO

Mark J. Levy

From Where I Have Come To I Don't Know Where, © 2000, Studio City Branch of the Los Angeles, CA, Public Library, 64" × 237"

Martin Fine

Liturgical Environments Company

Holy Spirit, faceted stained glass (dale de verre), Our Lady Star of the Sea Catholic Community, Grosse Pointe Woods, MI, 80'w × 12'H (peak) × 3'H (sides); font area, carved glass, 20'w × 8'H

Trinity windows, leaded glass (antique mouthblown), Servite Center for Life, Ladysmith, WI, each: 4'w × 12'H

Twelfth Station of the Cross, carved glass, Addolorata Villa, Wheeling, IL, 12"H × 12"w

Photos: Theresa Krauski

Ellen Mandelbaum

Glass Landscape, 2000, leaded stained glass window, upper level with view of buildings of Charleston, entry hall, South Carolina Aquarium, Charleston, SC, 30'H × 18'w, architects: Eskew + Architects

Marilyn Ott

Franz Mayer of Munich, Inc.

Glass wall executed in the technique of "floatglass painting," sandblasting, ceramic melting color, computer preparation, photochemical processes, British Embassy in Moscow, Russia, artist: Alexander Beleschenko, architect: Ahrends, Burton & Koralak

Detail of stained glass window with Luther's original text, mouthblown glass, enamel paint, lead, Lutheran church in Coburg, Neustadt, Germany, artist: Anne Hitzker

Running Figures, executed in the technique of "floatglass painting," Sportarena Department Store, Stuttgart, Germany, artist: Sabine Kammerl, architect: Heinz Maier

Lexicon, glass facade, sandblasted, tempered, Department for Waste Disposal, Munich, Germany, 270'L, artist: Heiner Blum, architect: Ackermann + Partner

Meltdown Glass Art & Design LLC

Feeling Fall (detail)

Feeling Fall, 1999, cast glass sculptural wall, American Express Corporation, 96"H × 420"W

Photos: Richard Abrams

Michael Davis Stained Glass Inc.

Panel detail

Sliding doors in overlap position

Panel detail

Sliding doors used to separate living room from music room, full view of doors in fully closed position

Photos: Elizabeth Felicella

Pearl River Glass Studio, Inc.

Chandelier #2,
3.5' × 2' × 1'

Gretchen Haien

Garden Figure, 36" × 20"

Andrew Young

Prayer and meditation windows, 4' × 12'

Andrew Young

Michael F. Pilla

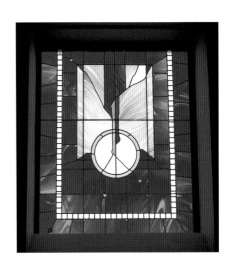

Pentecost, rose window, Saint Ambrose Catholic Church; top: *Celestial Being*, clerestory, Saint Ambrose Catholic Church

Maya Radoczy

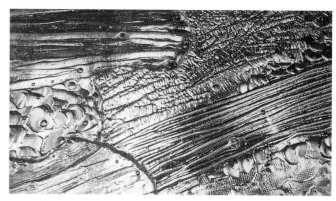

Strata (detail)   Maya Radoczy

Strata, April 2000, bas-relief cast glass doors, REI flagship store, Denver, CO   Dick Springgate

Blair Reed

Abstract design, 2000, glass, Hyatt Hotel, 9'H × 30'W

Wetland scene, 1995, glass, Henry Ford Hospital, 6'H × 68'W

Photos: Glen Calvin Moon

Helle Scharling-Todd

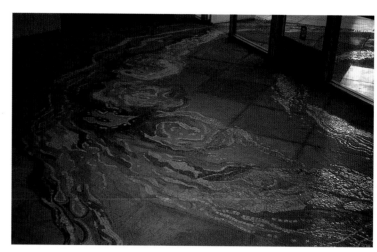

Water Lines, wall and floor mosaics, 1989, Port Hueneme Prueter Library, 200' sq.

The Human Web, painted glass, Junior College, Denmark, 126' sq.

Water Lines (detail)

Michael Shields
Matthew Durbin

Bronze Memorial Sculpture, 1999, etched and polished double-flashed glass, 74"DIA

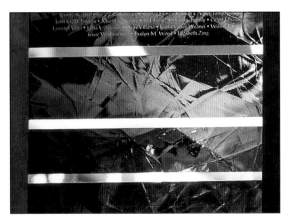

Jeff G. Smith

Resurrection Window, view from Reservation Chapel, St. Albert the Great Catholic Church, Austin, TX, 24.25' × 24.25'

Detail view from Reservation Chapel

Overview from sanctuary

Detail view from sanctuary

Jeff G. Smith

An Evolution of Flight, private library and gallery, four of seven windows, each: 36" × 53"

Left two of seven windows

Exterior view

Arthur Stern

The St. John Millennium Cross Window, exterior view, leaded handblown glass with different densities of gray plate glass and beveled glass prisms, PeaceHealth Medical Center, Longview, WA, 24' × 24'

Blake Praytor

Architectural Glass

Arthur Stern

Interior view from atrium balcony, PeaceHealth Medical Center, Longview, WA,
American Institute of Architects and the Interfaith Forum on Religion, Art & Architecture design award winner

Angelika Traylor

Holmes Regional Medical Center, Melbourne, FL

Spring (detail)

Winter (detail)

Photos: Randall Smith

Architectural Glass

VitraMax Group

Cast glass bathroom vanity with integrated sink

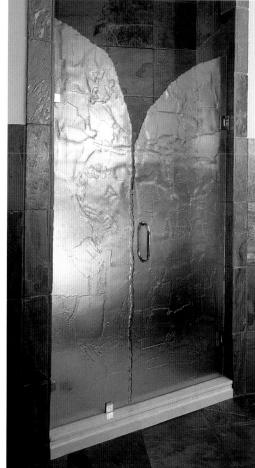

Champagne caddy, cast glass with copper leaf

Photos: Doug Decker

Cast glass shower enclosure with tile pattern

Daniel Winterich

 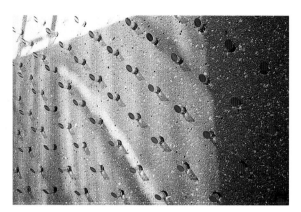

Solar Matrix, 2000, public art award, Microsoft Silicon Valley Campus, Mountain View, CA, 40' × 20' × 12', architect: Quezada Architecture

Michael O'Callahan

Joy Wulke

Where Earth Meets Sky, 1998, glass, water, stainless steel, light, Chicago, IL,   Joy Wulke
5'H × 5'W × 5'D

Frozen Fountain, Wave Window, Sconces, glass, light,   Joy Wulke
fabric, Malibu, CA; 24'H × 40'W × 6'D

Frozen Fountain, Wave Window, Sconces, night view   T. Charles Erickson

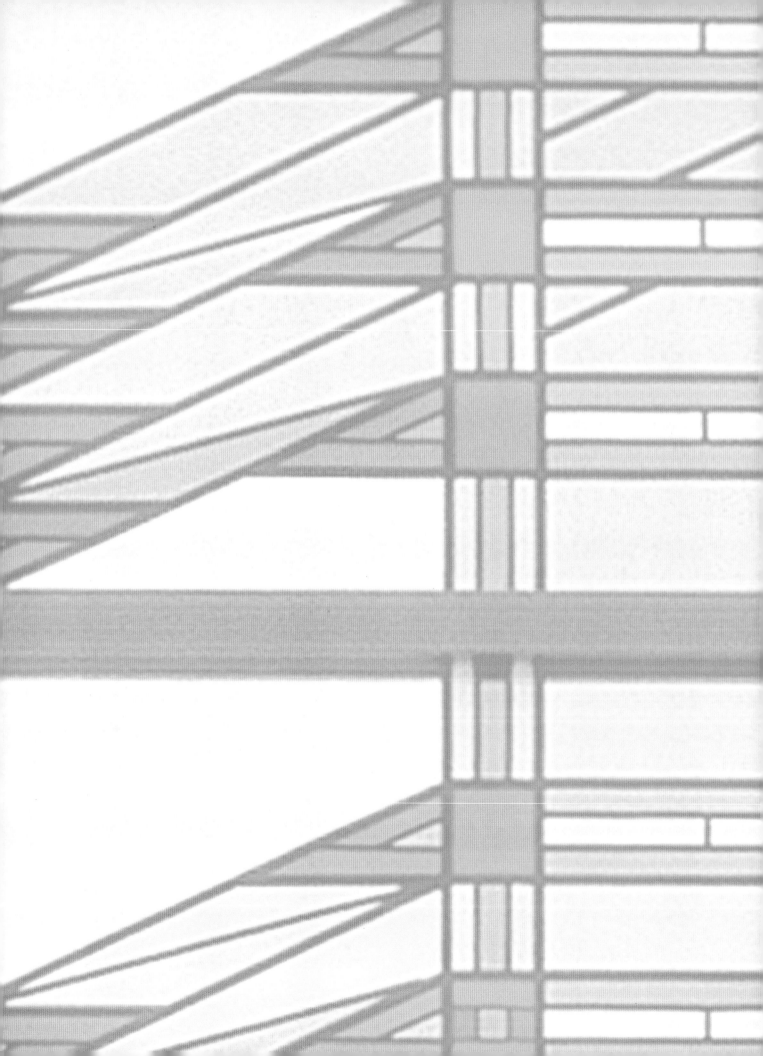

Architectural Elements

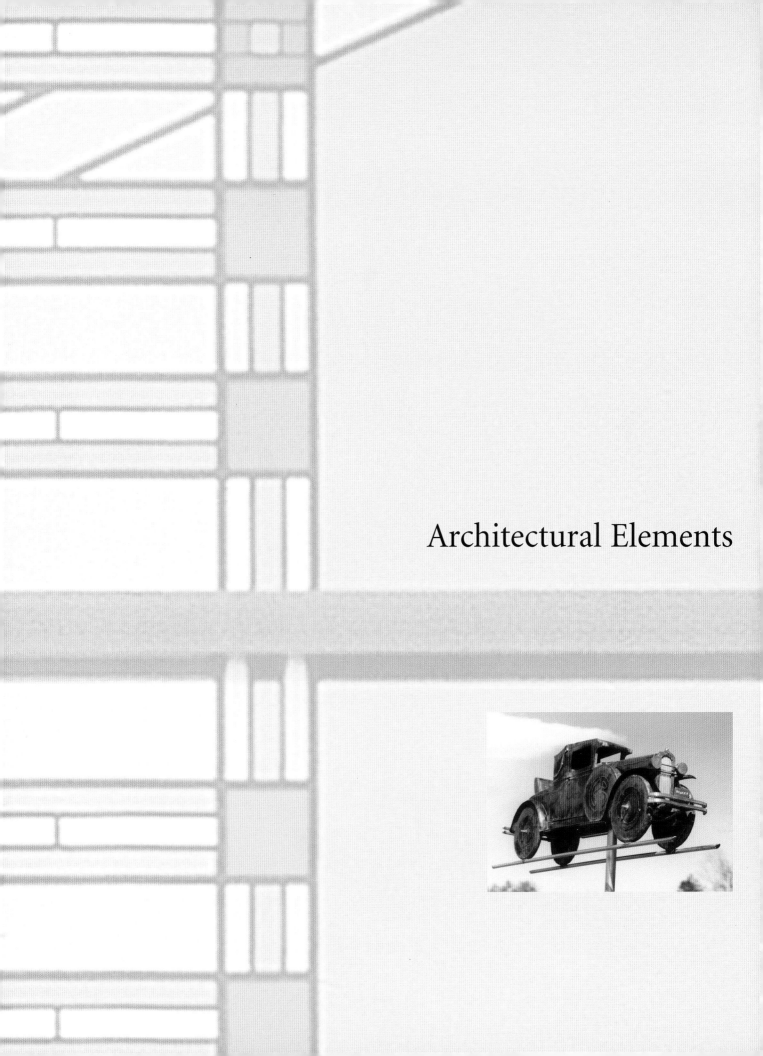

Shawn Athari

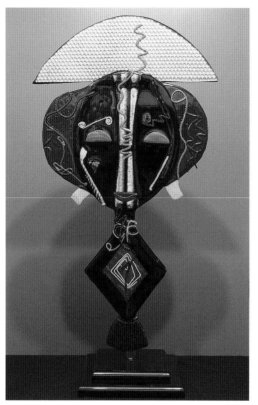

Kota Mask, contemporary African sculpture replication, re-formed, layered and fused molten glass, 9" × 30", 8" stand

Plank Mask, contemporary African sculpture replication, re-formed, layered and fused molten glass, 21" × 43" × 5"

Fireplace, total area: 10' × 20'; sconce, multiple layers of fused or formed glass, 9" × 13" × 4"

Photos: Robert Baumbach

Architectural Elements

Shawn Athari

French doors, painted, fused, blown, sandblasted and fabricated glass, 8'w × 7'H

Robert Baumbach

glass door

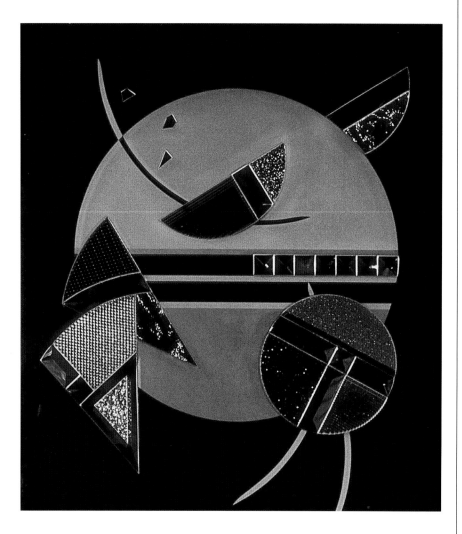

ARTISTS
Ellen Abbott
Marc Leva

DESCRIPTION
Front door, etched glass with
laminated clear textured glass,
64"H × 22"W

YEAR
2000

SITE
Private residence, Houston, TX

TIMELINE
5 to 6 weeks

"After selecting the basic line drawing for his door, this client allowed us total freedom to fabricate it however we thought best, declining even a rendered version of the drawing. As a result, we made decisions as we went along, changing things as needed, never planning out the details in advance. It was a more spontaneous fabrication, with the extra freedom giving the whole thing a sense of adventure. We think it is one of our best works. The client thought so, too, and we are now working on seven windows for his home, using the same techniques."

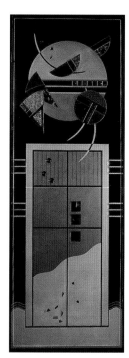

favorite commissions

Richard Altman

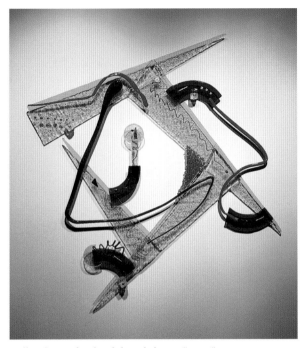

Wall sculpture, fused and shaped glass, 24" × 24"

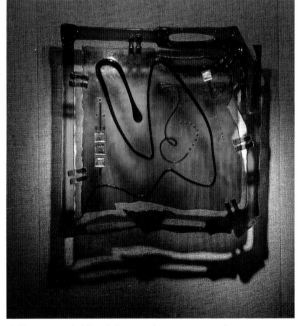

Ceiling-suspended fused glass panels, corporate conference room, 20" × 20"

Fused glass lighting elements, corporate headquarters

Photos: Gregg Mastorakos

marquetry

ARTIST
Kerin Lifland

DESCRIPTION
Paneled study with marquetry, various woods, 12'ʜ × 20'ᴡ × 18'ᴅ

YEAR
1999

SITE
Los Angeles, CA

TIMELINE
16 months to fabricate

"Aside from an ideal client, the most enjoyable aspect of this commission was the chance it gave me to integrate my love of drawing and painting with my woodworking skills. I not only learned the technique of marquetry, but I was able to appreciate firsthand the achievement of the 15th-century Italian masters of intarsia, whose work incorporated the studies of perspective and chiaroscuro together with the more narrative elements of their subject matter. Marquetry demands great patience and challenges the creative attention span, but it is ultimately very rewarding and I would jump at an opportunity to do more."

favorite commissions

Travis Tuck Metal Sculptor

Velociraptor Weathervane, residence of Steven Spielberg, East Hampton, NY, 48"L   Mark Lovewell

Vintage "Graham" Automobile Weathervane, 24"L

Dragon Weathervane, 23K gold leaf, 48"L

Beehive Weathervane, 23K gold leaf, 29"L   Mark Lennihan

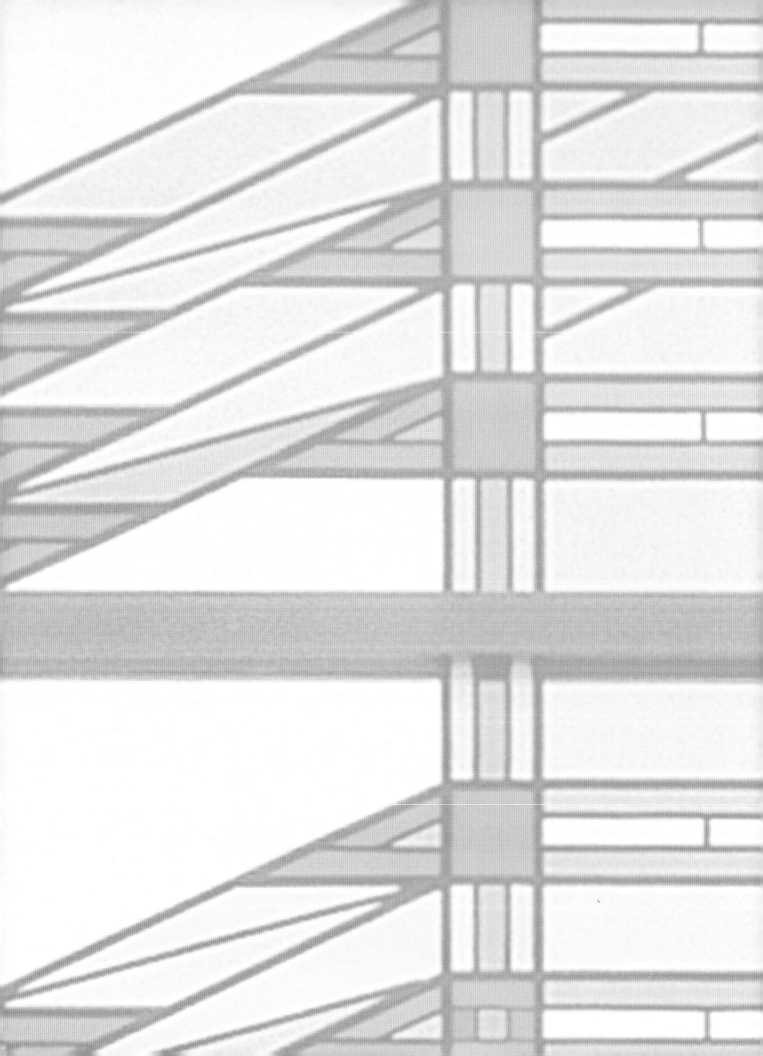

Murals & Trompe L'Oeil

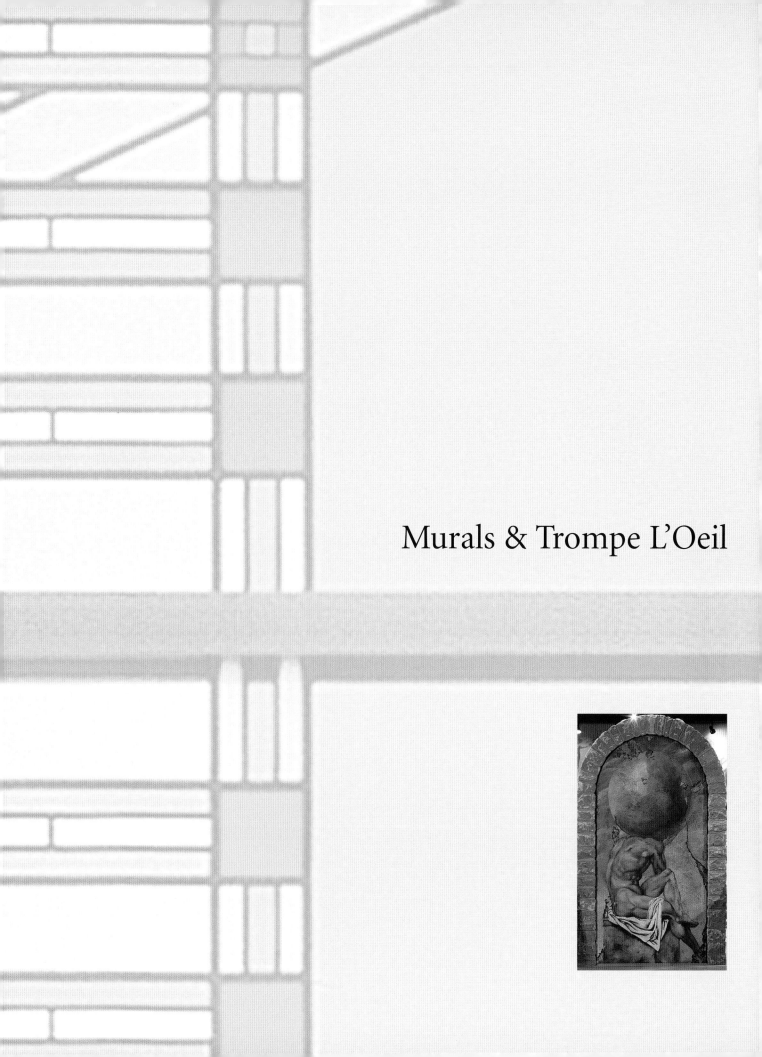

The Art Studio/Fine Art Murals

Atlas, 1998, oil on cracked plaster on plywood, retail men's clothing store, 9'H × 5'W

Temple of Athena, 1999, acrylic on curved drywall, private residence, 12'H × 14'W

The Great Age of Travel, 2000, acrylic on curved drywall, conference center, 10'H × 18'W

Photos: Roy White Photography

G. Byron Peck/City Arts

Metro Center mural, Washington, DC, 15' × 60'

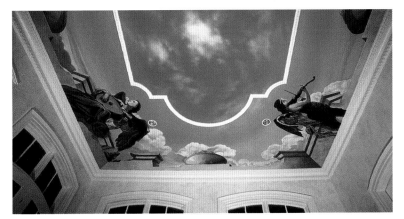

Music room mural, McLean, VA, 16' × 30'

Byron Peck

Stone Mill Elementary School mural, Bethesda, MD, 6' × 8'

Greg Staley

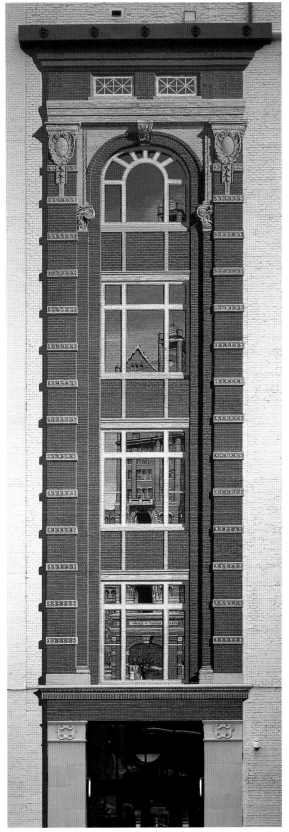

Miller Building mural, Knoxville, TN, 90' × 21'

Robert Batey

Wolfgang Gersch

Ceiling and wall mural, 2000, airbrushing, acrylic paints, mixed media, private residence, San Francisco, CA, ceiling: 20' × 40', wall area: 40' × 9'

Wolfgang Gersch

Kerin Lifland

Musical Instruments, 1999, marquetry panel, various wood veneers, 31"H × 55"W

Paneled study with marquetry, 1999, various woods, Los Angeles, CA, 12'H × 20'W × 18'D

Photos: Douglas Hill

Meamar

Ceiling dome fresco

Wall mural

Living room fresco (detail)

Living room fresco, private home, Saratoga, CA, 25' × 18'

Meamar

Bedroom mural, 10' × 22'

Wall mural

Ceiling fresco, private residence, CA

Mural over fireplace mantle, 18' × 10'

New World Productions

A Little Monkey Business (detail)   Eric Michael Hilton

A Little Monkey Business (detail)   Eric Michael Hilton

A Little Monkey Business, 2000, silicate paints on masonry, Sarasota, FL, 62' × 90'   Greg Wilson

John Pugh

Study with Sphere and Water, University Center, UNF, Jacksonville, FL, 12' × 30'

Neil Rashba

Woman in Café, Los Gatos, CA, 7' × 5'   Brian Brumley

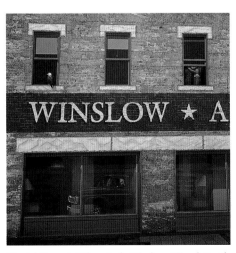

Slowin' Down to Take a Look, Winslow, AZ, 23' × 40'

Moss Canyon, Hall residence, Morgan Hill, CA, 20' × 14'

Brian Brumley

Susan Richter Todd

Hudson Valley, six panels, 6.67' × 18'

Humpback Whales, 8' × 40'

Photos: Richard Dentch

Elizabeth Thompson

The Debraake and the Twin Capes, 1997, acrylic on vinyl, Cape May Ferryboat, 8' × 37'

Carson Zullinger

Oakavenga Delta, 2000, oil on canvas, Metropolitan Life Building, New York, NY, 7' × 21'

James Dee

interior mural

ARTIST
Anne Marchand

DESCRIPTION
Dining room mural, acrylic
and latex paint, 6' × 11'

YEAR
1999

SITE
Godes residence, Washington, DC

TIMELINE
2 weeks

"The most exciting aspect of working on this wall was combining styles and techniques with muralist Freya Grand. The result was a blend of abstract design with landscape elements. The client wanted an abstract design that would bring her love of gardening into her living space and create an inviting place for dining. The play of abstract shapes immersed in the grassy spaces challenged my notions of real-world form versus enigmatic shapes to evoke mystery and poetry. When applied to the wall, the glazing technique that I had developed in earlier acrylic paintings gave the piece a depth and richness of soft color that thrilled me."

favorite commissions

Sheryl VanderPol

Old World fruit still life on commercial ceramic tile

Transformed commercial sink

Wall mural

Trompe l'oeil shutters, pillars and archway view

Photos: Greg Page/Page Photography

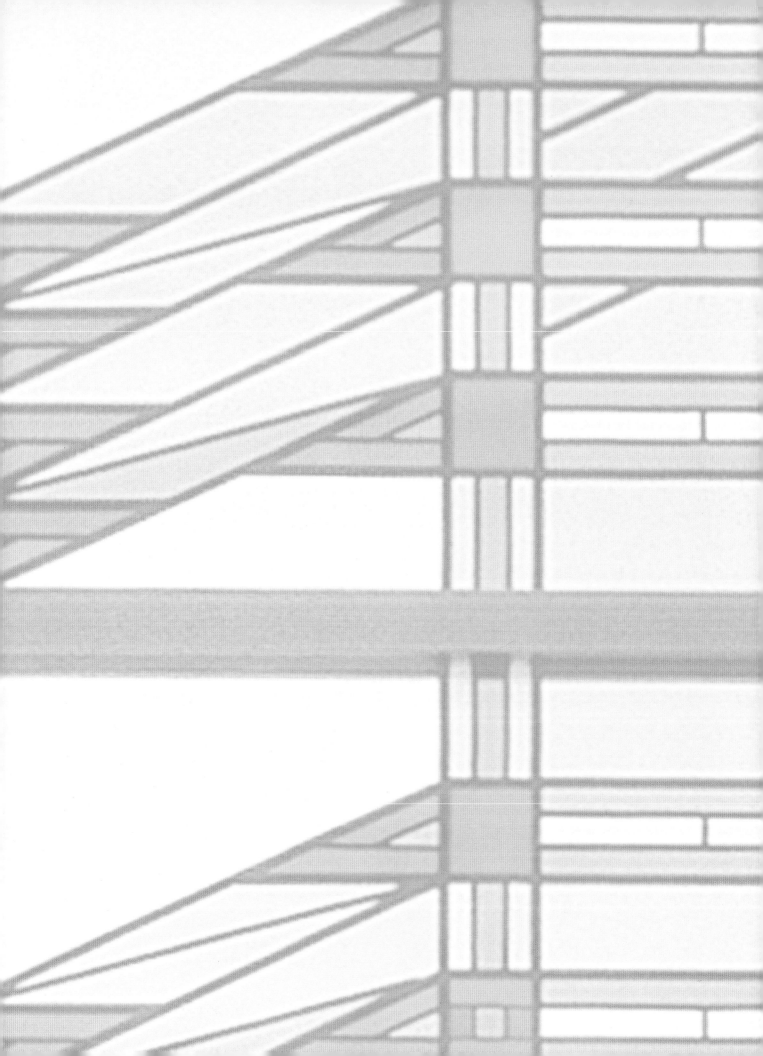

Atrium Sculpture

Airworks Inc.

Trees of Knowledge, wire screen, copper, aluminum, Lexan, sunscreen, 14'w × 16'D × 26'H

Trees of Knowledge

Parhelion (detail), coated sunscreen, fiberglass bar, 10 units, each: 24'w × 6'H × 1"D

Rob Fisher

Weather or Not, 2000, The Penn Stater Conference Center Hotel

Tracy Hanselman

Patterns of Nature, 2000, stainless steel and aluminum, Presidential Towers, Chicago, IL, 11'H × 12'W × 2'D

Saverio Truglia

Patterns of Nature

Saverio Truglia

Jonathan Clowes Sculpture

Confluence, 2000, mahogany and painted aluminum, 10.5'H × 2.5'W

Jeffrey Baird

Atrium Sculpture

Jill Casty

Jeremy Elliott

Trent Foltz

One part of a three-part installation for Northwest Plaza, St. Louis, MO, layered Plexiglas, painted aluminum, 1' × 10.5' and 2' × 18', total width: 8'; inset: *Sunrise/Sunset*, entry sculpture, City of Montclair, CA, painted aluminum, Plexiglas, 20'H × 13'W

Rich Griendling

University of Kentucky Children's Hospital (detail)

University of Kentucky Children's Hospital, 1998, plaster, steel, oils and light, life-size

Nolin Rural Electric Cooperative, 1998, plaster, steel and light, life-size

Spine Surgery, P.S.C., 1992, plaster and steel, life-size

John Charles Gordon Studios, Inc.

3-Part Wood, Sharp Healthcare Corporate Offices, San Diego, CA, mahogany and stained glass, each piece: 6' × 18' × 6"

DNA Action, The Schaetzel Center for Health Education, Scripps Memorial Hospital, La Jolla, CA, aluminum, bleached Irish linen, 10' × 10' × 80'

Photos: Departure Studio

Robert Pfitzenmeier

Petals, 1999, polychromed aluminum and stainless steel,
Texel Corporation, Reston, VA, 12'H × 26'W × 12'D

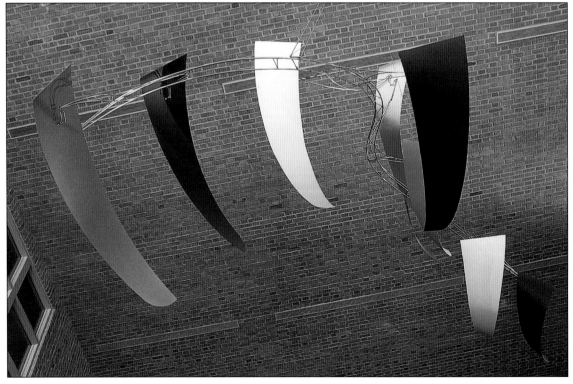

Blue Blossoms, 1999, polychromed aluminum and stainless steel, Pharmacia Upjohn, Peapack, NJ, 16'H × 15'W × 9'D

Timothy Rose

Water/fish/bird, full view, mobile construction, 2000, South Carolina Aquarium, Charleston, SC, 180' × 15' × 9'

Water/fish/bird (detail)

Water/fish/bird (detail)

Photos: Kim Gissendanner

Sable Studios

Dawn of Spring's Bouquet, 2000, acrylic, City Hall, Hayward, CA, 15' × 15' × 18'

Photos: Paul Sable

Spectral Spiral, 1998, acrylic, Lucent Technologies, FL, 10' × 10' × 16'

Sky Ballet, acrylic, Metro Plaza, San Jose, CA, 4' × 6' × 17'

Spectral Arc, 1998, acrylic wall hanging, Lucent Technologies, FL, 4' × 5' × 11'

Joy Wulke

Hell's Fire, 1995, glass, stainless steel, light, Joliet, IL, five units, each: 4' × 14' × 14'

Spirit Flight, 1996, fabric, stainless steel, Middletown, CT, 30'H × 60'W × 60'D

Photos: Joy Wulke

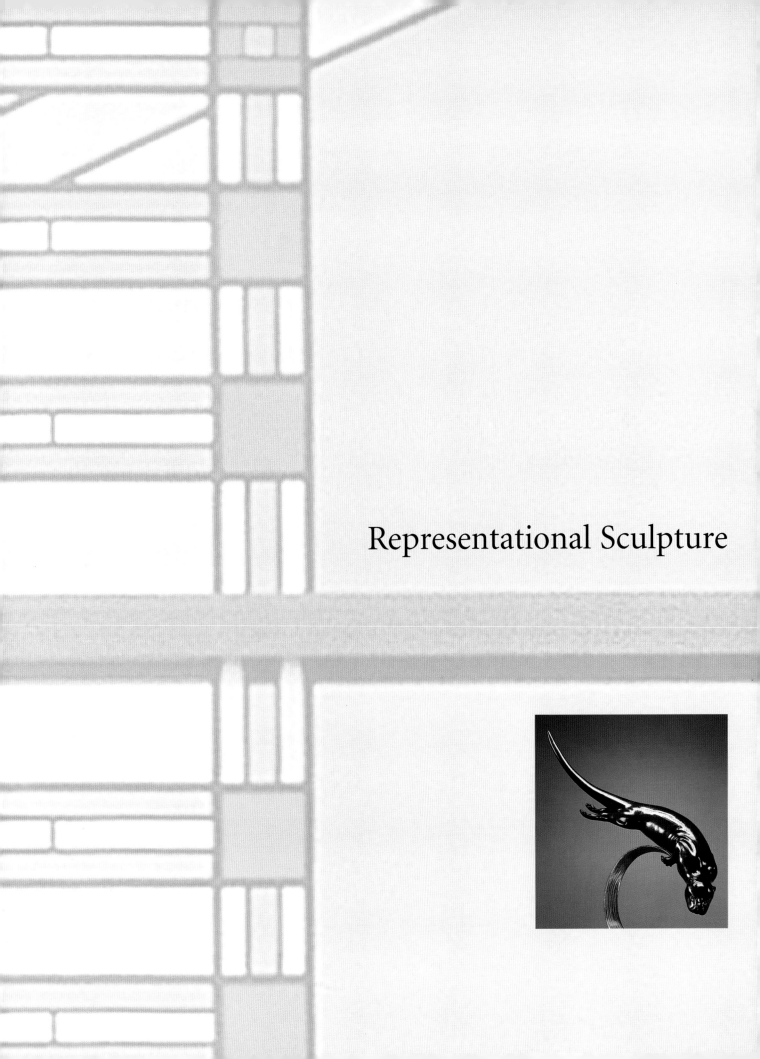

Representational Sculpture

James Barnhill

Robin (detail), bronze, 39"H

Representational Sculpture

Barney Boller

Blindsided, 2000, bronze, stainless steel, 92" × 40" × 36", edition of 8

Torpedo, 1999, bronze, 24" × 36" × 24", edition of 20

Longneck Battle, 2000, bronze, 14" × 13" × 13", edition of 30

Photos: Storm Photo

Eric Boyer

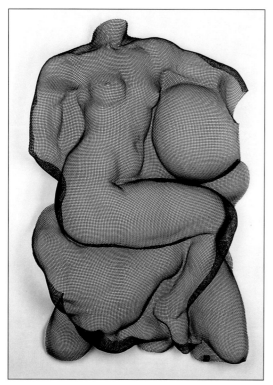

Casseiopeia, steel wire mesh, 30"H × 18"W × 4"D

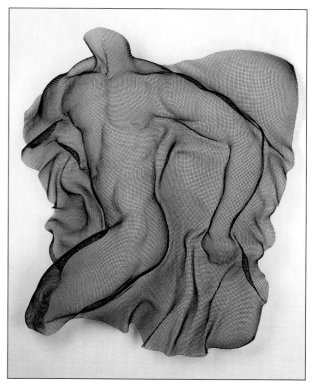

Running Draped Male Torso, steel wire mesh, 22"H × 20"W × 4"D

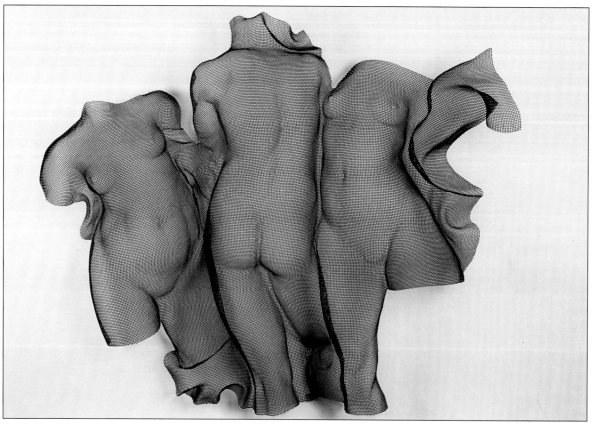

Three Graces, steel wire mesh, 20"H × 30"W × 5"D

Photos: Jeff Baird

Ann L. Deluty

Red Shell, 1998, tiger eye alabaster on marble base, 18"H × 8"w × 7"D

Orange Delight, 1999, translucent alabaster on marble base, 18"H × 11"w × 9"D

Whales, 1999, cockscomb alabaster on marble base, 10.5"H × 17.5"w × 10.5"D

Catherine K. Ferrell

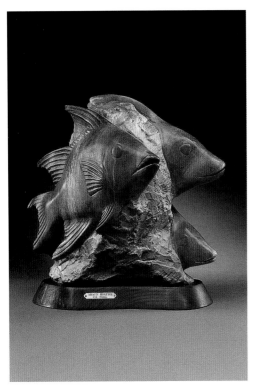

Abaco Hogfish, bronze, 14" × 14" × 8"

Just Kidding Around, bronze, 17" × 11" × 17"

Rejoice, bronze, edition of 20, 16" × 10" × 10", larger sizes available

Elizabeth Guarisco

Power Player, bronze, 21" × 24" × 12"

The Wind & The Arabian Stallion, bronze, 11" × 11" × 10"

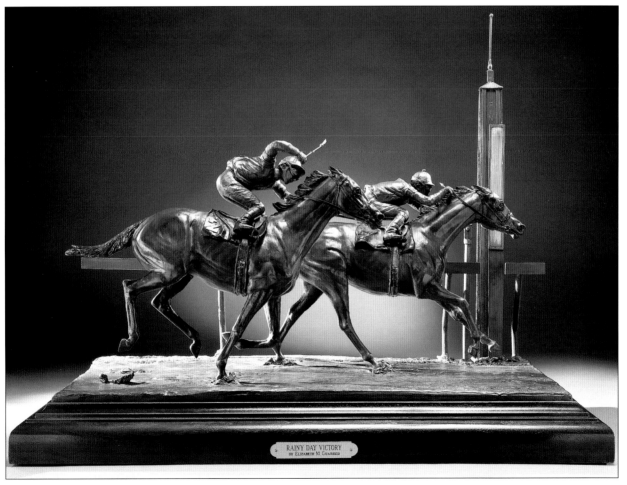

Rainy Day Victory, bronze, 19.5" × 24" × 14"

Robert Holmes

She Dances, 42" × 34" × 5" (30" base)

On Thin Ice, 72" × 106" × 115"

Rhapsody, 96" × 48" × 42"

Just Dancing, 124" × 36" × 28"

Representational Sculpture

Barry Woods Johnston

My Future Prince, 2000, bronze

Photos: Barry Woods Johnston

John Kennedy

Mother and Child, 2000, Oxford Museum,
Oxford, England, 7'H

Scott Van Dyke

Metamorphosis, 1999, Barbara Sinatra Children's
Center, Palm Desert, CA, bronze, 7'H × 12'W

Bradley Hanson

Amore, 1999, bronze, 7'H

Bradley Hanson

Tuck Langland

Resting Dancer, life-size bronze, edition of 7

Dance of Awakening Day, bronze figure, 44", edition of 10

Memory: though they are gone, their impressions remain, bronze, 8.5', edition of 7

Solitude, bronze, 50", edition of 10

Jafe Parsons, Loveland, CO

Alan LeQuire

Athena Parthenos, 1982-1990, gypsum, fiberglass and steel, 42'ʜ

Swimmers, 1989, bronze, 5'ʜ

Flying Torso, 1994, bronze, 64"ʜ

Carrie, 1997, bronze, life-size, edition of 6

Bj. Michaelis

Mommy, do you know about the birds & bees?, bronze, 9"ʜ,
limited edition of 35

Mommy, do you know about the birds & bees?

Let's go fly a Kite, 1999, bronze, Bethany Lutheran Village, Dayton, OH,
45"ʜ

Hometown Girl, 1999, bronze,
Englewood, OH, 5.5'ʜ

Photos: Larry E. Michaelis

aerial sculptures

ARTIST
Jill Casty

DESCRIPTION
Fifteen sets of Plexiglas
and painted aluminum aerial
sculptures for three different
site locations

YEAR
2000

SITE
Northwest Plaza, St. Louis, MO

COMMISSIONING AGENT
Westfield Corporation

TIMELINE
3 months

"This site's problems turned out to be a positive stimulus for pleasing aesthetic solutions. Three rectangular courts were a real challenge — huge, heavy gray grids were overhead, and a hectic melange of colors, shapes and materials were all around.

How to go serene but strong enough? Plexiglas. It's festive yet soft, with soothing colors — just the right calming, humanizing presence in that visual din. For enough size for a definite impact, I used pairs of vertical groupings of Plexiglas up to 18 feet long. But to play against the heavy, busy surroundings, I fragmented each grouping into separated segments of varying lengths, getting a light, openwork counterpoint."

favorite commissions

R.W. McBride

Flushed Out II and III, 32" wingspan

Incomprehensible Circumstance, 82" wingspan

Buffalo Keeper, 32"ʜ

Play Time, 10'ʜ

Photos: Jeffery Dow Photography

National Sculptors' Guild

Spring Plumage, bronze, Leigh Yawkey Woodson Museum, Wausau, WI, 60"H, edition of 12, sculptor: Kent Ullberg

Jafe Parsons

Polished Performance, City of Paramount, CA, 60"H, sculptor: Dee Clements

Julia Clements

Windsong, bronze, 96"H, edition of 10, sculptor: Leo E. Osborne

Chris Sherman

Freedom Series, set of three bronzes, 67"H, edition of 10, sculptor: Denny Haskew

Mel Schockner

Rite of Passage, City of Avon, CO, 1.6 life-size, edition of 5, sculptor: Sandy Scott

Jafe Parsons

ARTIST
Michele vandenHeuvel

TITLE
Kimo

YEAR
1999–2000

DESCRIPTION
Bronze sculpture, 5.5'h seated

SITE
Kimo Park, Albuquerque, NM, and Washingtonian Plaza, Gaithersburg, MD

COMMISSIONING AGENT
City of Albuquerque, NM, and City of Gaithersburg, MD

TIMELINE
Approximately 8 months for both projects

"This project was most enjoyable for me because it gave me the opportunity to place *Kimo,* the large bronze cat seated "human-style" on a park bench, in two different locations. One edition was placed in my hometown of Albuquerque, NM, and the other was placed in Gaithersburg, MD. Both places totally fulfilled for me what I feel sculpture, and public art in particular, are all about — work that is joyful and touchable and therefore hopefully unites us as a community. I knew I had accomplished the goal of my sculpture when I saw the community appeal of this piece in two very different settings — everyone wants to sit with Kimo, to touch him and visit with him and each other."

favorite commissions

Meltdown Glass Art & Design LLC

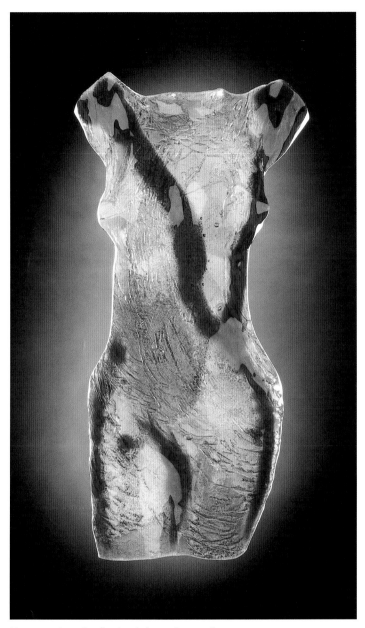

Torso, cast, draped and painted glass, 30"H × 16"W

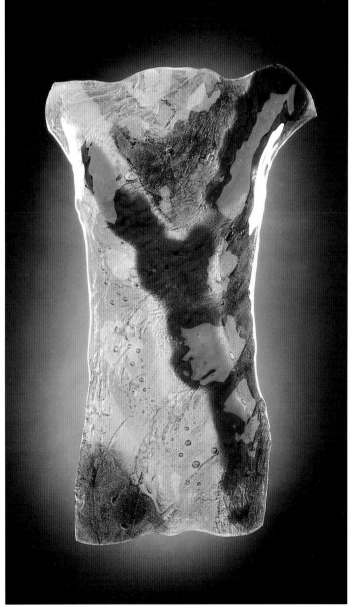

Torso, cast, draped and painted glass, 35"H × 18"W

Photos: David Hedrich

Martha Pettigrew

Bison, bronze, commissioned by The Irvine Company, Newport Beach, CA, 8'H, edition of five

Running Horse, bronze, commissioned by J.P. Morgan Investment Management, Inc., Gale and Wentworth, LLC, Somerset Financial Center, Bedminster, NJ, 88"H × 150"L, edition of five

Peter Jacobs

Delmar Pettigrew

Catch of the Day, bronze, 19"H × 26"L, edition of 15

Catch of the Day

Not Speaking, bronze and steel, 60"H, edition of 15

ARTIST
Martha Pettigrew

DESCRIPTION
Bronze sculpture for Pereira Bonita
Canyon Redevelopment, 96"H × 120"L

YEAR
2000

SITE
Corner of MacArthur and Bonita Canyon
roads, Newport Beach, CA

COMMISSIONING AGENT
EPT Landscape Architecture, agent
for Irvine Community Development
Company

TIMELINE
1 year

"This was the first major commission I received. It would not have happened if I hadn't placed an advertisement in *The Architect's Sourcebook 12*. Having this commission on my resume has been helpful in receiving other commissions, including a recent project for the J.P. Morgan Company."

favorite commissions

Paula Slater Sculpture

Life is a Journey, life-size clay sculptures to be cast in bronze, Desert Dreams, Fountain Hills, AZ

Craig Eve

Spiritual Warrior, limited-edition bronze, 28"H

Gentle Wisdom, life-size bronze, also available as 22"H limited-edition bronze

David L. Phelps

Voyagers, 1994, bronze, 8" × 49" × 9", also available as a large-scale bronze

Nancy, 1999, bronze, 35" × 123" × 73", also available as a smaller bronze

Jane Rankin

Join the Parade, life size, limited edition of 10

Morris the Dragon, 4'h × 5'w × 7'l, limited edition of 7

Toadly Cool, life size, limited edition of 20

Jacqueline L. Spellens

Nkanyit, alabaster, two-thirds life-size   Lang Photography

Zapotek, Siena marble, three-quarters life-size   Lang Photography

The Bath, Utah alabaster, one-half life-size   Jacqueline L. Spellens

Gerald Siciliano

Associates Sculpture, bronze and steel, American Axle & Manufacturing Company, life-size

History Panel I, stainless steel, American Axle & Manufacturing Company, 4' × 10'

Taracor Fine Art Consulting

Out of the Blue, bronze, 50"ʜ × 44"ᴡ × 39"ᴅ, edition of 18, artist: Ken Rowe   Christopher Marchetti

Spring Songs, bronze, 5.5'ʜ, edition of 15, artist: Bob Piercey   Al Abrams

Ellen Tykeson

Treasure, 2001, heroic-scale bronze, Southwest Community Church, Palm Desert, CA, male figure: 6.75'H, overall size: 12'H × 9'L × 4'D

Photos: David Simone

Bruce Wolfe

St. Francis, original clay, to be bronzed for Santa Barbara Mission, 7.5'ʜ

Classic medallion in bronze commemorating Edward Ageno, 28"ᴅɪᴀ

Clay study, head of Ann as reference for bronze of Mary and Ann, life size

Eve (maquette), bronze, study for life size, 24"ʜ

Bruce Wolfe

St. Jude, 2000, bronze, antique ivory patina, St. Mary's College, life size

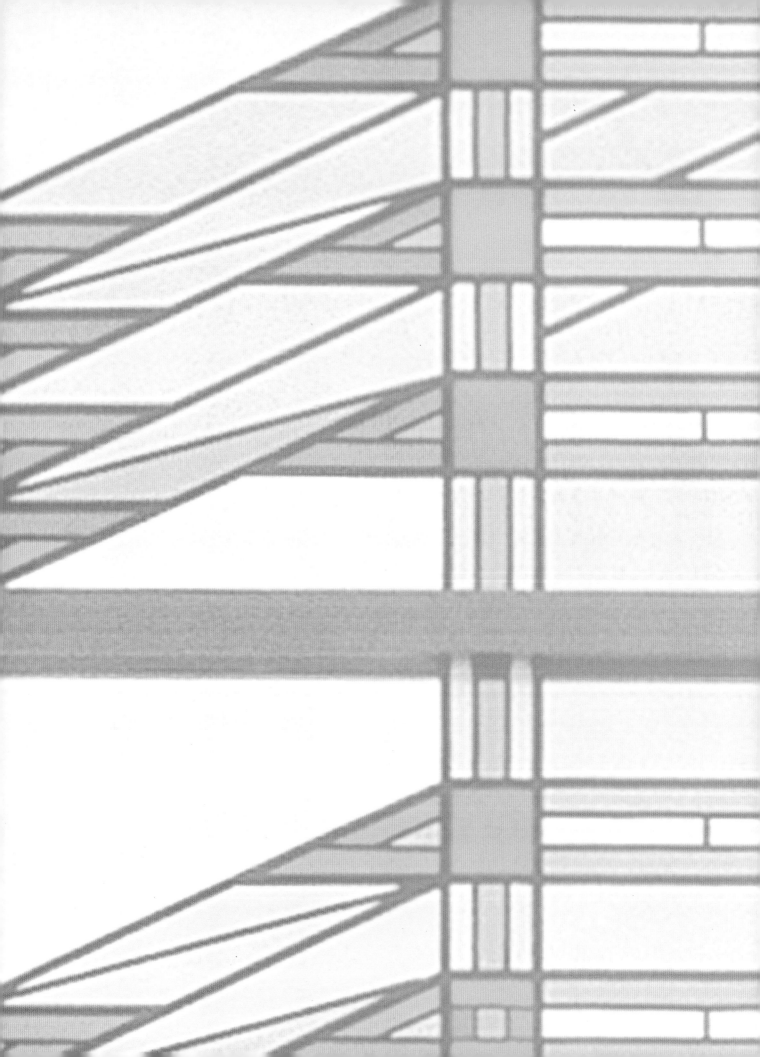

Non-Representational Sculpture

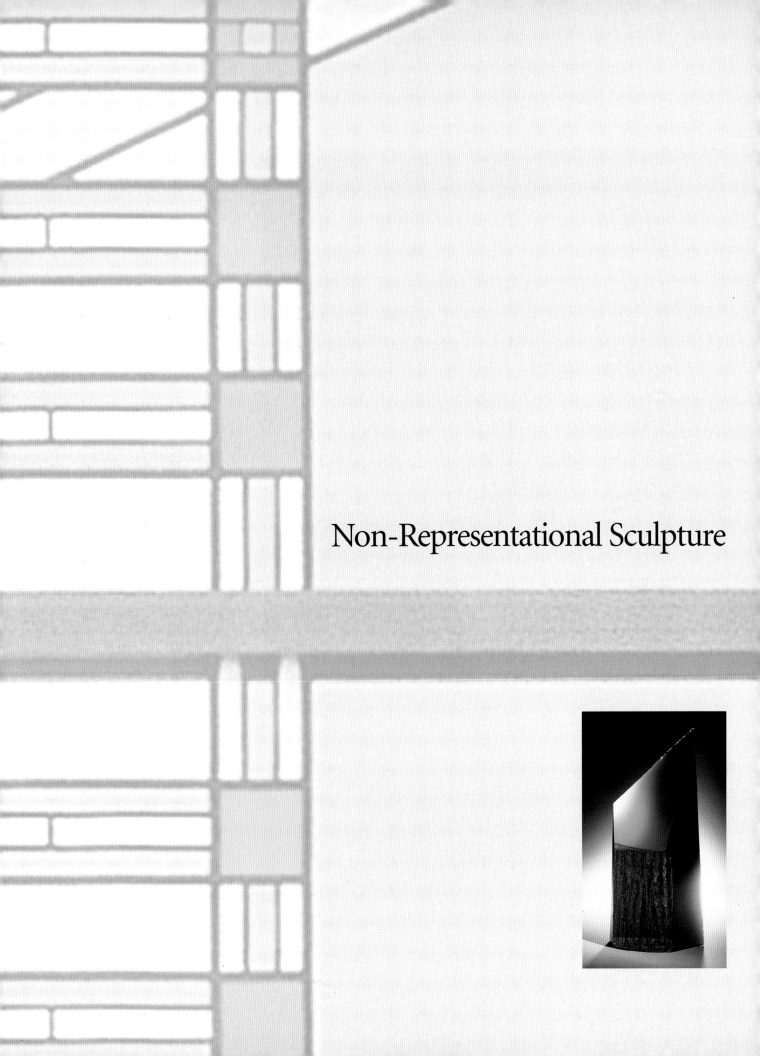

sculpture

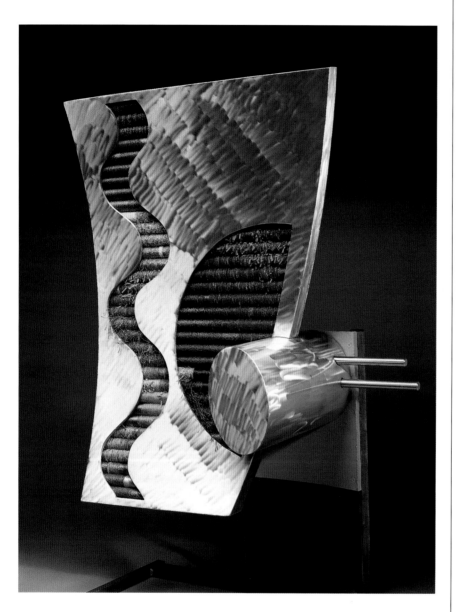

ARTIST
Myra Burg

TITLES
Galactic Curve (left) and
Japonaise (below)

YEAR
2000

DESCRIPTION
Wall sculptures of natural and synthetic
fiber, twigs, jute and burnished aluminum;
Galactic Curve: 3' × 4' × 18"
Japonaise: 3' × 6' × 5"

SITE
Universal Studios Japan, Osaka, Japan

COMMISSIONING AGENT
Universal Creative

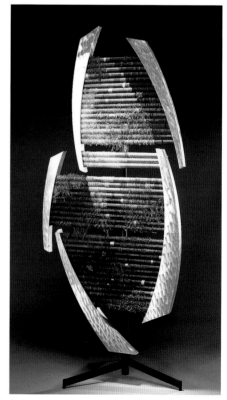

"Usually, my work and color are fitted to the surrounding space. This project was unusual in that the client treated me like royalty, fitting their interiors and colors around my choices. One of the designers came to my studio and helped me with the color and material selection. The two of us spent four hours clipping two samples of each of several hundred colors that went into the work. These two sample kits enabled the team in Japan to work with color months before my wrapping process began. They treated me like a celebrity, and I was deeply honored."

favorite commissions

Archie Held Studio

Entry, 1999, bronze and water, 162"H × 61"W × 23"D

Jay Graham

Barbara Butler Artist-Builder

The Canyon Perch, 2000, 25.5'ʟ × 20.5'ᴡ × 27'ʜ (including 8'ʜ tree stump)

The Atherton Clubhouse, 1999, 14.5'ʟ × 6'ᴡ × 17'ʜ

The Hillside Hamlet, 1999, 46'ʟ × 40'ᴡ × 17'ʜ

Photos: Teena Albert

Non-Representational Sculpture

Michael D. Bigger

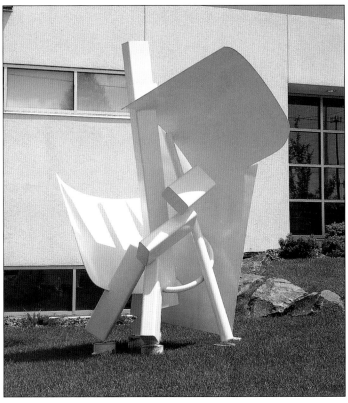

OZONA, 1997, welded steel coated with polyurethane, Minneapolis, MN, 12'ʜ

MARFA, 1998, welded steel coated with polyurethane, El Paseo, Palm Desert, CA, 8'ʜ

POR TIERRA, 2000, welded steel coated with polyurethane, Minneapolis, MN, 16'ʟ

Photos: M.D. Bigger

Rita Blitt

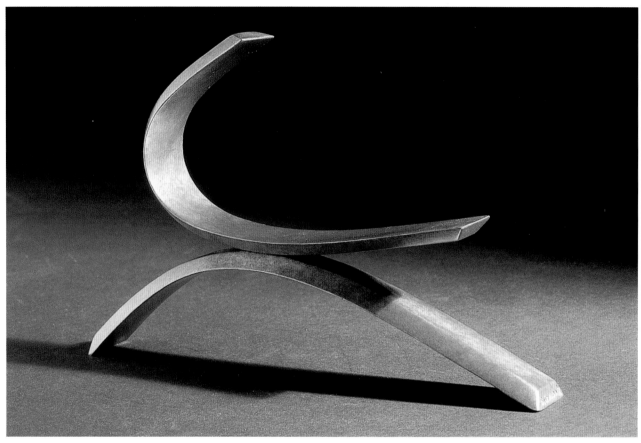

Passionate Gesture II, 2000, bronze

Passionate Gestures, 2000, bronze; opposite page: *Passionate Gesture I,* 2000, bronze

Photos: Joe Schopplein

Jeanine Briggs

Wired, 2000, metal, wire, wood

Shifting Gears, 2000, metal

Southwest I, 2000, wood

Photos: Maximage

Riis Burwell

Entropy Series #42, 1999, bronze, 48" × 20" × 8"

Syncronetic Variation #2, 2000, bronze, 12" × 12" × 36"

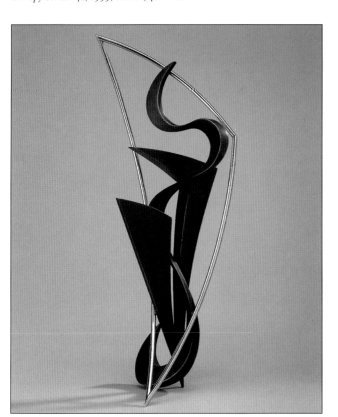

Syncronetic, 1998, bronze, 24" × 10" × 8"

Entropy Series #37, 2000, bronze, 42" × 32" × 10"

Photos: Bruce Shippee

L.T. Cherokee

Face Off, resin-bonded concrete, 7.5' × 5' × 3'

The Threat©, bronze, 7' × 4' × 4.6', edition of 7

The Dreamer©, bronze, stone, stainless steel, 56" × 13" × 7", edition of 7

Non-Representational Sculpture

Jeremy R. Cline

Birds of Paradise, blown glass, 33"H to 38"H

Photos: Latchezar Boyadjiev

Richard Erdman

Spring, 1996, Portuguese marble, Four Seasons Park, Singapore, 10' × 4' × 3'

Richard Erdman

Aria, 2000, Pakistan onyx, private collection, 35" × 20" × 18"

Rinehold Kohl

Passage, 1985, travertine, PepsiCo Sculpture Gardens, Purchase, NY, 25' × 16' × 8'

Richard Erdman

Lois Key Giffen

Mother with Baby, kinetic sculpture, 14" × 20" × 8"

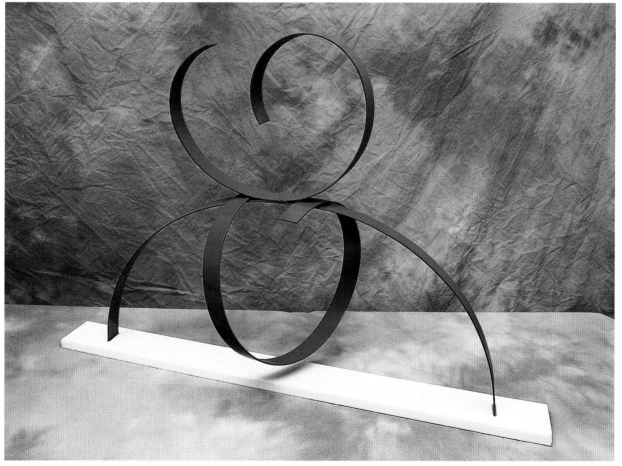

Big Blue, steel, marble, 30" × 24" × 4"

Photos: Bill Keogh

Brower Hatcher

Fan, 1999, glass, stainless steel, iron, 144" × 36" × 72"

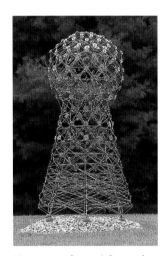

Tower, 1999, glass, stainless steel, iron, 120" × 60" × 60"

Wave, 1999, glass, stainless steel, iron, 264" × 72" × 40"

Radial Light, 2000, glass, stone, stainless steel, 168" × 48" × 96"

Photos: Sarah Carmod·

Helaman Ferguson, Sculptor

Eightfold Way, white marble, black serpentine, hyperbolic tiling, 6' × 6' × 6', 3 tons

Jon Ferguson

Four Canoes, linked Klein bottles, red and black granite, rusticated hexagon plaza, 6' × 25' × 29', 12 tons

Sam Ferguson

Michael Jacobsen

Interactive: Flight of Fantasy, 2000, granite, 112"H × 54"W × 32"D

Michael Jacobsen

Norma Lewis

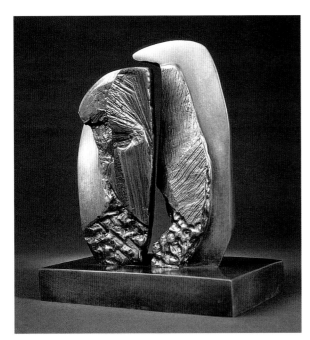

On Ice, bronze, 45"H

Seadance, bronze, 32"H

Calypso, bronze, 44"H

Photos: Bob Kohlbrener

James C. Myford

Sing, 2000, aluminum, 10' × 10' × 3'

Rising Forms, 1999, painted aluminum, 10' × 3' × 3'

Single Elongated Form, 2000, painted aluminum, 35" × 6" × 5"

Family, 1999, aluminum, 9' × 4' × 3'

James C. Nagle

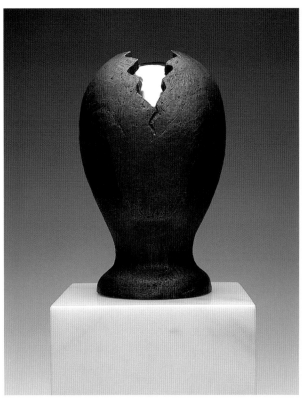

Split Personality, bronze, total size: 18"H

Having A Ball, bronze, total size: 15"H

Auspicious Offering, alabaster, bronze, juniper,
23"H × 18"W × 12"D

Photos: Craig Smith

Henry B. Richardson

Tikkun, hollow fractured glass, 6'DIA, 5000 lbs.   M. Hershman

Coming of Age, 1999, solid fractured glass, 5'DIA, 8000 lbs.

Non-Representational Sculpture

Joel O'Dorisio

Wild Cherry, 1999, cast glass, 18" × 12" × 6"

Birch, 2000, cast glass, 20" × 14" × 4"

White Pine Spire, 1998, cast glass, 24" × 14" × 7"

Photos: Frank Burkowski

ARTIST
Richard Erdman

TITLE
Passage

YEAR
1983-1985

DESCRIPTION
Italian travertine sculpture,
25' × 16' × 8'

SITE
The Donald M. Kendall Sculpture
Gardens at PepsiCo, Purchase, NY

COMMISSIONING AGENT
PepsiCo, Inc.
(Donald M. Kendall, CEO)

TIMELINE
2 years

"The single most interesting — and daunting — aspect of creating the sculpture *Passage* was its size. In every aspect of the project, from cutting the original block in Italy to transporting the finished sculpture to New York, meticulous and creative attention had to be given at each turn.

A 300-ton, 26' x 16' x 9' block of travertine was felled from the Tivoli quarry — twice, since the first attempt resulted in cracks. Initial shaping in the quarry was required to reduce the weight to a buoyant 120 tons, allowing for the sculpture's transport on a special 74-wheel rig to my Carrara studio.

After 20 months of carving, a virtual house was built around the complete sculpture for its transatlantic passage to the PepsiCo gardens. Upon arrival in New York, a midnight ride of the crate through Manhattan made for a hair-raising evening, and the longest tire change I have witnessed.

Final installation required two cranes, while two years of work rested in the fingertips of the crane operators. My relief upon the successful completion of this project was surely proportional to its weight in tonnage!"

Thomas Alex Osika

Reflection, 1998, bronze, private collection, Greenwich, CT, 8'ʜ, edition of five

Dryad, 1999, bronze, private collection, Greenwich, CT, 5'ʜ, edition of seven

Arisaema (maquette), 1999, black walnut, private collection, Washington, DC

Tree of Life (maquette), 2000, black walnut

Pozycinski Studios

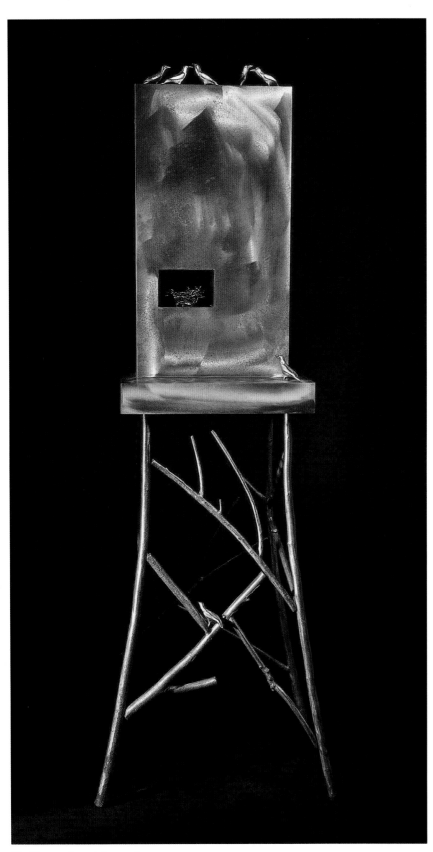

Rhino Cabinet, 20" × 12" × 3.5"

The Nest, 61.5" × 16.5" × 14.5"

Fish Fountain, 63" × 24" × 12"

Kevin B. Robb

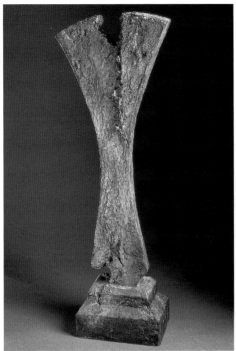

Dead Sea Series B, 1999, cast bronze, 28" × 8" × 5"

John Bonath

Falling Blocks, 2000, fabricated bronze, 40" × 21" × 18"

John Bonath

Toy Blocks II, 1999, stainless steel, 121" × 40" × 32"

Kevin B. Robb

Swan Dance, 2000, stainless steel, 94" × 36" × 29"

Kevin B. Robb

Brian F. Russell

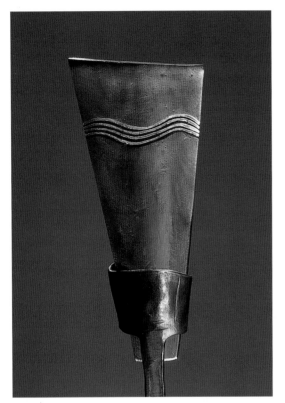

Red Wedge (detail), 2000, forged bronze and cast glass,
12" × 30" × 72"

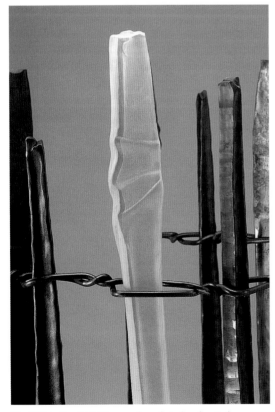

The Will to Live (detail), 1999, forged steel and cast glass,
30" × 30" × 72"

Red Bone 1, 1999, forged steel and cast glass, 14" × 30" × 84"

Richard Taylor

When I Lift You Up, 2000, aluminum, Imron, Mount Vernon, IL, 11' × 6' × 5'

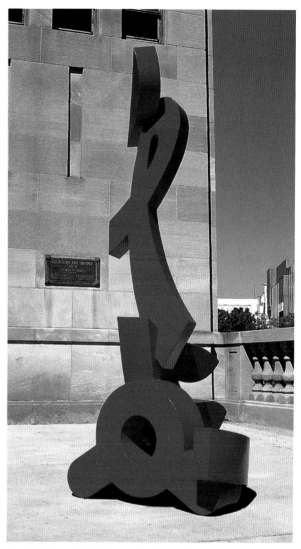

You Rise Above the World, 1999, aluminum, Imron, Milwaukee Riverwalk, 11' × 5' × 4'

As Rock to Hope, 2000, aluminum, Imron, 3.5' × 10.5' × .5'

Photos: Richard Taylor

James Thomas Russell

Counterpoint, © 1985, polished stainless steel, Big Canyon Country Club, Newport Beach, CA, 11'w

Eternal Spring, © 2000, polished stainless steel, Enlight Corporation and the City of Santa Fe Springs, Santa Fe Springs, CA, 14'H

Millennium, © 1999, polished stainless steel, Westborough Corridor, City of South San Francisco, CA, 12'H

John Wong

Non-Representational Sculpture

James Thomas Russell

Voyage to Excellence, © 1999, polished stainless steel, Western Oregon University, Monmouth, OR, 14'H   Sharon Shute

Strong-Cuevas

Tower, 1994, bronze, green patina, 20" × 15" × 14"

Lightning I, "Jazz," 1992, bronze, antique black patina, stainless steel, glass eye, 27" × 11" × 10"

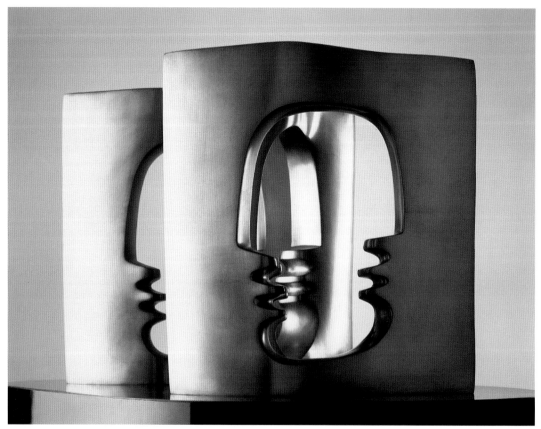

Arch II, Set V (small), 1989, bronze, light antique black patina, 13" × 22" × 17"; opposite page: *Look Twice,* 1997, stainless steel, one moving element, 8.5' × 8.5' × 5'

Photos: Renate Pfliederer

Non-Representational Sculpture

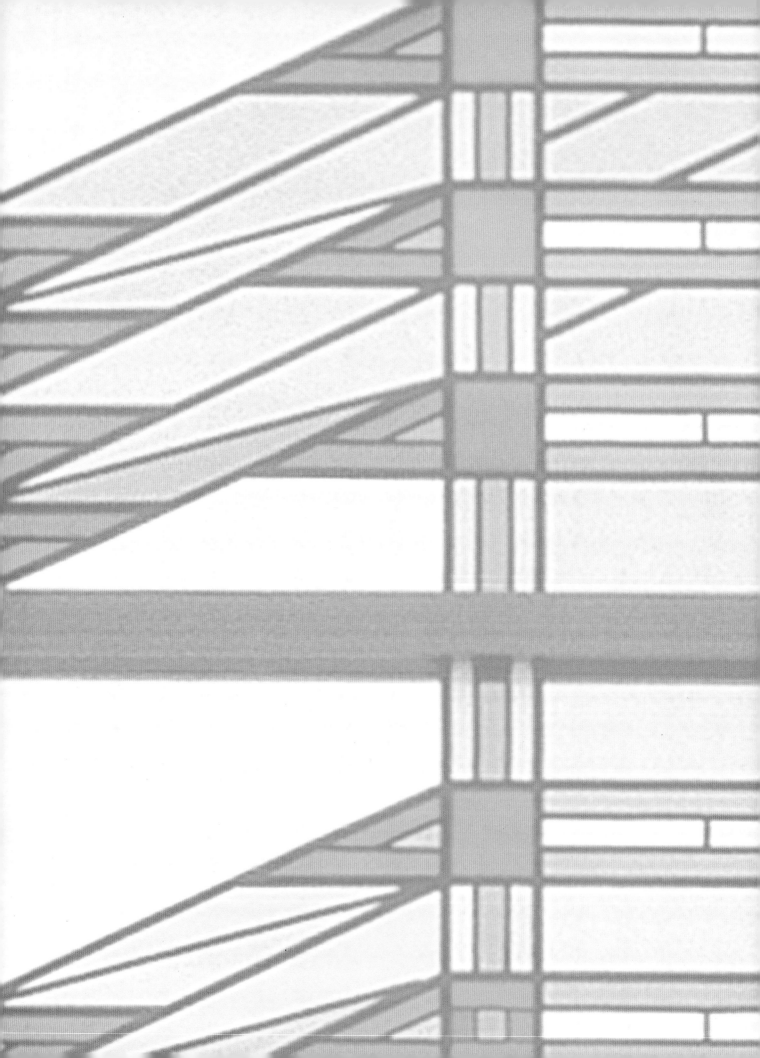

Public Art

Dana Lynne Andersen, M.A.

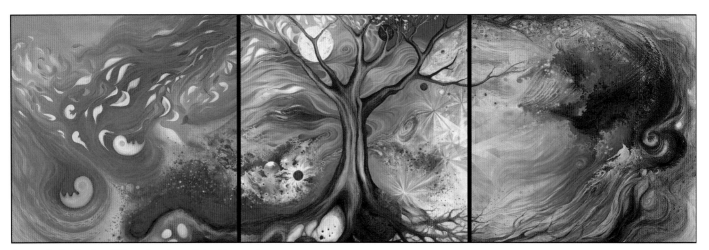

Autumn in the Garden of Eden, triptych, total size: 8' × 24.5'

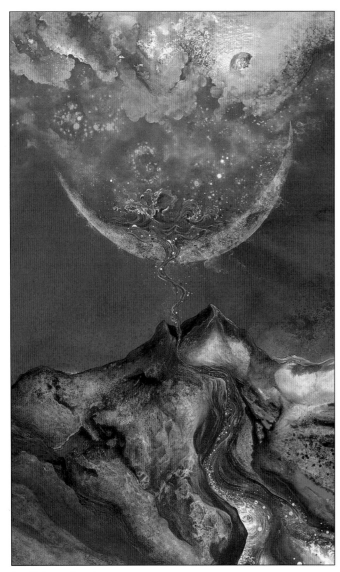

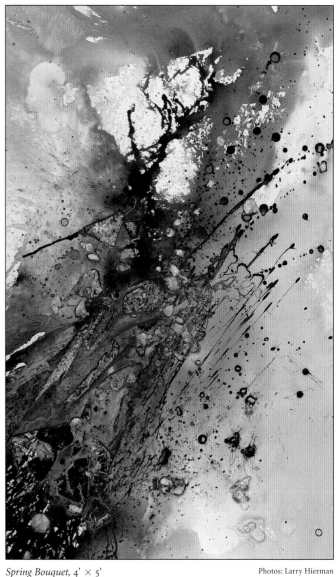

Swadisthana, 4' × 5'

Spring Bouquet, 4' × 5'

Photos: Larry Hierman

Tobey Archer

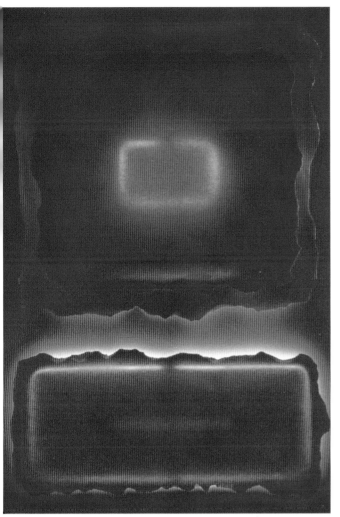

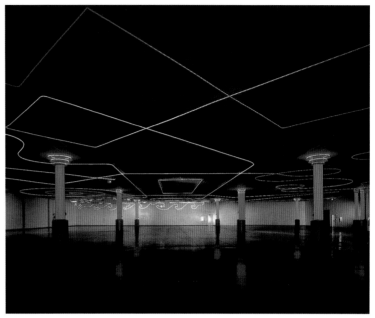

Calypso, 1998, Public Art and Design Program, The Great Hall, Port Everglades Terminal 2, Fort Lauderdale, FL, 26,200' sq.

Chuck Wilkins

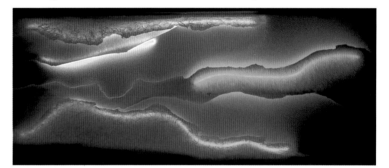

Homage, neon, sculpted papers, Lucite, 45" × 31" × 5"

Dawn Horizon, neon, sculpted papers, Lucite, 23" × 58" × 5"

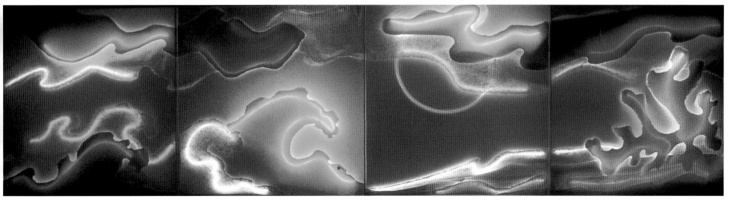

Atlantic Illuminations Quartet, Florida Atlantic University, Florida Art in State Buildings Program, each section: 4' × 4' × 5"

Matthew A. Berg V

Children of the World, 2000, stainless steel, glass, Indianapolis, IN, 16'DIA, 18'H (including pedestal)

Bear, 1997, steel, Minneapolis, MN, 25'H × 26'L × 7'W

Children of the World

Photos: Robert Ruldolph

Leslie C. Birleson

Tumbleweed, Red Rock Country Club, Las Vegas, NV, 8' × 22" × 11"

Traveling Light, large-scale installation, Sacramento International Airport, 180'ʟ × 12'ʜ

Glen Korengold

Found Beacons, indoor installation, Sacramento Metropolitan Utilities District, 15'ᴡ × 40'ʟ

Crystal Wall, M. Heller Collection, Sacramento, CA, 12 stacked cubes, each: 1'

Jeffrey Cooper

Olde Florida Portico and *Two Manatees Bench*, Jan Kaminis Platt Library, Tampa, FL

William C. Culbertson

Time Piece, 1994, Granite Thoro System, Garland, TX, 20' × 4' × 4'

The Shepard Historical Columns

The Shepard Historical Columns (detail)

The Shepard Historical Columns (detail), 1999, mixed media with neon lighting, five pieces, each: 8' × 2' × 2'

Bill FitzGibbons

Daystar Arch, 1999-2000, jet airliner wings, fiber optics, mixed media, San Antonio International Airport, San Antonio, TX, 40'h × 35'w

Douglas Olmsted Freeman

The Fountain of the Wind (detail), Duluth, MN, 35' × 35'

The Fountain of the Wind (detail), Duluth, MN

Photos: Jerry Mathiason

Stephanie Gassman

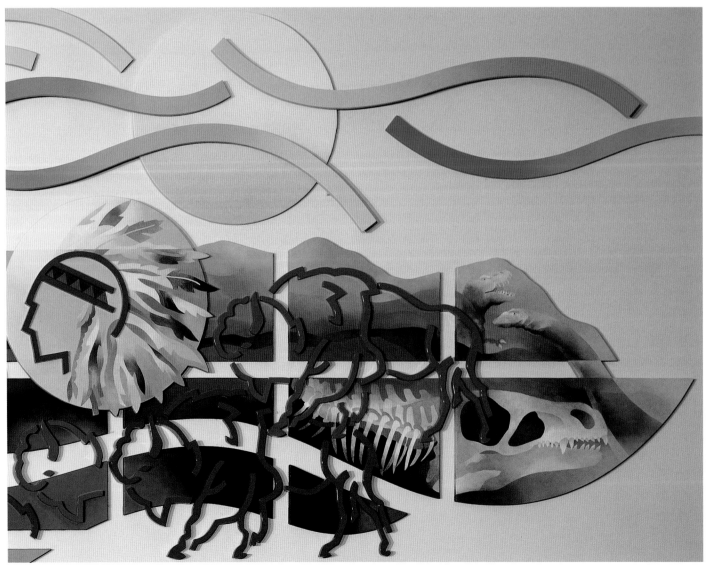

Wall relief (full view and detail), 2000, Montana State University-Great Falls, 8'ʜ × 30'ᴡ × 3"ᴅ

Photos: McMillan Studio

Public Art

George Mossman Greenamyer

Atlantic City Air, Victorian airplane detail, 1999, painted aluminum, each wind indicator: 20'H × 12'L × 4'W

Atlantic City Air, contemporary and mid-1940s airplanes, Atlantic City Airport, South Jersey Transportation Authority, New Jersey State Council for the Arts

Photos: Beverly Burbank

Jon Barlow Hudson

Fire in the Hole!, © 2000, stainless steel, Civic Center Plaza, Omaha, NE, 12'DIA

Caduceus Fountain, © 1998, granite, water, glass block, fiber optic light, stainless steel, Ohio Arts Council, 40'L × 18"H × 29"D

Cloud Hands, © 1994, granite and stainless steel, Europos Parkas Sculpture Park, Vilniaus raj., Lithuania, 11' × 10' × 10'W

Photos: Jon Barlow Hudson

Gregory Johnson

Byron, 26"H × 10"W × 12"D

Storyteller's Circle, woman: 6'H, children: 3'H and 4'H

Cumming-Forsyth Heritage Gardens, 30' × 30' base, 14'H; inset: *Suggested Presence of Missing Soldier*

LepoWorks, Inc.

Photos: Michael J. Ayers

John Medwedeff

Smysor Plaza Fountain, 1999, forged and fabricated bronze, Murphysboro, IL, 10' × 6' × 6'

Jeff Bruce

Trena McNabb

Thank you for your Service, transparent overlapping images painted in acrylic on canvas panels

Thank you for your Service (detail), Lopez Nursing Home, Veterans' Administration Art in State Buildings Program, Land O'Lakes, FL, seven equilateral triangles, total size: 39" × 184" × 2"

Photos: Tommy McNabb

Public Art

Peter W. Michel

Fathers and Sons, © 1999, painted aluminum, Chicago Navy Pier, 10'H × 10.5'DIA

Mind Folk, © 1996, painted wood, Clinton, NY, 94"H × 58"DIA

Standing Tall — A Community Totem (detail), © 2000, painted wood and steel, Chicago Navy Pier, 19.5'H × 8'W × 8'D

Photos: Peter Michel

Bruce A. Niemi

Tall Ship II, © 1999, stainless steel, on exhibition, Skokie, IL, 17' × 9' × 8'   Suzi Niemi

Seven, Seven, Seven, © 1999, stainless steel, on exhibition, Waukegan, IL, 14.5' × 5' × 4'   Suzi Niemi

Emergence III, © 1999, bronze, on exhibition, Palm Desert, CA, 14.5' × 5' × 7'   Bruce Niemi

Kia Ricchi

Full Fathom Five, 2000, concrete, steel, 21' × 10' × 6'

This Forest Primeval, 1999, concrete, steel, 14' × 10' × 6'

sculpture

ARTIST
Brower Hatcher

TITLE
Starman in the Ancient Gardens

YEAR
1990

DESCRIPTION
Stone, bronze, stainless steel and
aluminum sculpture, 40' × 12' × 12',
in a 100' × 100' plaza

SITE
Walnut Towers Plaza,
Philadelphia, PA

COMMISSIONING AGENT
Philadelphia Redevelopment Authority
and Walnut Towers Associates

TIMELINE
1 year

"*Starman* was an opportunity to create a civic monument that uses traditional features of
the city, while working with these elements to create a futuristic icon. *Starman* was also my
first opportunity to design and build the setting that, within the scope of the project, most
advantageously complements the focal work. With this project, I was able to closely collab-
orate with a distinguished architectural firm, and to work with a sophisticated engineering
group.

This project significantly altered the level of professionalism of my work and opened doors
for future, more intensive, collaborations."

favorite commissions

Heath Satow

Whole Wheat, 2000, steel, stainless steel, 21' × 8' × 10'

Children at Play, 1997, stainless steel, five figures, each approximately 12' × 5' × 2'

Alien Skin Table, 1999, steel, stainless steel, dyed resin, 3' × 5' × 12'

Waterfall Wall, 1999, copper, etched glass, water, stone, 9' × 12' × 4'

Photos: JWest Productions/James West

John C. Sewell

Three Graces, bronze indoor/outdoor fountain, 32"H × 14"W × 14"D

Two Leaves, bronze fountain, 57"H × 16"W × 12"D

Cat, bronze fountain, St. Louis University, 62"H × 18"W × 15"D

Alvin Sher

Oculus, 2000, welded aluminum, Mitchell College, New London, CT, 14'H

Mano Siebal, 1992, welded aluminum, College of Santa Fe, 12'H

Luis Torruella

Serie en Amarillo, painted aluminum, 6'ʜ

Regata, painted aluminum, Wyndham Hotel, Old San Juan Bay Marina, 41' × 16' × 15'

Reflejo Melódico, painted and brushed aluminum, Performing Arts Center, San Juan, PR, 37' × 12' × 12'

Photos: Johny Betancourt

Luis Torruella

La Marcha de las Siluetas, painted aluminum, San Juan, PR, 260'L × 10'H × 1'W

Ave de Paraíso, painted aluminum, 36" × 15" × 14"

Bailoteo, painted aluminum, Museo de Puerto Rico, 8' × 7' × 6'

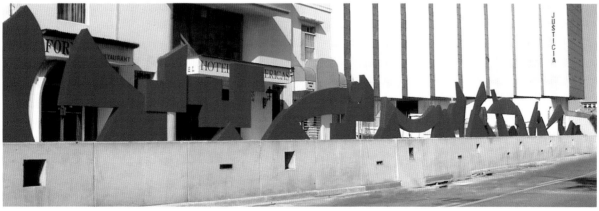

La Marcha de las Siluetas, painted aluminum, San Juan, PR, 260'L × 10'H × 1'W

Michele vandenHeuvel

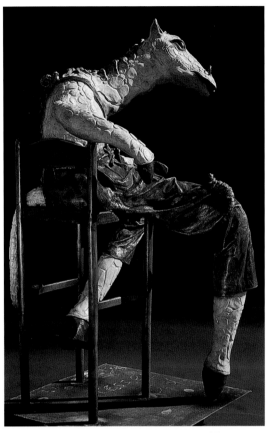

Papa Jan G. Raffe (side view), 1999, bronze, Bernalillo County Courthouse, Albuquerque, NM, 62"H × 34"W × 36"D

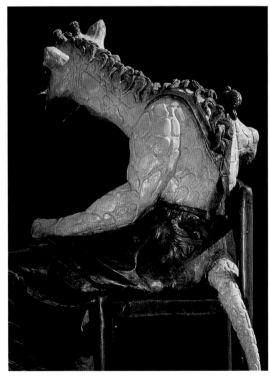

Papa Jan G. Raffe (back view)

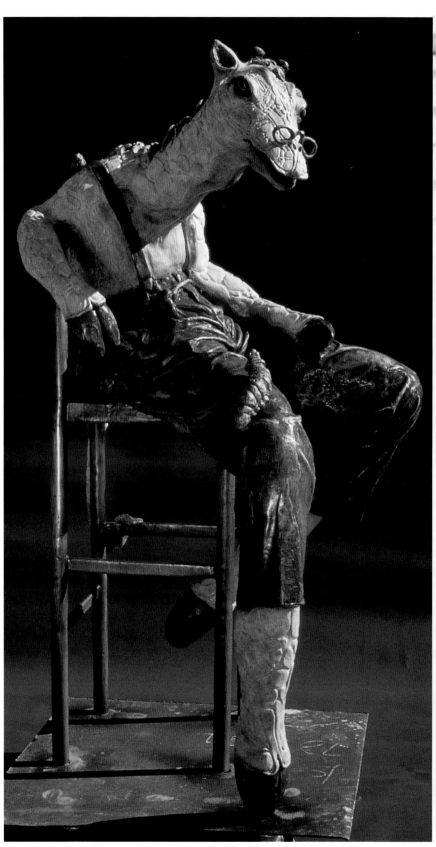

Papa Jan G. Raffe (front view)

Photos: Joseph G. VanDenHeuvel

John Wehrle

Pump Jacks and Cows, Valencia Town Center, 6' × 30'

Kenna Love

Century Xing, 2000, west view, gateway, Richmond, CA, 24,000' sq.

Malcolm Lubliner

Century Xing, 2000, east side detail, Richmond gateway

Malcolm Lubliner

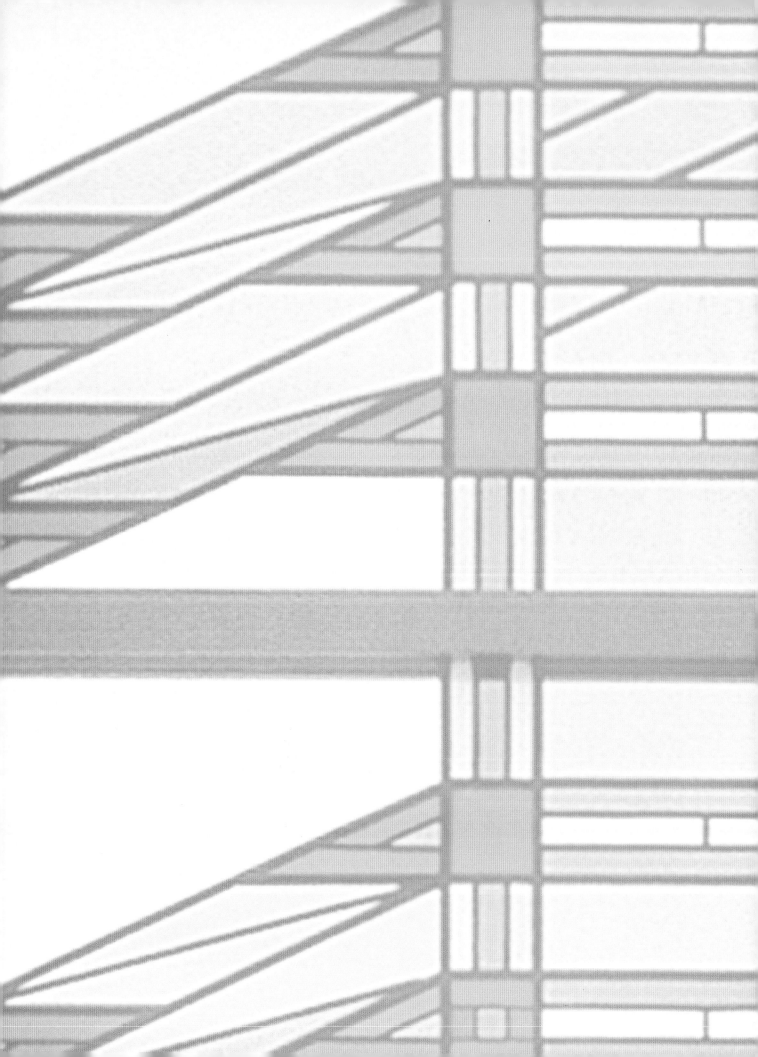

Liturgical Art

Art as Servant

Altar, maple, glass, perforated aluminum, mica sheeting; right: processional cross, carved maple pole and sculpted base, inlaid lapis lazuli, mica in fused glass, crystal glass, gold leaf, Epiphany Lutheran Church, Chandler, AZ

Singing Sky, mosaic and sculptural multilayered and mixed-media wall depicting a family in relationship with God, Epiphany Lutheran Church, Chandler, AZ, 12'H × 28'L

Beyer Studio, Inc.

Creation, 2000, St. Joseph's Roman Catholic Church, Beltsville, MD, 12'DIA

Bramante Studio

Contemporary Station of the Cross

Pieta

Beginning of Life Hangings

Fredric B. DeVantier

The Evangelists (St. Luke detail)

Chalice, 1994, sterling silver, sodalite, St. Stephen's Episcopal Church, Schenectady, NY, 9"ʜ

The Evangelists, 1999, brass vase, cherry stand, Trinity Lutheran Church, Wellsboro, PA, vase: 13.25"ʜ, total size: 50"ʜ

Photos: Robert Hirsch III

Erling Hope

Processional Cross #35, 2000, maple, walnut, pigment, 16" × 16"

Texture #1: How Words Work, 2000, mahogany, brass escutcheon pins describing a poem written in braille, 11.5" × 9.5" × 2.5"

Processional Cross #34, 1999, carved Baltic birch ply, vitreous mosaic tile fragments, gold leaf, pigment, 18" × 30"

Bill Hopen

St. Joseph, clay in progress

Blessed Mother Maria De Matius, patinaed bronze over a wrought iron and copper repoussé bench   Steve Rasmussen

Woman of the New Covenant, patinaed bronze, natural sandstone, 6'   Steve Rasmussen

Juanita Y. Kauffman

Ascent: Blue River (detail), 1999, Princeton University Chapel, lower third of one of two paintings on silk, 25'ʜ × 5'ᴡ

Threshold, 1997, Princeton University Chapel, right panel of one of two paintings on silk, 25'ʜ × 5'ᴡ

J. Kenneth Leap

Peter Groesbeck

Isaiah 40:31, Masonic Home Chapel, 10′ × 15′

Peter Groesbeck

restoration

ARTISTS
Conrad Schmitt Studios, Inc.

DESCRIPTION
Restoration of decorative scheme
and murals with paint, stencil,
glaze and gold leaf

YEAR
1998

SITE
Basilica of St. Josaphat,
Milwaukee, WI

TIMELINE
13 months

"The investigation, documentation and restoration of the interior of the Basilica of St. Josaphat was a privilege because of the magnificence and spirituality of the space, as well as the strong support for the restoration from the church, its stewards and the community. The months of work had further meaning for Conrad Schmitt Studios because the interior decoration of the basilica has been at the hands of the studio since 1926 when, along with Roman artist Gonippo Raggi, the company was commissioned to create the original decorative scheme and murals."

favorite commissions

McMow Art Glass, Inc.

Interior curtain wall separating the sanctuary from the Meditation Chapel, stained glass, Church of the Epiphany, Pt. Orange, FL, 12' × 20'

3,000th Anniversary of Jerusalem, stained glass, Temple Emanuel, Palm Beach, FL, 6' × 7'

Jesus Calms the Storm, figurative stained glass window inspired by the artwork of Julius Schnorr von Carolsfeld (published in *Die Bibel in Bildern*, 1860), Memorial Presbyterian, West Palm Beach, FL

Photos: Kim Sargent

Pante Studio

Cranes, 1992, bronze, Le Gru, Torino, Italy, life size

Franco Maria Vignati, Italy

Crucifix, 1985, bronze, Resurrection Catholic Church, Destin, FL, 5'H

Bruno Flaim, Italy

Presentations Gallery
Synagogue Arts & Furnishings

Donor recognition wall; wood, copper, acrylic, light, Woodbury Jewish Center, Long Island, NY

Ark doors, collar and eternal light; copper, onyx, Congregation Micah, Brentwood, TN

Holocaust memorial; photographs, wood, acrylic, light, Woodbury Jewish Center

Sanctuary and lobby renovation including overall design, congregational seating, Torah ark, eternal light, menorahs, bimah chairs, Torah holders, reading table, lectern, flower holders, donor walls; Sutton Place Synagogue/Jewish Center to the United Nations, New York, NY

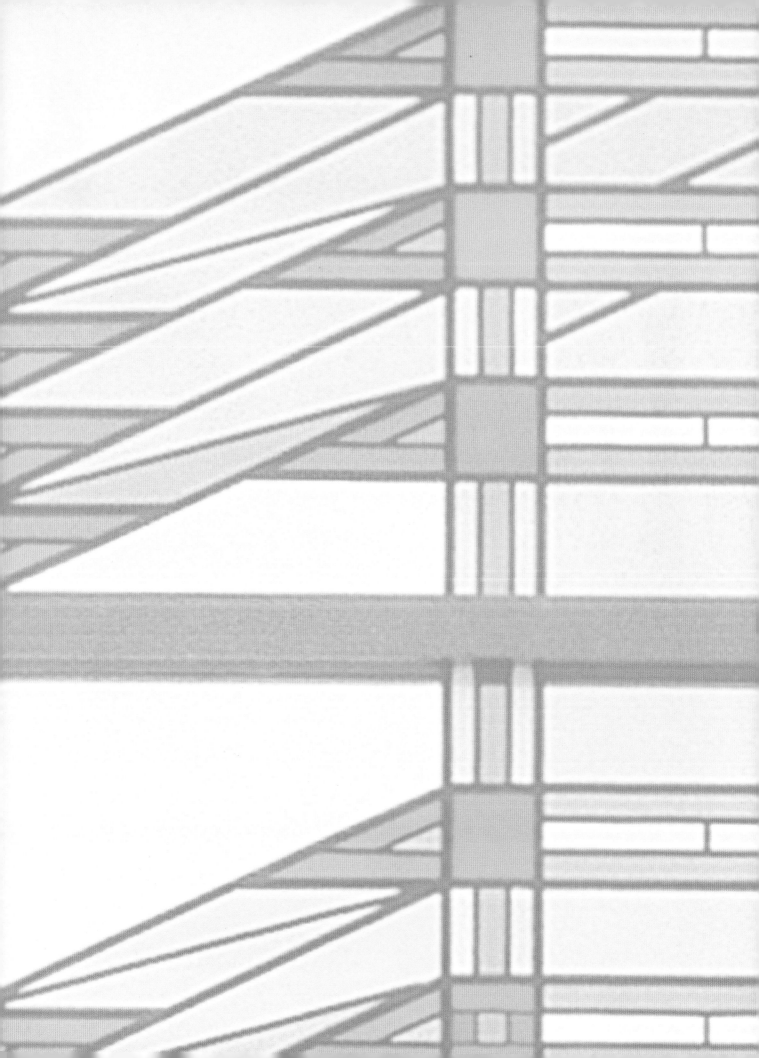

Furniture & Furnishings

Badman Design

Festive Mirror, 2000, aluminum, clay, various metals, epoxy, Sanders Restaurant, 4' × 4'

The View, 2000, heated copper, epoxy, private collection, 6' × 2'

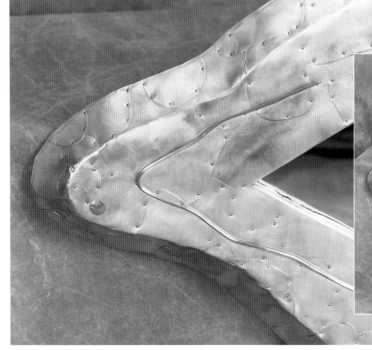

Photos: Bob Caulfield

Diamond, 2000, satin-finished aluminum with brass, private home, 4' × 2.5'

Robert L. Cooper

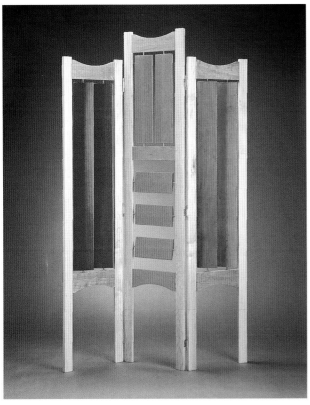

Space Divider, maple, faux dyed maple

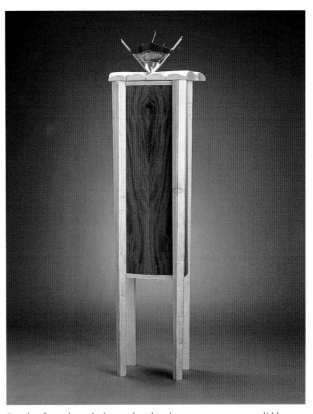

Royalty, figured maple, brass-glazed mahogany, quartz gem, solid brass

Flamingo, natural maple, faux dyed maple

Bar, dyed maple, Saints Brewery Co.

Photos: Bill Nellans

tile fireplace

ARTIST
Elizabeth MacDonald

DESCRIPTION
Ceramic tile fireplace, 16' × 5.5' × 7"

YEAR
1991

SITE
Private residence, Sherman, CT

TIMELINE
4 months

"When I was approached to create tile for the facade of the fireplace, I suggested a small work, echoing the shape of the wall. However, during meetings with the owners, architect, builder and mason, our conversations led us to the final design — part architecture, part sculpture and part painting. This became a truly collaborative venture, filled with the energy that develops in a shared vision. I am especially proud of this fireplace project."

favorite commissions

Feral Design

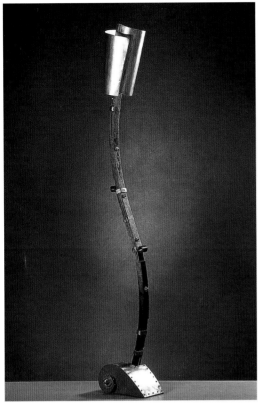

Margot, floor lamp, 6'H

Aengus MacGiffin

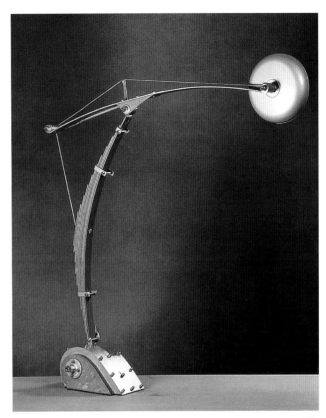

Dock, floor lamp, 55"H

Aengus MacGiffin

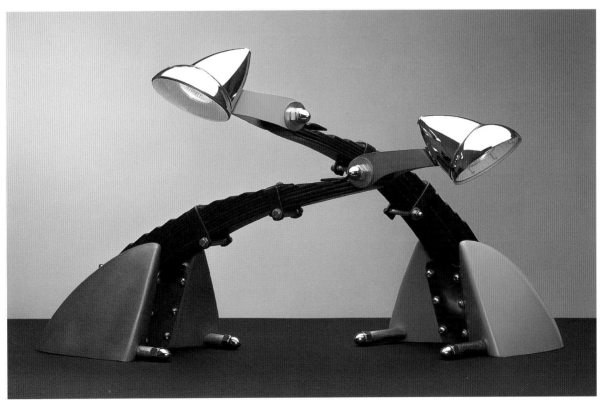

Jet desk lamps, 15"H × 24"L

Pierre LeProvost

Hammerton

Citadel Chandelier, Chateau Collection

Hammerton

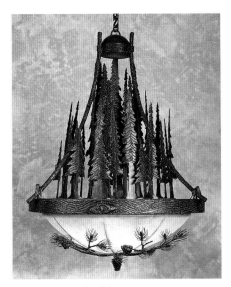

Grand Summit Chandelier,
Mountain Moose Collection

Rosendal Outdoor Sconce, Chateau Collection

Acorn Outdoor Sconce,
Mountain Moose Collection

Timber Creek Pine Floor Lamp,
Mountain Moose Collection

Scratching Bear Accent Table, Mountain Moose Collection, limited edition

Peter Kaufman

Elliptical drop leaf table, cherry, 30"ʜ × 48"ᴡ × 72"ʟ

Paired tables, ash burl and white oak, each: 30"ʜ × 54"ᴡ × 54"ʟ

Elliptical arch and built-in cabinetry, cherry

Lightspann Illumination Design, Inc.

Chandeliers, Grand Lux Café, Las Vegas, NV, 60"H × 48"w

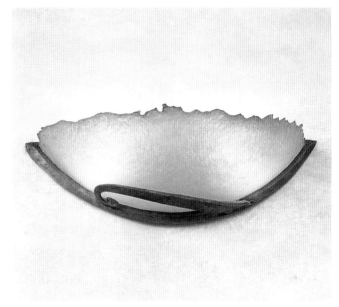

Botanica sconce, 5"H × 17"w

Southend chandelier, 48"H × 48"w

Mia Tyson, Inc.

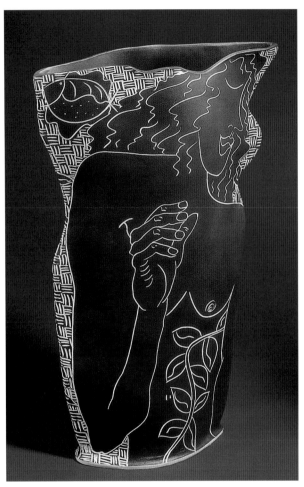

Complete Woman, 2000, porcelain, 32"H × 20"W × 6.5"D

Contemplation, 2000, porcelain, 26"H × 17"W × 5.5"D

The Lady In The Moon, 2000, porcelain, 8"H × 18"W × 1.5"D

Photos: Pat Staub Photography

Rob Peacock

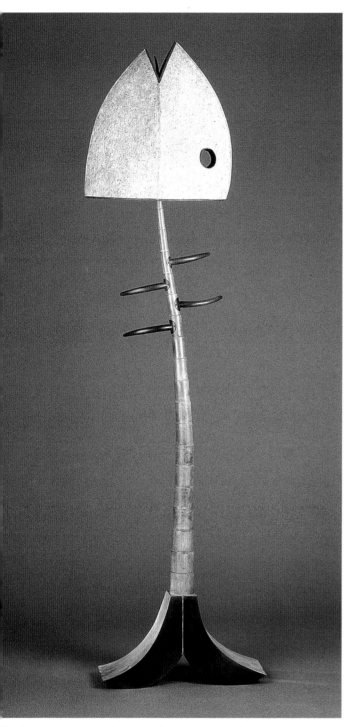

Fish Lamp, 2000, patinaed brass with rice paper shade, 20" × 8" × 78"

Pigeon Stool, 2000, patinaed brass, 17" × 18" × 48"

Photos: Doug Garrabrant

Binh Pho

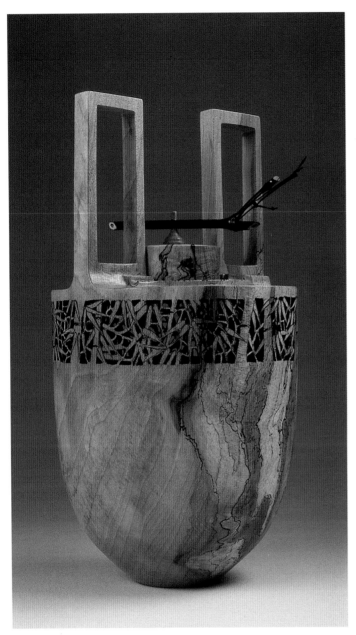

Bamboo Basket I, 2000, maple, black bamboo, 12"H × 7"DIA

Bamboo Basket II, 2000, birch, black bamboo, 12"H × 7"DIA

Photos: Binh Pho

William Poulson

Table lamp, sculpted wood, bent glass, granite,
27" × 19.5"DIA

Mike Rothwell

Limited-edition folding screen, sculpted cherry, art glass,
70" × 60" × 12"

Robert Arnold

Tissiack, Yosemite art glass mural, 8.5' × 14.25'

Mike Rothwell

Martin Sturman

Table base, 2000, stainless steel, 27"H × 26"W × 26"D

Table base, top view

Wall sculpture, 2000, stainless steel, special commission for Hyatt Hotel, 79"H × 21"W × .13"D

Photos: Barry Michlin

Ted Box Limited

Wave Table with Rock, solid birch veneers, American white ash, 26"H × 48"DIA

Swimming Upstream (Shelves with Fish), solid birch veneer shelves with pine fish

Reclining Conch, solid birch veneers, eastern pine and ash, 39"H × 81"W × 14"D

Tuska Inc.

Illuminates Bath Screen, wood and fabric, two panels, each: 62" × 20"

Lee Thomas

Rick Van Ness

French Horn Monument, 1996, 12" × 30" × 12"

Photos: © Rick Van Ness 2001

Composition Grande with sphere nightlights and lit tables, 2000, 14" × 14" × 70"

Coronet Verde with cymbal and blown glass torchiere, 1997, 8" × 8" × 34"

Trombone Floor Sculpture with lit table, 2000, 12" × 12" × 70"

ARTIST
Binh Pho

DESCRIPTION
Wood table of eucalyptus, gum burl
and maple burl, 29"H × 32"W × 27"D

YEAR
2000

SITE
Collection of Mr. Wornick,
St. Helena, CA

TIMELINE
1 week

"This table, a collaborative project between myself, Steve Sinner and Leonard Hartline, was
the result of a desire to display a unique piece of wood art at the Collectors of Wood Art
booth at SOFA Chicago in November of 2000. It received many accolades from attendees.
Originally intended as a temporary object, the table was rebuilt for Mr. Wornick immediately
following the show, and was installed in his collection within a week. Each of these tables
has its own characteristics depending on the burls used."

David Woodruff

Nature's Windows vase, manzanita and ebony, 13"H × 7"W

Natural edge vase, white oak and ebony, 12"H × 6.5"W

Rimmed hollow-formed bowl, oak and ebony, 7"H × 13"W

Photos: McNabb Studio

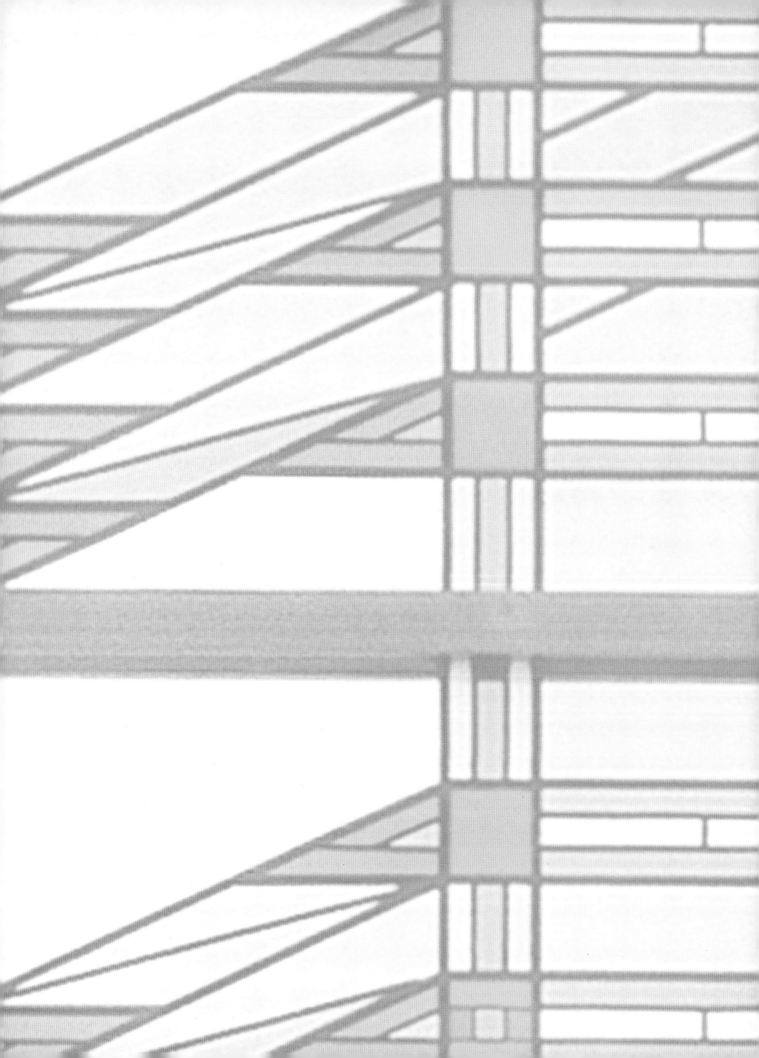

Paintings, Prints & Drawings

Sharron Bliss

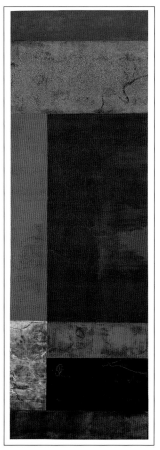 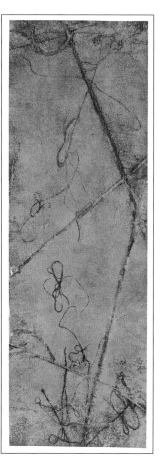

Sarah's Song I (left) and *Sarah's Song VII* (right), limited-edition iris prints,
paper size: 37" × 17.5", image size: 30" × 10"

Amber Light II, limited-edition iris print,
paper size: 35" × 35", image size: 24" × 24"

Photos: Don Felton, ALMAC

Bob Brown

#46 *Russian Olive,* 1999, acrylic, 30" × 36"

#52 *Yolavivia Drive,* 2000, acrylic, 30" × 36"

Fran Bull

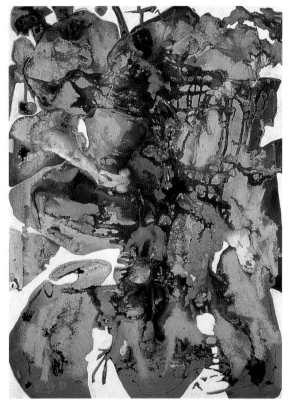

Child of Ice, Magdalene series, 1993, acrylic on canvas, 90" × 65"

Clarissa, Magdalene series, 1993, acrylic on canvas, 90" × 65"

Sylvia, Magdalene series, 1993, acrylic on canvas, 90" × 65"

Sylvia (detail)

Photos: Erik Landsberg

Bridget Busutil

Tree No. 2, 1998, oil on canvas, 60" × 30"

Reflections, 1996, oil on canvas, 20" × 24"

Still Waters, 1996, oil on canvas, 48" × 70"

Steven Carpenter

Blue River, 1999, pastel

Summer Meadow, 2000, pastel

Photos: Petronella J. Ytsma

Pamela Cosper

Fear No Evil, oil
Lisa Vitale

Behind Closed Doors, acrylic
Tomiko Gumbleton

Garden Trellis, acrylic
Lisa Vitale

Karl Dempwolf

Poppy Splendor, 2000, oil, 42" × 42"

Lengthening Shadows, 2000, oil, 16" × 20"

Sunset Drama, 2000, oil, 20" × 24"

Photos: Karl Dempwolf

Norman Foster

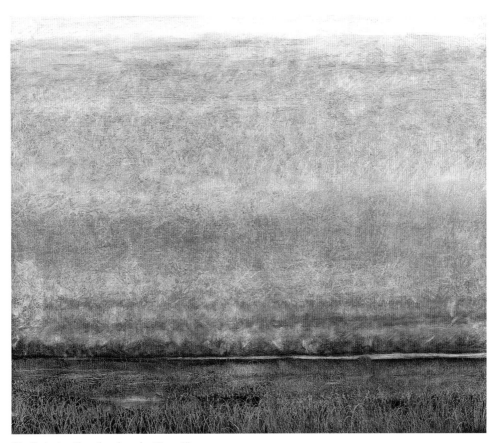

The Sheltering Sky, oil on board, 56" × 48"

Wind and Rain, Winter, oil on board, 48" × 36"

Photos: Patrick Tregenza

Niki Gulley

Fall Color, 2000, pastel on paper, 20" × 36"

Arboretum Path, 1999, pastel on board, 19" × 25"

Photos: Scott Williams

Yoshi Hayashi

Water Lily Pond, 1997, gold, silver leaf and oil paint, 42" × 96"

Full Moon, 2000, gold, silver leaf and oil paint, 48" × 72"

Photos: Ira D. Schrank

Steve Heimann

Keeper of the Code, 2000, oil on canvas, 12" × 16"

Sooth Sayer, 1997, oil on canvas, 16" × 12"

Patricia B. Ingersoll

Running Vines, 1998, oil on canvas, 54" × 76"

The Clearing, 1998, oil on canvas, 54" × 76"

Photos: Jack Ramsdale

Caroline Jasper

Aquavitae, © 1999, oil, 24" × 30"

Railed Ascent, © 1999, oil, 36" × 24"

Past Presence, © 2000, oil, 30" × 40"

Photos: Daniel Whipps, Baltimore

Marlene Lenker

Mesa, © 2001, 20" × 20"

Sunset Vista, © 2001, 20" × 20"

Desert Vista, © 2001, 48" × 72"

Anne Marchand

Paris Rooftops, 2000, oil on canvas, 36" × 48"

Seventeenth Street & Massachusetts Avenue, 2000, oil on canvas, 36" × 54"

Photos: Greg Staley

Paintings, Prints & Drawings

Anne Marchand

Rolling Deep into Existence, 2000, oil on canvas, 28" × 34"

Shimmering at the Edge, 2000, oil on canvas, 48" × 48"

Photos: Greg Staley

Stephanie L. Nadolski

Mayan Relics – Chac, mixed-media monotype, 24" × 24"

Dan Beigel, Annapolis, MD

Mayan Temples – Tikal, commissioned monotype, 20" × 34"

Perfect Image, Des Plaines, IL

Canyon Passages – XXII, mixed-media monotype, 38" × 30"

Perfect Image, Des Plaines, IL

Canyon Passages – XXIII, mixed-media monotype, 36" × 30"

Perfect Image, Des Plaines, IL

Marlies Merk Najaka

Nancy Egol Nikkal

Dream Painting, 1996, collage and acrylic on paper, 22" × 30"

Parade, 1994, acrylic on paper, 46" × 54"

Photos: Jon Ferrentino

Joan Osborn-Dunkle

Let Not Your Heart, mixed media on canvas, 47" × 37"

Foiled Copper, mixed media on paper, total size: 51" × 78"

interior mural

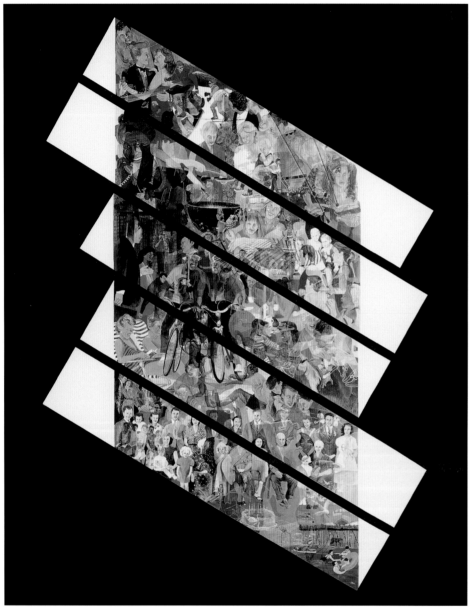

ARTIST
Trena McNabb

TITLE
We're a Family

YEAR
1993

DESCRIPTION
Wall pieces of acrylic on cotton duck canvas, 186" × 144" × 2"

SITE
AT&T Family Federal Credit Union (Truliant Federal Credit Union), Winston-Salem, NC

TIMELINE
9 months

"This commission is my favorite because I was able to work with the art committee when the building was in the planning stage. I began to paint as they began to build. The large two-story lobby wall had originally been designed to have a brick pattern run though it as it did on the outside walls. I asked them not to do that because it would compete with the angles I had designed for the piece. We were able to select lighting that would show the work off best and have that invisibly built into the ceiling. The lobby piece is so well lit that it shows from the interstate as people drive by."

favorite commissions

Bob Russo

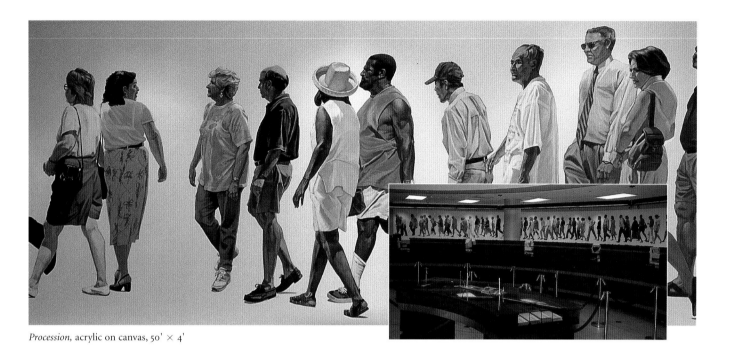

Procession, acrylic on canvas, 50' × 4'

Bibb Graves Bridge, acrylic on canvas, 80" × 54"

Susan Sculley

Coral Haze, 1994, oil on canvas, 36" × 36"

Cynthia Howe

Mango Sky, 1999, oil stick on canvas, 12" × 12"

Dan Kuruna

Orange Sky, 1999, oil stick on canvas, 22" × 38"

Dan Kuruna

Susan Sculley

Pathway, 1991, oil on canvas, 21" × 50"

Dunes on the Lake, 1996, oil stick on canvas, 18" × 21"

Photos: Cynthia Howe

Dane E. Tilghman

The Hot One

Harp on It

Man and His Horn

Boat Man

garden mural

ARTIST
Claudia Wagar

DESCRIPTION
Two garden murals, enamel
on PVC board, each: 3' × 8'

YEAR
2000

SITE
Sonoma, CA

TIMELINE
4 months

"These privately commissioned murals represented a new challenge because the shape was unusual and the materials were new to me. I knew the murals would be placed in direct sunlight so, in a never-ending effort to find a slow-fading paint and a permanent archival support, I chose to use sign painters' enamel on PVC board. Since enamel is so quick drying and sticky, I was forced to begin a whole new style of painting that I have found to be very successful."

favorite commissions

Claudia Wagar

Sunflowers, 2000, watercolor, 19" × 21", giclée available any size

Tannia, 1999, watercolor, 21.5" × 31"

Pinot Noir II, 2000, watercolor, 24" × 18", giclée available any size

Photos: Ken Wagar

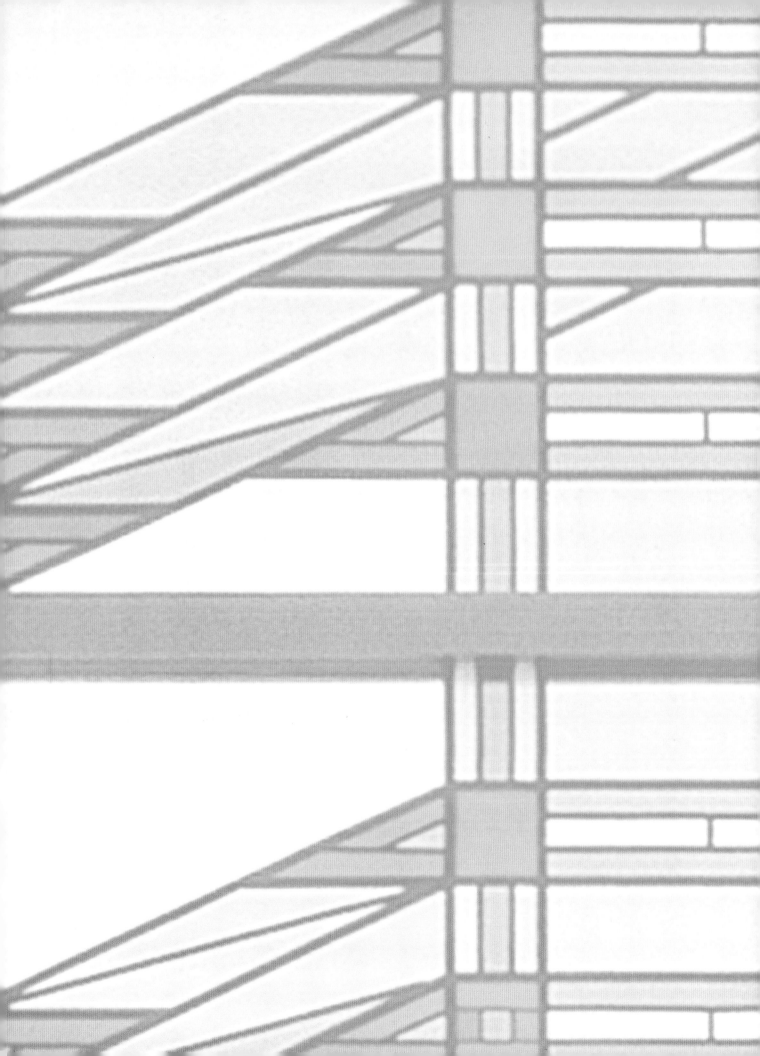

Fine Art Photography

Babs Armour

Watching All The Girls Go By, highly saturated color print on archival paper, sizes up to 40" × 60"

Allan Bruce Zee Fine Art Photography

Twin Lakes, Oregon

Japanese Garden, Portland, Oregon

Echoes, Chaco Canyon, New Mexico

Oaxaca, Mexico

Allan Baillie

Inner Solitude, 1999, Cibachrome print, 14"ʜ × 11"ᴡ

Cali Gorevic

Father Tree, giclée print

East of West Thumb, giclée print

Skeleton Tree, giclée print

Grace, giclée print

photography

ARTIST
Julie Betts Testwuide

DESCRIPTION
Two large iris giclée prints/pastels,
image size: 20" × 20",
framed: 36" × 36"

YEAR
2000

SITE
Savannah Westin Golf Club,
Savannah, GA

COMMISSIONING AGENT
Soho Myriad Gallery, Atlanta, GA

TIMELINE
Approximately 2 weeks

"My sole reason for being part of GUILD sourcebooks is to reach out to design firms and art galleries for business. Sarah Hall at Soho Myriad in Atlanta works extensively with designers and directly with large design projects. As soon as she received *The Designer's Sourcebook 15,* she commissioned me to create artwork for a new Marriott in Tampa, FL. This led to the Savannah Westin Golf Club's need for beach-themed artwork. My goal has been to get more exposure in public spaces where there is high-end traffic and potential art collectors. GUILD sourcebooks are helping me accomplish this goal."

favorite commissions

Juliearts.com

Boats, Nice, France

Emily's Letter from Paris

The Lido, Venice

Gondola, Venice

Karl P. Koenig

Pitcorthie Parasite Tree, © 2001, gumoil photographic print, 12" × 12"

Ranchos de Taos Church, © 2001, gumoil photographic print, 12" × 12"

Thames Barrier, © 2001, gumoil photographic print, 28" × 19"

George Thomas Mendel

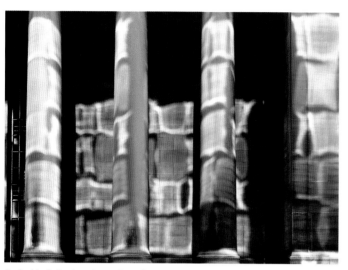

Bathed in Reflection, Carnegie Mellon Institute

San Felipe de Neri, Albuquerque, NM

R & R Hall, Cleveland, OH

NeoGraphique

Blue Window, limited-edition giclée

Blue Stairs, limited-edition giclée

Green Stairway, limited-edition giclée

Mexican Stairs, limited-edition giclée

NeoGraphique

Three Calla Lilies, limited-edition giclée

Calla Lily, limited-edition giclée

Joyce P. Lopez

Feather Series #11, archival inkjet photo, 22" × 17"

Matthew O'Shea

Birds Out of Trees

Poplars

Branches Into Water

Round the Block 2

Christopher Petrich

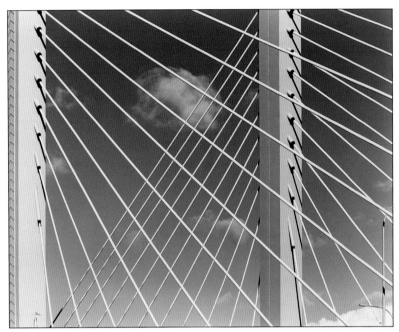

Cable Stay Bridge, Thea Foss Waterway, Tacoma, 2000, silver gelatin print, 8" × 10"

White Shadows, Sheraton Hotel, Tacoma, 2000, silver gelatin print, 8" × 10"

Plastic Bag, Wind and Shadow, Seattle, 1979, silver gelatin print, 8" × 10"

Christopher Petrich

Green Point from Garage at 62 Island Blvd., Fox Island, 1994,
silver gelatin, 8" × 10"

Cedar & Periwinkle, Fox Island, 1991, silver gelatin, 8" × 10"

Fan Light over Green Point, Fox Island, 2000, silver gelatin, 8" × 10"

Talli Rosner-Kozuch

Three Sunflowers, 1996, sepia-toned Polaroid film, 8" × 10" and up

Amarylis At Night, 1996, sepia-toned Polaroid film, 8" × 10" and up

Tulips, 1998, sepia-toned Polaroid film, 8" × 10" and up

Talli Rosner-Kozuch

Sunflowers in the Morning, © 1999, 16" × 20", other sizes available

Tulips Dewdrops, © 1998, 20" × 20", other sizes available

Gary San Pietro

Blue in Green

Rhapsody

Overture

Fine Art Photography

Thea Schrack Photography

Return to Hog Island, 2000, limited-edition print, 10" × 25"

Zen Rocks, 1999, limited-edition print, 12" × 25"

Lighthouse, 2000, limited-edition print, 10" × 25"

Wayne Williams Studio

Turtle Islands, 2000, photographs and iris prints up to 40"w

Moonglow, 1999, photographs and iris prints up to 40"w

Shevaun Williams

Scone Palace, Scotland, © 2000

St. Peters, Italy, © 2000

Ibaraki, Japan, © 2000

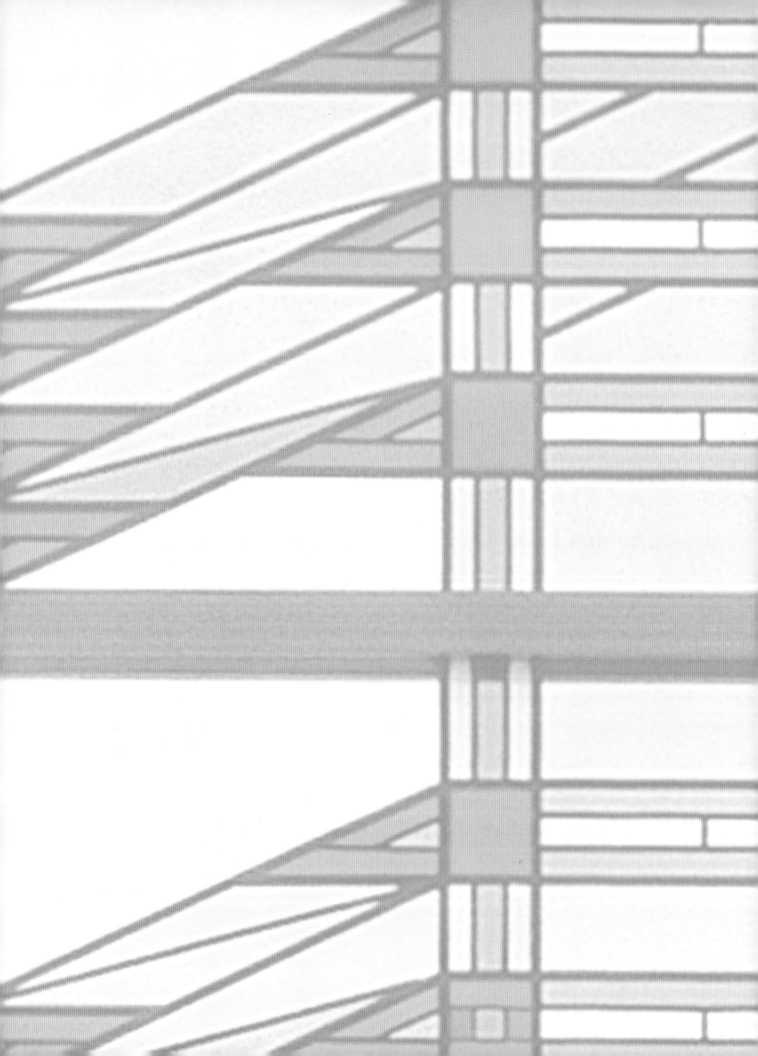

Art for the Wall
Metal

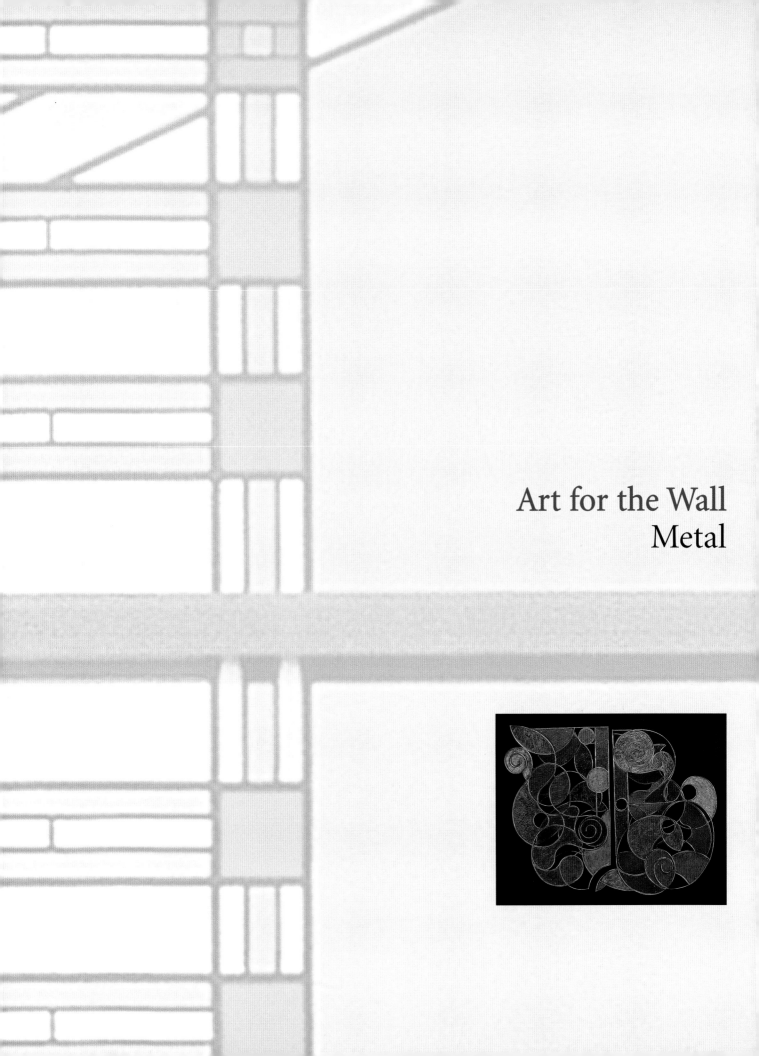

David M Bowman Studio

Wallpiece 00.08, patinaed brass, 21" × 48"

Wallpiece 00.17, patinaed brass, 19" × 56"

Art for the Wall: Metal

Linda M. Leviton

It Takes Two, 1999, copper, oil, patina, 46"ʜ × 58"ᴡ × 4.5"ᴅ

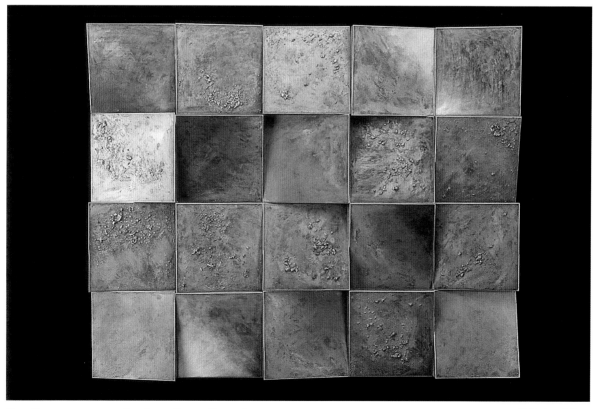

Green Peace, 2000, copper, oil, patina, 32"ʜ × 40"ᴡ × 3"ᴅ

Photos: Jerry Anthony

wall sculptures

ARTIST
Martin Sturman

DESCRIPTION
Fifteen stainless steel wall-hanging sculptures ranging in size from 4.5'H to 6.5'H

YEAR
2000

SITE
McGraw-Hill Publishing Company, Columbus, OH

COMMISSIONING AGENT
ArtSouth, Philadelphia, PA

TIMELINE
12 weeks

"I was initially contacted by ArtSouth as a result of my page in *The Designer's Sourcebook 13*. I was able to create images of children and young adults who are the direct beneficiaries of my client's publications. All sculptures are in the large employee cafeteria, so the employees interact with art and their intended audience on a daily basis.

favorite commissions

Art for the Wall
Mixed Media

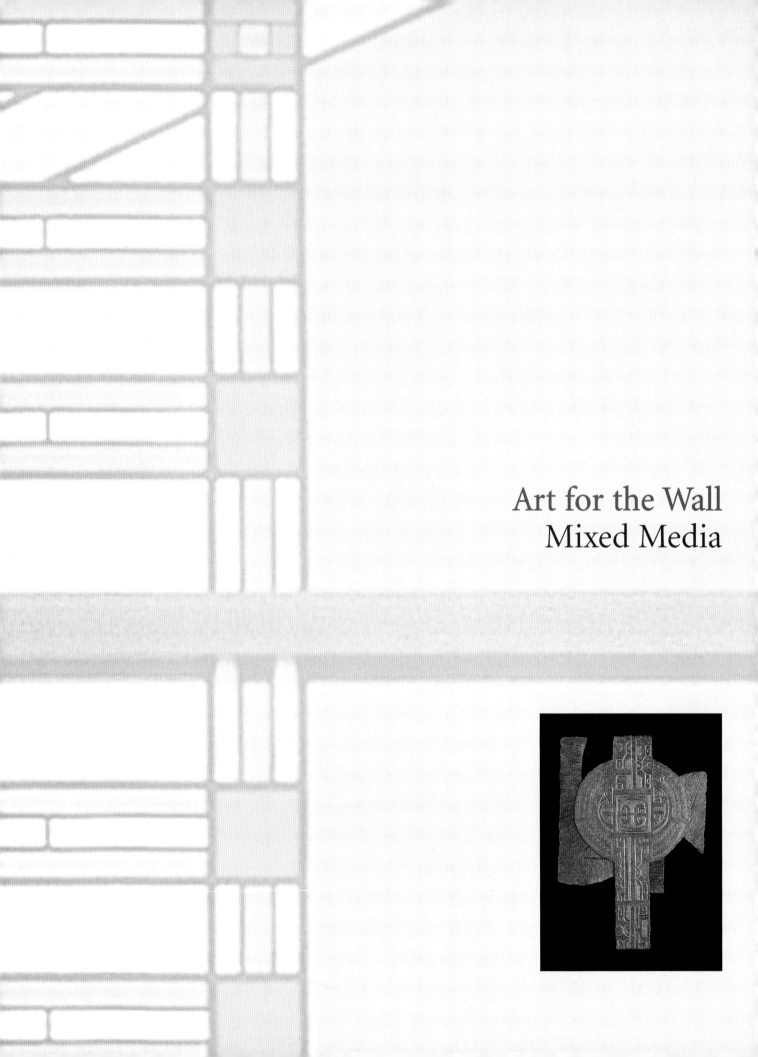

Barbara Brotherton

Deko Kioku, 2000, wood, poured stone, copper leaf, acid patina, 39"H × 39"W

Pathways, 1999, wood, poured stone, silver leaf, acid patina, U.S. Ambassador's residence, Nicosia, Cyprus, each panel: 54"H × 36"W

Helene's Peace, 1999, wood, poured stone, silver leaf, acid patina, St. Vincent Hospital, Indianapolis, IN, 36"H × 30"

Gretchen Lee Coles

Plan for Nuevo Bosque, 2000, carved wood, willow, paper, 30"H × 29"W × 7.5"D

Eugene Sladek, College of DuPage

Alonzo Davis

Bamboo Bundle IV (detail), mixed media on bamboo, 10"H × 48"W × 5"D

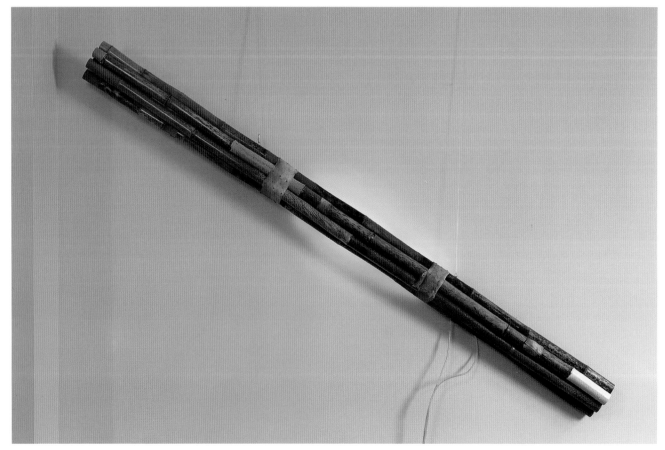

Palos de Azul, mixed media on bamboo, neon, 10"H × 96"W × 6"D

Joan Giordano

New Wave, handmade paper, copper, wax, 16"H × 24"W × 8"D

Dancer #3, copper cable, lead, handmade paper, 26"H × 12"W × 6"D

Secret of the Scroll, handmade paper, copper cable, 96"H × 22"W × 8"D

Photos: D. James Dee

Ione

The Family, woodcarving, 28"H × 22"w

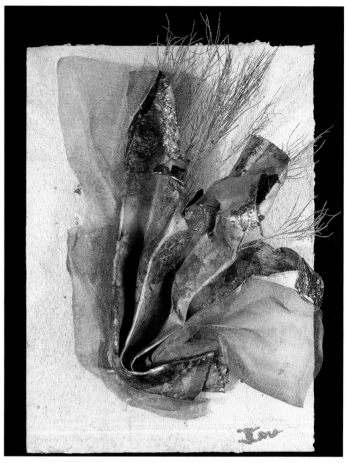

Fancy Fan, mixed media, 40"H × 30"w

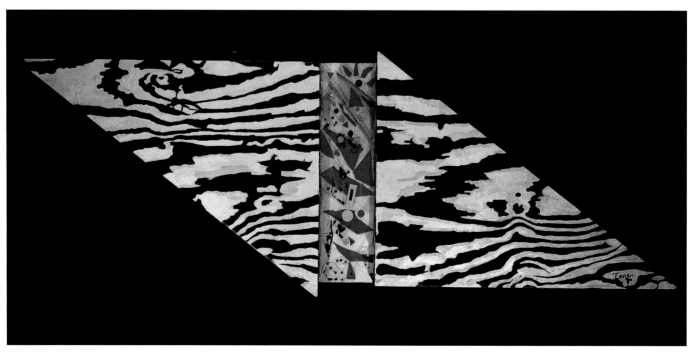

Stellar Abstraction, mixed media, 30"H × 96"w

Jacques Lieberman Editions

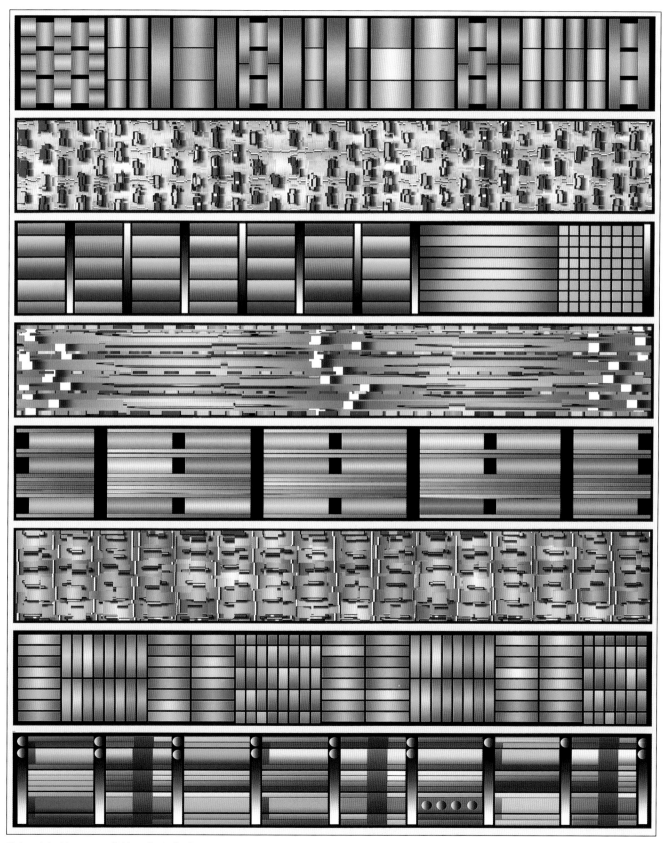

Eight original images, available as limited-edition prints on rag paper, 26"· × 22" to 50" × 40"; on tiles, 4" × 4" to 16" × 16" individually (any size for murals); or sublimated onto fabric

wall sculpture

ARTIST
Ellen Kochansky

TITLE
Graduation

YEAR
2000

DESCRIPTION
Memorabilia from Bridgette Lacher's childhood, including currency from travels, cat tags, a sailing award plaque, notes to her mother, a favorite book, original photographic film, carved print blocks, report cards, magazine cover, watch, 18" × 18" × 3"

SITE
Private residence, Billy and Dana Lacher, Greenville, SC

TIMELINE
3 months

"Art heaven is great people wanting to pay you for the work you most yearn to do.

A watershed piece of mine went to live in a beautiful, high-traffic public building. Life was good. A talented young student saw it and loved it and offered her services for a summer as an unpaid intern, just to see more of what I did. Life was very good. When her parents commissioned me to design a personal sculptural work for her graduation gift, I felt I had reached a sort of peak.

Bridgette Lacher came from a very supportive family. She's disciplined, perceptive and visually astute. Her doting mother encouraged those qualities, collecting every precious fragment from her adventurous and well-traveled childhood. The sculpture that resulted represents a real loving and creative collaboration between us, full of archives and connection … my favorite things."

favorite commissions

Ellen Kochansky

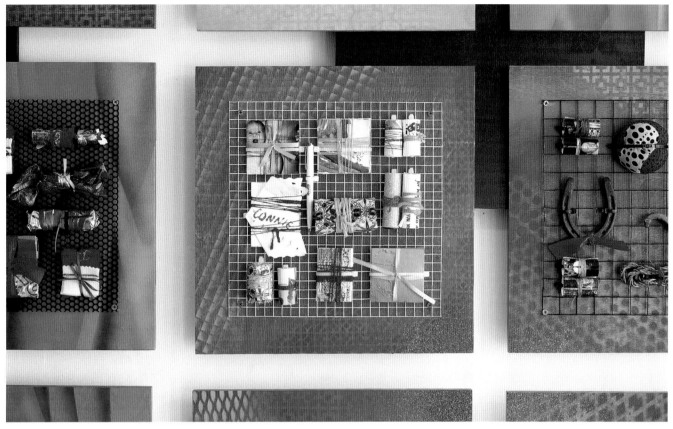

Garden Party (detail)

Garden Party, 2000, mixed media, wrapped personal mementos from Bank of America regional associates and facility partners, Gateway Center, Charlotte, NC, 24' × 6' × 4"

Photos: Mitchell Kearney, Charlotte, NC

Frances G. Pratt

Counterpoint, 1992, mixed media, 40" × 33" × 6"

Iridescent Crescent, 1998, mixed media, 12" × 14" × 3"

Pas de Deux, 2000, mixed media, 24" × 50" × 3"

Pat Musick

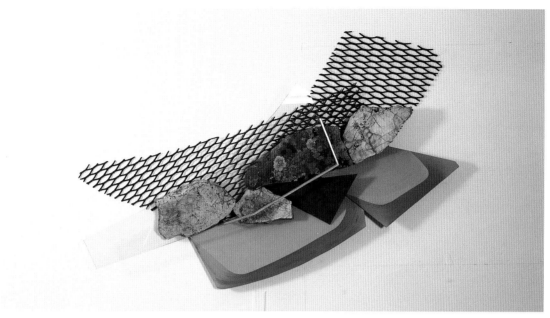

EPILOGUE 25, wood, canvas, stone, steel, glass, acrylic, 57" × 85" × 9"

EPILOGUE 6, wood, canvas, steel, hydrocal, acrylic, 72" × 84.75" × 18"

Luminous Artworks

Pier, three-dimensional wall sculpture, neon, Plexiglas, wood, paint, 52" × 96" × 10"

Tide Pool, freestanding sculpture, neon, Plexiglas, Cabrillo Marine Aquarium, 5' × 7' × 10'

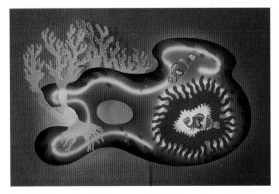

Sea Garden, wall sculpture, neon, Plexiglas, 22" × 42" × 6"

Rainbow Doorway, architectural element, 2000, glass, neon, aluminum, Club Sushi, 10' × 8' × 9"

Photos: Larry Lytle

Art for the Wall: Mixed Media

Stephanie Schirm

Yoga Under the Sun, 1998, paint and fabric tapestry, Georgetown, ON, 8' × 2'

Mother's Love, 2000, paint and fabric collage, Guelph, ON, 25" × 14"

Photos: Trina Koster

Naomi Tagini

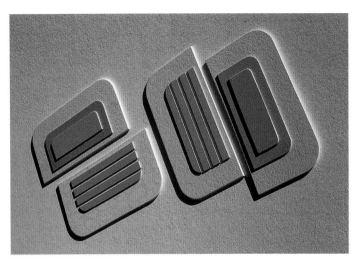

Palm Beach, 2001, wood, each piece: 13.25" × 6.5"

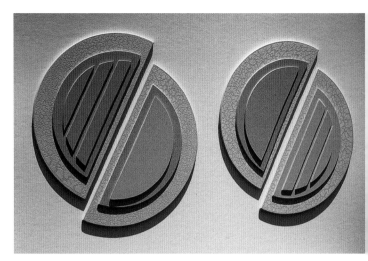

Sunset, 2001, wood, each piece: 13.25" × 6.5"

Vermont, 2001, wood, each piece: 13.25" × 6.5"

Retro, 2001, wood, each piece: 13.25" × 6.5"

Photos: Claudio Tagini

Art for the Wall: Mixed Media

Alice Van Leunen

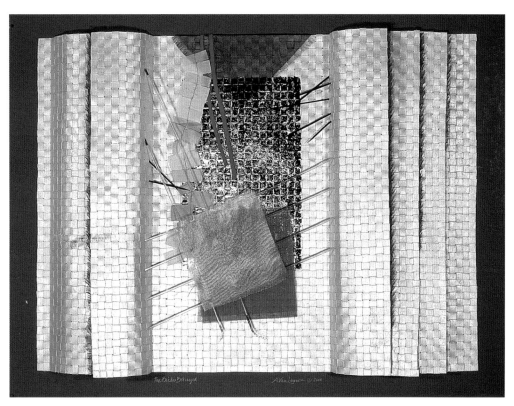

The Bride Betrayed, 2000, mixed media, woven paper, 32" × 40" × 3"

Veiled Threats, 2000, mixed media, woven paper, 32" × 40" × 1"

Susan Venable

Sol La Mar, University of Mexico, 3.5' × 4.5'

Sunset Samba, 3' × 3'

Canyon Canto VI, 5' × 15'

Photos: William Nettles

Art for the Wall: Mixed Media

Nancy J. Young

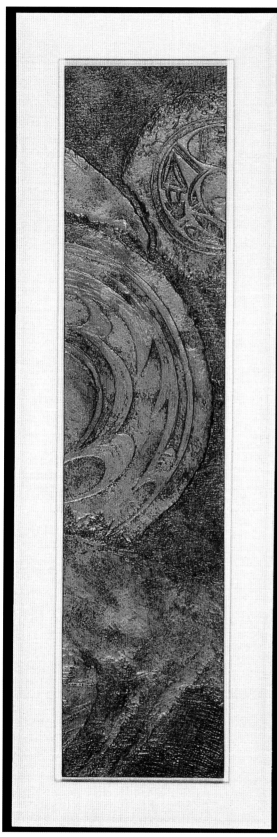

Sonata, mixed media, 36"ʜ × 31"ᴡ

Meditation, mixed media, 40"ʜ × 16"ᴡ

Serenade for Two, mixed media, 43"ʜ × 32"ᴡ

Photos: Pat Berrett

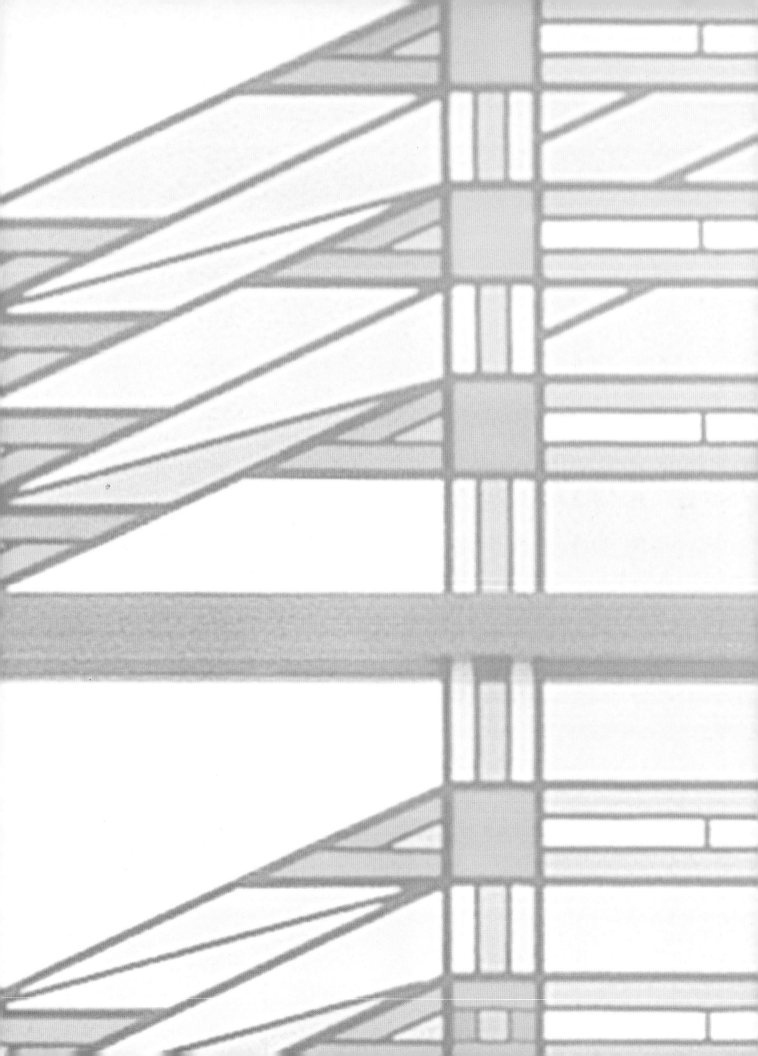

Art for the Wall
Paper

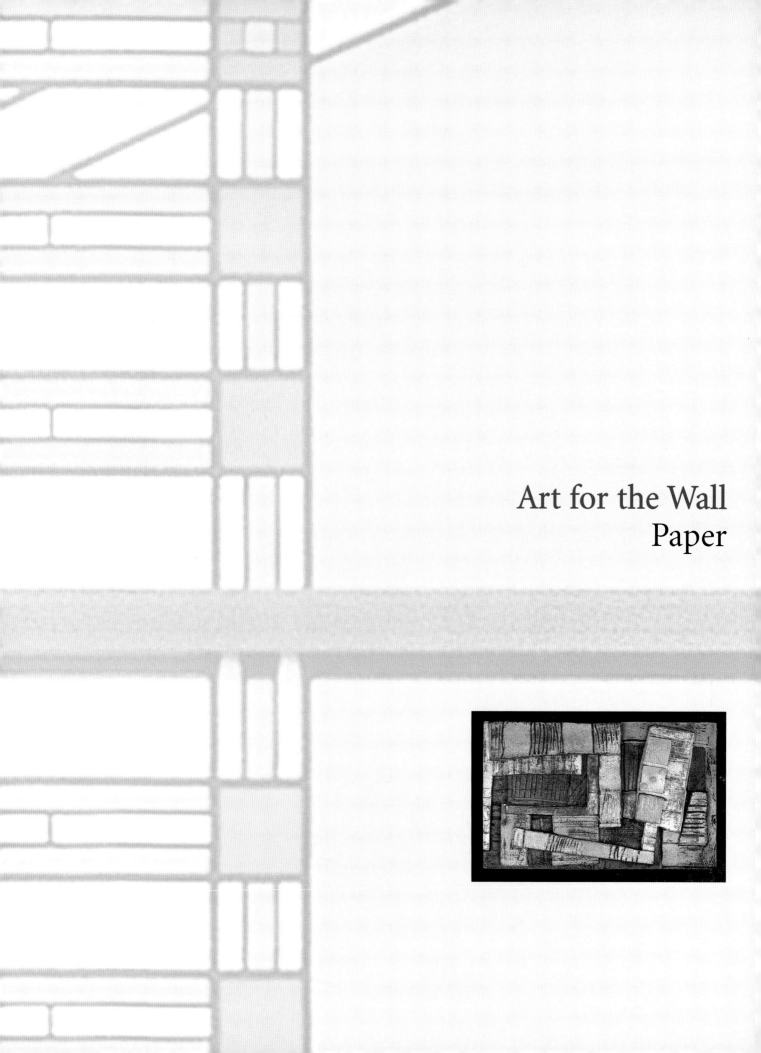

Barbara Fletcher

Tropical Scene, 2000, cast paper, 16" × 20" × .5"

Bathroom fish installation, 2000, cast paper, private home

Monkeys, 2000, cast paper, 16" × 20" × .5"

Photos: Gordon Bernstein

Ellen Mears Kennedy

Blue Arc 1998, left view, handmade paper, 41"H × 55"w × 3"D

Blue Arc 1998, right view

Red/Blue Triangle 2000, left view, handmade paper, 36"H × 44"w × 3"D

Red/Blue Triangle 2000, right view

Photos: PRS Associates

Joan Kopchik

Sanctuary, cast handmade paper and pigments, 18"ʜ × 30"ᴡ × 6"ᴅ

From the Floor of an Ancient Sea, cast handmade paper, pigments, shale, 18"ʜ × 36"ᴡ × 2.5"ᴅ

Photos: John Woodin

Christina Roe

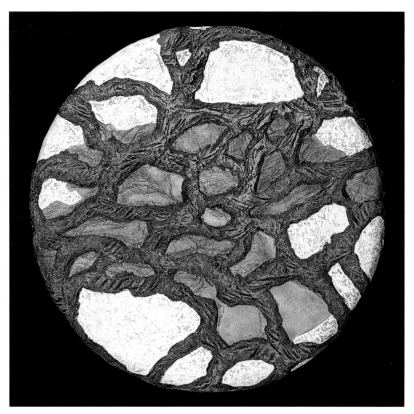

Organic Tracery, papier mâché, 22.5"DIA

Macanese Textures, cast paper, 23" × 37"

Photos: Rich Miller

Priscilla Robinson

Garden Series 70, acrylic, handmade paper, 19" × 19"

Earth Beat, acrylic, handmade paper, fiberglass, 61" × 16" × 5"

Portal, acrylic, handmade paper, 48" × 60"

Susan Singleton

Private collection, Orcas Island, WA, 48"H × 36"w

R. Semple

Ziggurat artworks, Sprint Federal Headquarters, Washington, DC, each: 17"H × 17"w

R. Greenhouse

Golden Ziggurat, Sailfish Point Club, Hutchinson Island, FL, 86"H × 42"w

M. Brennan

Art for the Wall
Fiber

David B. Brackett

Twin Conception, cotton, painted and supplemental warps, screenprinting, 85" × 132"

Three Stages, cotton, rayon, painted and supplemental warps, screenprinting, 80" × 106"

Photos: David B. Brackett

Laura Militzer Bryant

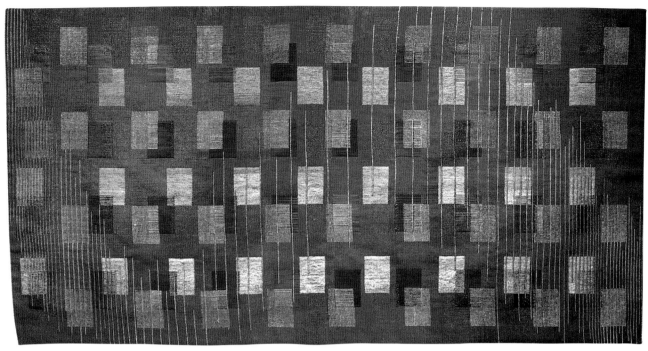

Sojourn, 1999, weaving, 36" × 69"

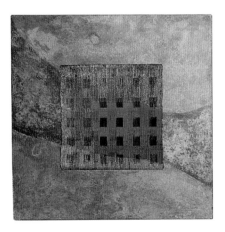  

River Run, 2000, weaving on copper, 42" × 64"

Photos: Thomas Bruce

Myra Burg

Quiet Oboes (detail, winter colors), 2000, wrapped fiber, 2" to 5"DIA

Quiet Oboes with Twigs and Jute (detail), 2000, wrapped fiber, twigs, jute, 2" to 5"DIA

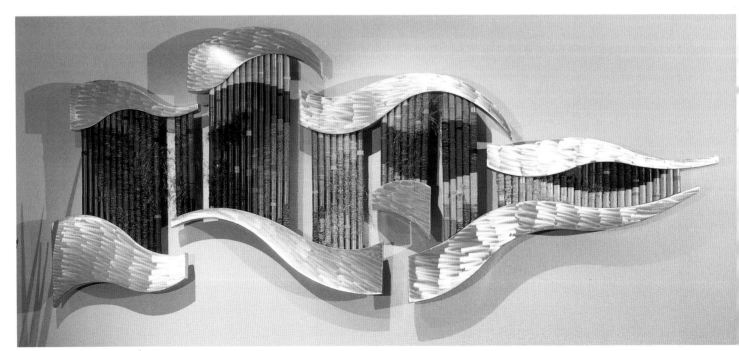

From the Deep, 1998, wrapped fiber, burnished aluminum, 96" × 36" × 5"

Photos: Ron Luxemburg

Robin Cowley

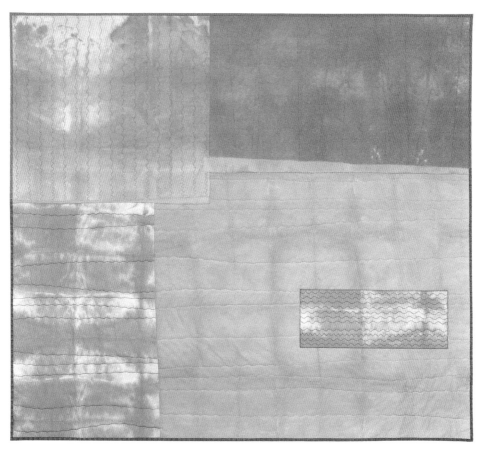

Out of an Orange Colored Sky, layered, stitched and hand-dyed cotton, 45" × 49"

Serene Spring, layered, stitched and hand-dyed cotton, two panels, each: 46" × 46"

Photos: Don Tuttle Photography

Graphics in Wool

Dance, 2000, available 40" × 60" and 60" × 76", artist: Dennis Downes

Nightfall, 2000, available 44" × 56" and 60" × 79", artist: Dennis Downes

Donna Durbin

Tropical Bloom, 2000, mixed-media tapestry, private residence, Houston, TX, 10'H × 7'w

Photos: Janet Lenzen

Marilyn Forth

Matin Jardin, batik, 42" × 59"

Coral Fantasy, batik, 45" × 72"

Photos: Anthony Potter

Art for the Wall: Fiber

Marilyn Forth

Tulips, batik, 25" × 35"

Anthony Potter

Tim Harding

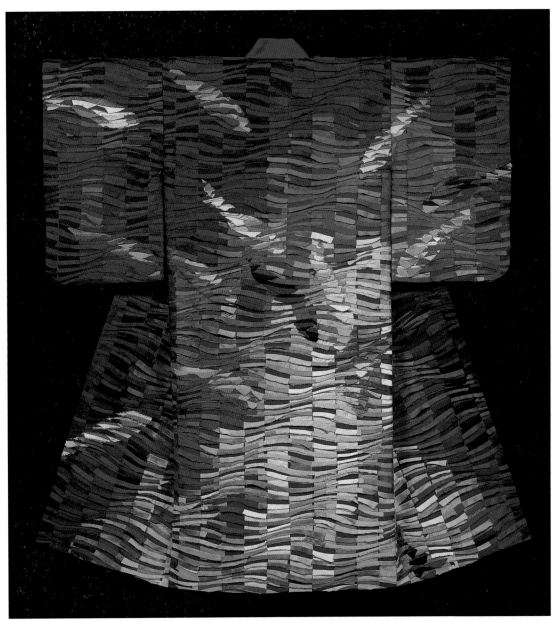

Koi Kimono, cut silk, 68" × 60"

Petronella Ytsma

Still Water Reflections, cut silk, 64" × 98"

Autumn Reflections Triptych, cut silk, 75" × 192"

Judy B. Dales, Quiltmaker

Fire on the Water, © 2000, pieced, appliquéd and machine-quilted cotton, chiffon and tulle, 65"H × 51"W

Photos: M3 Photographic

Lauren Camp, Fiber Artist

Heroes (*Leftovers* series), © 2000, dyed, painted, digitally printed and stenciled cotton and silk, acrylic paint, thread, 34" × 33"

Once (*Leftovers* series), © 2000, dyed, painted and digitally printed cotton, silk, canvas and linen, acrylic paint, thread, 46" × 34"

Photos: Hawthorne Studio

Verena Levine

Fish Market, 46" × 31"

Elephant Walk, 25" × 37"

Photos: Mark Gulezian

Linda Filby-Fisher Quilt Artist

Rising, Celebration of Life series, international and handpainted fabrics, photo transfers, embroidered text, fetishes, 47.75"w × 59.25"L, reversible

Hope, Celebration of Life series, international and handpainted fabrics, metallic and silk threads, embroidered text, 68"w × 47"L, reversible

Photos: P-TN/Eric Berndt

Joyce P. Lopez

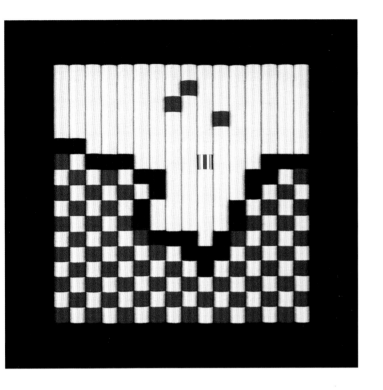
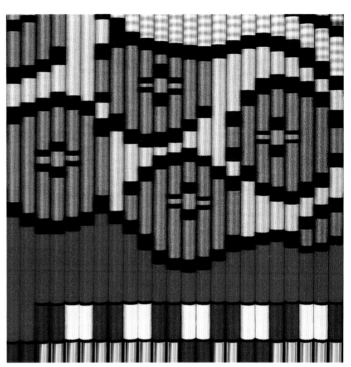

Auspicious Techno Bento — Ginza Sector, 2001, steel and thread sculpture, 31" × 62" × 2"

Photos: Mark Belter

ARTIST
Charlene Marsh

TITLE
Muncie Through the Seasons

YEAR
1997

DESCRIPTION
Gold thread and hand-dyed wool tufted onto a cotton backing, 53" × 124"

SITE
Installed above the stairwell in the Cantina, Minnetrista Cultural Center, Muncie, IN

TIMELINE
4 weeks to fabricate

"This was a very exciting project to work on because Muncie is my hometown. I was able to design a piece that featured the prominent architecture, culture, history, monuments, flora and fauna that had made an impression on me when I was growing up, as well as features I discovered in the course of my research. I was able to include elements of my own family's history, memorializing their standing in the community. During my research for this project, I was given access to papers and spaces that are not normally available to the public, and I had a wonderful time exploring them. I gained new insight and a better appreciation of my hometown, and was pleased to have the opportunity to give something back to the community that gave me my start in life."

favorite commissions

Charlene Marsh

Mermaid Under the Sea

Mermaid Under the Sea, © 2000, gold thread, hand-dyed wool, silk and cotton tufted onto a cotton backing, sculpted for three-dimensional effect, Howard Hughes residence, Nashville, IN, 43" × 106" × 2"

Photos: Kendall Reeves, Spectrum Studio

Barbara McQueeney

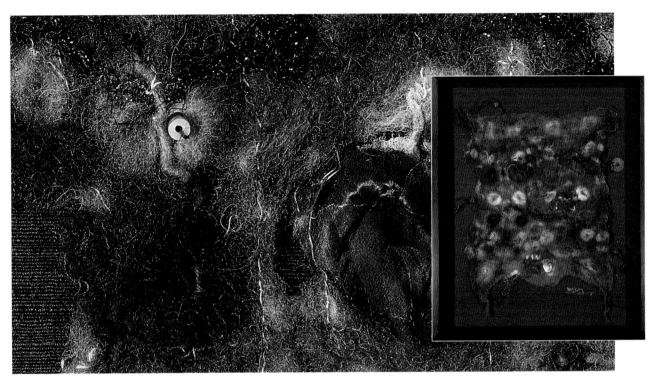

Coming Undone, dyed wool and silk, found objects, 15.5" × 18.5"

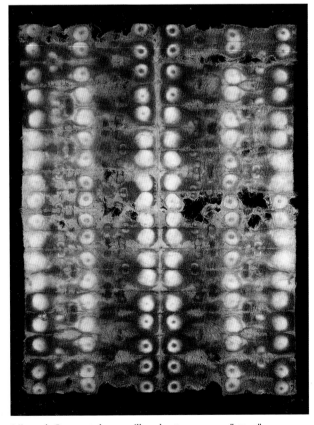

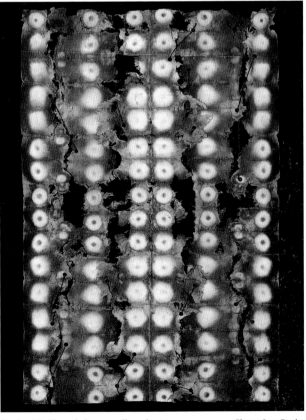

Minerva's Cerement, dyes on silk and cotton paper, 27" × 34"

Sewing My Shroud, dyes on silk and cotton paper, 25" × 34.5"

Photos: Steve Beasley

Kim H. Ritter

Organic Energy

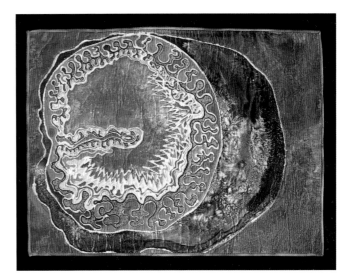

Geode

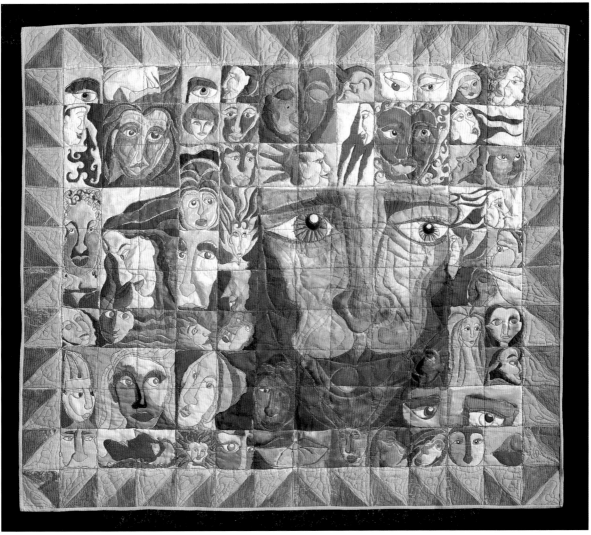

Face Value

Photos: Michael McCormick

Judy Speezak

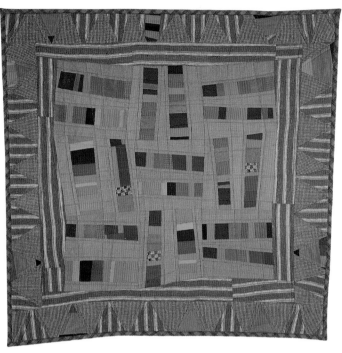

Spontaneous Construction #1: Stripes, 2000, cotton wall quilt, 37" × 35"

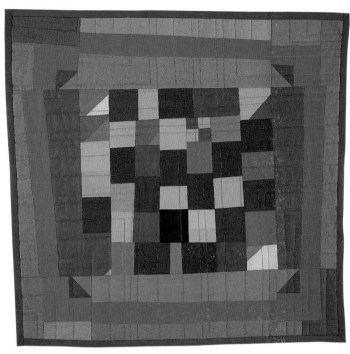

Spontaneous Construction #3: Four-Patch, 2000, cotton wall quilt, 25" × 27"

Spontaneous Construction #2: Medallion, 2000, cotton wall quilt, 41" × 47"

Photos: Karen Bell

Art for the Wall: Fiber

Karen Urbanek

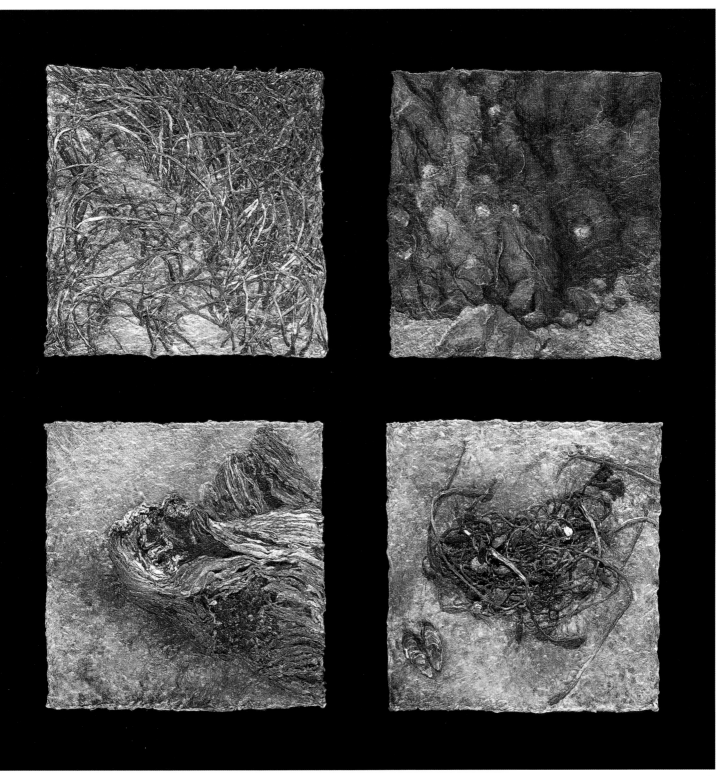

(coastal)² *1-4,* 2001, natural dyed silk fiber, polymer medium, four works, each: 15"H × 15"W

Don Tuttle Photography

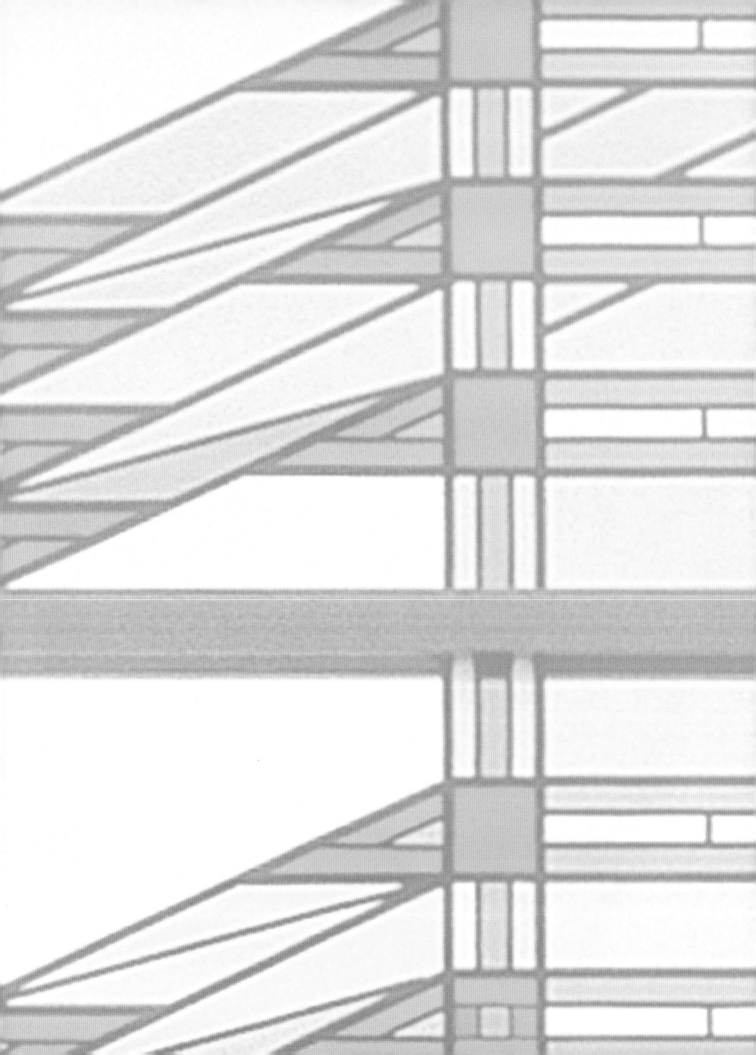

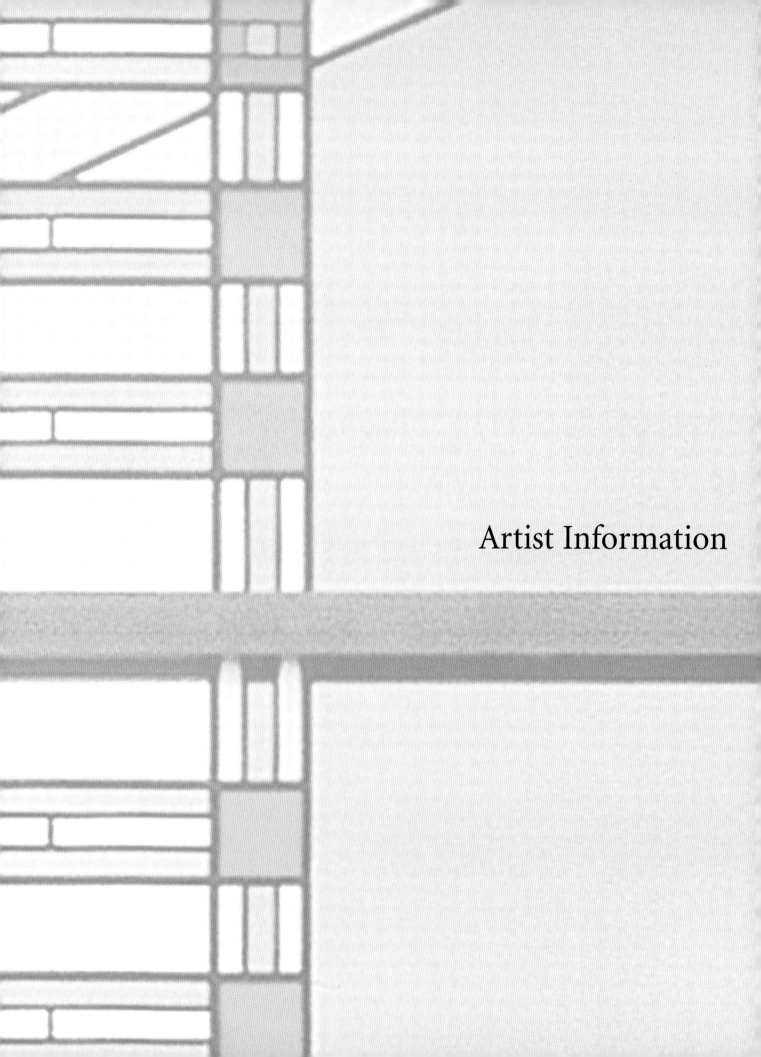

Artist Information

In the pages that follow, you will find additional information on the artists featured in THE SOURCEBOOK OF ARCHITECTURAL & INTERIOR ART 16.

This Artist Information section is arranged in alphabetical order according to the heading on the artist's page. Under that heading (displayed here in a gray band) is the contact information for the artist, as well as additional details on the artist's materials and techniques, commissions, collections and more. References to past GUILD sourcebooks are also included so that you can further explore the breadth of a particular artist's work.

The gray band at the top of each artist's listing also includes references to the pages in the book where you can see images of his or her work.

As you explore THE SOURCEBOOK OF ARCHITECTURAL & INTERIOR ART 16, use the Artist Information section to enrich your experience. If something intrigues you while perusing the sourcebook — a shape, a form, an exotic use of the commonplace — please give the artist a call. Serendipity often leads to a wonderful creation.

Ellen Abbott
Marc Leva   PP. 52, 106

Custom Etched Glass
1330 Lawrence
Houston, TX 77008
TEL   713-864-4773
FAX   713-869-5721
E-mail: **ellen@emstudioglass.com**
E-mail: **marc@emstudioglass.com**
Web: **www.emstudioglass.com**

This art team produces architectural glass for residences and corporate interiors using sandblasting, laminating and related techniques. Their artistry and attention to detail attract a national and international clientele. They also work in the pate de verre cast glass method, creating footed bowls and small sculptures.

RECENT PROJECTS: "Modern Masters," Home and Garden Television, March 2000

PUBLICATIONS: *Glass Craftsman*, October/November 1999; *Etched Glass — Techniques and Designs*, 1998; *The Art of Glass*, 1998

GUILD SOURCEBOOKS: *THE GUILD 4, 5; Architect's 7, 8, 10, 15*

Airworks Inc.   P. 126

George Peters
Melanie Walker
815 Spruce Street
Boulder, CO 80302
TEL/FAX   303-442-9025
E-mail: **airworks@concentric.net**

As a collaborative team, George Peters and Melanie Walker create works that address contemplation and celebration. Their site-specific sculptures and mobiles enliven, illuminate and soften architectural spaces with elegant simplicity and lightness. Both artists are proficient in a wide range of materials and processes, incorporating their unique visions into works that inspire kinetic and poetic play in aerial atrium spaces.

RECENT PROJECTS: University of Central Florida, Orlando, FL; University of Colorado Health Sciences Cancer Center, Denver, CO; Special Collections, University of Arizona, Tucson, AZ

COMMISSIONS: Tokyo Bay Hilton, Tokyo, Japan; University of Colorado, Colorado Springs, CO; Shriners Hospital for Crippled Children, Boston, MA; Desert Sage Library, Phoenix, AZ; Colorado Department of Education, Denver, CO

GUILD SOURCEBOOKS: *Architect's 13, 14, 15*

Mary Lou Alberetti   P. 32

Alberetti Studios
16 Possum Drive
New Fairfield, CT 06812
TEL   203-746-1321
E-mail: **MLALB@aol.com**
Web: **www.southernct.edu/~alberett/**

Mary Lou Alberetti's hand-carved ceramic reliefs draw their inspiration from summers in Italy and the artist's study of classical architecture. Her single or combined units are wired for installation. Commissions are welcomed.

COLLECTIONS: Fuller Museum of Art, Brockton, MA; Mint Museum of Art, Charlotte, NC; HBO World Headquarters, New York, NY; Reese, Lower, Patrick & Scott Ltd., Architects, Lancaster, PA; Cultural Commission, City of New Haven, CT

EXHIBITIONS & AWARDS: Mastercraftsperson, honorary lifetime member, Society of Connecticut Crafts

PUBLICATIONS: *Architectural Ceramics* by Peter King; *Sculptural Clay* by Leon Nigrosh

GUILD SOURCEBOOKS: *Designer's 14, 15*

Allan Bruce Zee
Fine Art Photography   P. 297

Allan Bruce Zee
2240 Southeast 24th Avenue
Portland, OR 97214
TEL   503-234-3211
FAX   503-236-2973
E-mail: **zeebliss@spiritone.com**
Web: **www.allanbrucezee.com**

For 31 years, his unique vision, extraordinary range of imagery and impeccable printing technique have contributed to the enthusiastic response nationally and abroad to the photography of Allan Bruce Zee.

Imagery includes interpretive landscape; abstract textures; international travel; and oriental, impressionistic and architectural motifs.

Sizes range from 10" x 14" to 40" x 60".

Slide or color copy portfolios are available.

COLLECTIONS: IBM, AT&T, Merrill Lynch, Sloan Kettering Hospitals, World Bank

GUILD SOURCEBOOKS: *Designer's 14, 15*

Richard Altman   P. 107

Richard Altman Designs
974 East Divot Drive
Tempe, AZ 85283
TEL   480-831-0201
FAX   480-345-1084
E-mail: **richardaltman@yahoo.com**
Web: **www.richardaltman.com**

Contemporary style, vivid colors, texture and dramatic design are all hallmarks of Richard Altman's glass art. Applications of the artwork include wall panels, skylights, room dividers, wall sconces and sculptural elements. The glass can be mounted on walls, supported with custom metal stands for floor and table display or integrated into unique metal frameworks for large-scale installations. Stunning visual effects are created using combinations of glass particles, poured glass shapes and kiln-forming techniques.

Altman's work is well suited for custom residential projects as well as high-tech corporate environments and commercial projects including retail, restaurants and resorts.

Dana Lynne Andersen, M.A.   P. 204

Awakening Arts Studio
TEL   877-463-7443 (Toll free)
E-mail: **dana@awakeningarts.com**
Web: **www.AwakeningArts.com**

Dana Andersen's museum-quality paintings offer startling beauty and inspiring vision. Large in scale, yet intricate in detail and saturated with vibrancy, her works create worlds to enter and enjoy.

Andersen's refined style bestows an enduring beauty to a vision that is contemporary and compelling. Her paintings are alive with an extraordinary vitality and a spiritual quality that is universal and uplifting.

Her original work is featured in private, corporate and liturgical collections, and is also available as limited-edition archival prints on canvas or paper. In addition to a variety of custom sizes and materials, her studio also offers durable vinyl prints for atrium and outdoor use (up to 25' x 100').

Awakening Arts Studio welcomes commissions, collaborations and site-specific projects.

GUILD SOURCEBOOKS: *Designer's 15*

Tobey Archer   P. 205

Tobey Archer Studio
7618 NW 87th Avenue
Tamarac, FL 33321
TEL   **954-525-4344**
FAX   **954-525-4377**
E-mail: **TArcherArt@aol.com**

Whether intimate or monumental in scale, Tobey Archer's light sculptures energize the environment, creating a joyous luminescent atmosphere. The artwork is unique, highly visible and empowered with presence. The dramatic two-dimensional, three-dimensional, bas-relief, suspended or freestanding innovative light sculptures and architecturally integrated site-sensitive designs harmonize fiber optics and/or neon with a variety of materials.

Archer's award-winning artwork is found in museum, public and private collections worldwide.

Public art is approached through research and collaboration with design team members, the agency involved and the community. Archer's commissions are produced on time, within the budget and they are virtually maintenance free.

Archie Held Studio   P. 173

Archie Held
PO Box 70331
Point Richmond, CA 94807-0331
TEL   **510-235-8700**
FAX   **510-234-4828**
E-mail: **archieheld@aol.com**
Web: **www.ArchieHeld.com**

Archie Held works mainly in bronze and stainless steel, and many of his works incorporate water. His work incorporates richly textured surfaces and patinas. The piece displayed in this book was textured by hand.

RECENT PROJECTS: Orchard Hotel, San Francisco, CA; Harrah's Casino, Shreveport, LA; Booz-Allen & Hamilton, Cleveland, OH; Four Seasons, Kona, HI; First Republic Bank, New York, NY; SAP Technology, PA; Broadvision, Redwood City, CA; Alza Corporation, Mountain View, CA; Sephora Inc., San Francisco, CA; Louis Vuitton, San Francisco, CA

GUILD SOURCEBOOKS: *Architect's 6, 8, 12, 13, 14, 15*

Architectural Ceramics   P. 34

Elle Terry Leonard
401 Mango Avenue, Bay H
Sarasota, FL 34237
TEL   **941-952-0463**
FAX   **941-954-1721**

Architectural Ceramics has created distinct, custom works of art for both interior and exterior spaces since 1978. Inspired and diverse, specialties range from handmade tile and relief murals to ceramic, marble or glass mosaic. A full-service studio that works primarily with the trade, Architectural Ceramics produces site-specific commissions for corporate and residential clients worldwide.

Architectural Ceramics: Handbuilt beauty since 1978.

COMMISSIONS: Tampa International Airport, Worldgate Marriott Hotels, Kaiser Permanente, Johns Hopkins Hospital

GUILD SOURCEBOOKS: *THE GUILD 1, 2, 3, 4, 5; Architect's 6, 8, 9, 10, 11, 12, 13, 14, 15; Designer's 13, 14, 15*

Architectural Glass Art, Inc.   P. 54-55

Kenneth F. vonRoenn, Jr.
PO Box 4665
Louisville, KY 40204-0665
TEL   **502-585-5421**
FAX   **502-585-2808**
E-mail: **aga@unidial.com**
Web: **www.againc.com**

Architectural Glass Art, Inc., provides a complete range of services from design to fabrication to installation for a broad range of work (leaded, cast, laminated, printed and beveled). Kenneth vonRoenn's work is noted for its sympathetic integration with architecture and for his innovative application of new technologies.

The Orlando International Airport window measures 100' x 15' and is the end wall of a terminal. It is composed of antique, sandblasted and dichroic glass with laminated glass jewels.

Eleven glass columns, 10 feet tall and 2 feet in diameter, mark the two entrances to the School of Engineering at the University of Toledo. Within each column are eight vertical planes of glass with beveled glass and dichroic glass laminated onto each surface.

GUILD SOURCEBOOKS: *THE GUILD 4, 5; Architect's 6, 7, 8, 9, 10, 11, 13, 14, 15*

Architectural Glass Art, Inc.   P. 54-55

Kenneth F. vonRoenn, Jr.
PO Box 4665
Louisville, KY 40204-0665
TEL   **502-585-5421**
FAX   **502-585-2808**
E-mail: **aga@unidial.com**
Web: **www.againc.com**

Architectural Glass Art, Inc., provides a complete range of services from design to fabrication to installation for a broad range of work (leaded, cast, laminated, printed and beveled). Kenneth vonRoenn's work is noted for its sympathetic integration with architecture and for his innovative application of new technologies.

A recent project at Three First Union is composed of 52 fins of laminated glass with holographic film and dichroic glass. The fins rise 40 feet above the roofline on all sides of the building.

GUILD SOURCEBOOKS: *THE GUILD 4, 5; Architect's 6, 7, 8, 9, 10, 11, 13, 14, 15*

Babs Armour   P. 296

Babs Armour Photography
411 West End Avenue #8E
New York, NY 10024
TEL   **212-724-4028**
FAX   **212-787-8076**
E-mail: **bka411@aol.com**

In Babs Armour's extensive series of photographs of store windows, the worlds of fashion, architecture and city life are intertwined in a single, often humorous, image — the inside is joined with the outside, the real with the fanciful. Armour captures this interplay in the reflection on the windows' glass, then produces highly saturated color prints on archival paper in sizes up to 40" x 60". Her photographs have appeared in books and magazines and are in numerous residential and corporate settings.

COMMISSIONS: IDS Corporation (American Express Financial Services), Minneapolis, MN; private collections

EXHIBITIONS & AWARDS: First prize, Pilot Press Publication Contest, 2000; Artscapewest, San Francisco, CA, 1999; solo exhibition, Hindsgaul Mannequin Gallery, New York, NY, 1993; Grand prize, Kodak/*Daily News* national contest, 1990

Art As Servant — P. 232

Paul Kiler
17824 La Lima Lane
Fountain Valley, CA 92708-5326
TEL 714-848-5369

PO Box 4730
Santa Fe, NM 87502-4730
TEL 505-424-0868
E-mail: pkiler@earthlink.net
Web: www.art-as-servant.com

Paul Kiler desires that Art As Servant's creations enhance, encourage and draw people into worship and relationship with God through art. Working with a broad range of materials and techniques combined with excellent design, Kiler envisions and produces a wide variety of inspirational artwork for religious environments, including crosses, mosaics, stained glass, sculpture, altars and other implements.

COMMISSIONS: altarpiece sculpture, Pacific Southwest District Lutheran Conference; altar, Fountain of Life Lutheran Church, Tucson, AZ; sanctuary cross, Celebration Community Church, Foothill Ranch, CA; sanctuary cross, Community Christian Church, Yorba Linda, CA; complete worship environment, Epiphany Lutheran Church, Chandler, AZ

The Art Studio/ Fine Art Murals — P. 112

Carl White
Darren Schweitzer
2305 Fifth Avenue NW
Calgary, AB T2N 0T1
TEL/FAX 403-244-8686
E-mail: fineartmurals@home.com

Nicholas Jones
TEL 310-880-9393
E-mail: info@fineartmurals.com
Web: www.fineartmurals.com

The Art Studio/Fine Art Murals supplies original, hand-painted fine art murals for public or private spaces. The studio works to the highest professional standards to create custom artwork for specific environments — sensitive and unique designs in the true spirit of fine art from original concept development or works based on historical reference. The team has over 10 years of practical on-site experience working with clients, designers and architects.

COMMISSIONS: Sun Life Assurance Company; Hard Rock Cafe International; Second Cup Coffee Company; private residences in Canada, the U.K. and U.S.

GUILD SOURCEBOOKS: *Designer's 15*

Shawn Athari — PP. 104-105

Shawn Athari's, Inc.
14332 Mulholland Drive
Los Angeles, CA 90077
TEL 310-476-0066
FAX 310-476-9ART
E-mail: shawn@shawnathari.com
Web: www.shawnathari.com

Whether embracing an environment to create a statement through her work or borrowing from history to create a historical form in a contemporary manner, Shawn Athari has developed the skills and talents to do both successfully. Athari has been in the glass field since 1975 and through her vision she exemplifies good taste and sophistication.

Athari's work in this book is a continuation of her repertoire which ranges from Disney figures for Walt Disney Corporation to creating synagogue panels in excess of 240 sq. ft. Her work can be seen in many private and public collections.

COLLECTIONS: Pismo, Denver, CO; Glass Oasis, Aladdin Hotel, Las Vegas, NV; Wayside Gallery, Chatham, MA; Lynch & Kennedy, Skagway, AK; Adamms, Santa Monica, CA

Shawn Athari — PP. 104-105

Shawn Athari's, Inc.
14332 Mulholland Drive
Los Angeles, CA 90077
TEL 310-476-0066
FAX 310-476-9ART
E-mail: shawn@shawnathari.com
Web: www.shawnathari.com

Whether embracing an environment to create a statement through her work or borrowing from history to create a historical form in a contemporary manner, Shawn Athari has developed the skills and talents to do both successfully. Athari has been in the glass field since 1975 and through her vision she exemplifies good taste and sophistication.

In the French doors shown in this book, Athari manipulated the glass using cold, warm and hot glass techniques so as to create a body of work with unique depth of field and colors.

COLLECTIONS: Pismo, Denver, CO; Glass Oasis, Aladdin Hotel, Las Vegas, NV; Wayside Gallery, Chatham, MA; Lynch & Kennedy, Skagway, AK; Adamms, Santa Monica, CA

Eleen Auvil — P. 33

Stony Creek Studio
278 Corral De Tierra
Salinas, CA 93908
TEL 831-372-6991
FAX 831-484-9343
E-mail: auvil@redshift.com

Eleen Auvil's copper panels are meticulously crafted with cast lead and/or bronze, then enriched by patinas of washes, creating surprisingly unusual works of art.

Her widely collected bronze sculptures, ranging in size from one to ten feet, are inspired by flights of birds, ballet movements and the human form.

RECENT PROJECTS: Installation, Monterey Museum of Art, Monterey, CA

COMMISSIONS: Red Rock Country Club, Las Vegas, NV; many private homes

GUILD SOURCEBOOKS: *Architect's 15*

Badman Design — P. 246

David S. Badman
18 South Third Street
Grand Forks, ND 58201
TEL 800-552-2362
TEL 701-746-7300
E-mail: dave@badman.com
Web: www.badman.com

Originally a metalsmith and jewelry designer, David Badman has moved ahead with his home decor theme, adding mirrors of all shapes and sizes to his repertoire. The mirrors are framed in metal, glazed in subtle colors and earth tones and sealed for durability; some have the added element of terra cotta accents. Tables, wall art and wine racks are also available from Badman's studio.

GUILD SOURCEBOOKS: *Designer's 13, 14*

ARTIST INFORMATION

Allan Baillie P. 298

40 Waterside Plaza, 29G
New York, NY 10010
TEL 212-685-9858
Web: **www.guild.com**

Allan Baillie photographs from nature and shows the details of our world close up as well as distant vistas. His work in black and white is graphic, and can be printed with a rich sepia tone.

Prints are in limited editions and signed on the verso. They can be made any size and combined in sequence for large spaces.

More samples and price information are available.

EXHIBITIONS & AWARDS: Fine Art and Photography Shows, New York, NY; The Katonah Museum of Art; The Baltimore Museum; The Corcoran Gallery

Barbara Butler
Artist-Builder P. 174

Barbara Butler
325 South Maple Avenue #37
South San Francisco, CA 94080
TEL 415-864-6840
FAX 650-877-7223
E-mail: **barbara@barbarabutler.com**
Web: **www.barbarabutler.com**

San Francisco artist Barbara Butler creates vibrant, imaginative, uniquely functional works of art for the family backyard. Specializing in custom residential play sculptures, Butler's designs range from small carved and stained playhouses to large multi-tiered tree forts. Each structure is a beautiful extension of the home, providing "outdoor rooms" that stimulate physical and imaginative play.

COMMISSIONS: Disney, Kevin Kline, Bobby McFerrin, Robert Redford, Will Smith

PUBLICATIONS: *Architectural Digest, People, Sunset Magazine, The Treehouse Book*

GUILD SOURCEBOOKS: *Architect's 13, 14, 15; Designer's 13, 14*

Kathy Barnard P. 56-57

Kathy Barnard Studio
1605 Locust
Kansas City, MO 64108
TEL 816-472-4977
FAX 816-471-0984
E-mail: **KBarnardStudio@aol.com**

Kathy Barnard Studio designs and fabricates sculptural carved art glass, stained glass windows, deep-carved glass panels and murals. Her site-specific commissioned work is found in commercial, religious and private environments throughout the country. The love of nature, a commitment to the client's vision and a distinctive sense of design and detail are incorporated to produce representational and abstract installations in glass and granite.

GUILD SOURCEBOOKS: *THE GUILD 3, 4, 5; Architect's 8, 9, 10, 13*

Kathy Barnard P. 56-57

Kathy Barnard Studio
1605 Locust
Kansas City, MO 64108
TEL 816-472-4977
FAX 816-471-0984
E-mail: **KBarnardStudio@aol.com**

COMMISSIONS: Stillwater National Bank & Trust, OK, 2000; Mormon Temple, Houston, TX, 2000; First USA Bank, Wilmington, DE, 1997; East Lawrence Recreation Center, Percent for the Arts Project, Lawrence, KS, 1997; RLDS Temple and World Headquarters, Independence, MO, 1992; Jewish Community Center and Jewish Federation Headquarters, Overland Park, KS, 1988; Midland Theatre, Kansas City, MO, 1987

EXHIBITIONS & AWARDS: AIA Allied Arts and Craftsmanship Award, 1990

James Barnhill P. 138

206 South Chapman Street
Greensboro, NC 27403
TEL/FAX 336-275-7135

Working from the live model in the classical tradition, James Barnhill sculpts figures of quiet beauty and contemplation. The finished work is then cast in bronze.

COMMISSIONS: North Carolina Symphony, Raleigh, NC, 2000; Sisters of Divine Providence, Pittsburgh, PA, 2000; TWA Flight 800 Memorial, Montoursville, PA, 1999; Public Library, Hickory, NC, 1999; City of Mountain Brook, AL, 1997; Mission Memorial Hospital, Mission Viejo, CA, 1996; Booker T. Washington National Monument, Burnt Chimney, VA, 1996; City of Asheville, NC, 1996; Birmingham Botanical Gardens, Birmingham, AL, 1991

GUILD SOURCEBOOKS: *Architect's 7, 8, 11, 13, 15*

Matthew A. Berg V P. 206

Berg Studios LLC
1417 N. Harding
Indianapolis, IN 46202
TEL 317-974-1844
FAX 317-974-0845
E-mail: **bergstudio@aol.com**
Web: **www.bergstudios.com**

The monumental sculptures Matthew A. Berg invents are executed predominantly in steel and glass, occasionally incorporating wood. Intended for display outdoors where nature serves as a backdrop, pieces are inspired and based on natural forms. The play of natural light is important to the rhythm and balance that is envisioned for each piece — as daylight changes, the dynamics of the sculptures change. The effects of the natural elements upon the pieces add to that dynamic. With massive, identifiable forms, the sculptures cause curiosity, wonder and appreciation among public audiences captivated by the works' scale.

RECENT PROJECTS: Atrium fountains for St. Vincent Hospitals

COMMISSIONS: Galyan's Trading Company, Minneapolis, MN and Columbus, OH; Kiwanis International, Indianapolis, IN

Sandra C.Q. Bergér   P. 53

Quintal Studio
100 El Camino Real #202
Burlingame, CA 94010
TEL   650-348-0310
FAX   650-340-0198

Internationally exhibited and published, award-winning glass designer Sandra Bergér creates exceptional custom glass art and limited editions for corporate, public and private clients. Precision engineered, each glass sculpture or installation is effectively designed and executed.

Experienced and professional, worldwide service, timely delivery.

RECENT PROJECTS: "Video Magazine" for PBS

COMMISSIONS: Concert Theatre, Minot, ND; Tanforan Business Center, So. San Francisco, CA; White House, Washington, DC; Thermo King Corporation, Minneapolis, MN; other public and private commissions

PUBLICATIONS: *Designing Interiors* textbook; *Women in Design International; Facet Magazine*

GUILD SOURCEBOOKS: *THE GUILD 1, 2, 3, 4, 5; Architect's 6, 7, 8, 10, 11; Designer's 8, 11, 13, 14, 15; THE GUILD Hand Book 1998*

Beyer Studio, Inc.   PP. 64, 233

Joseph K. Beyer
9511 Germantown Avenue
Philadelphia, PA 19118
TEL   215-848-3502
FAX   215-848-3535
E-mail: **beyerart@bellatlantic.net**

Joseph K. Beyer's designs reinvent religious themes in a contemporary manner. Beyer Studio's 12 employees hold art degrees and assist in the design, fabrication and installation of new glass, restoration, framing consultation and industry-leading adaptive reuse of historic windows in new churches across the United States.

EXHIBITIONS & AWARDS: Best of Show, *Ministry & Liturgy Magazine* Visual Art Awards, 1999-2000; co-curator, "Philadelphia Stained Glass: A Continuing Tradition," Paley Gallery at Philadelphia University, 1999; Bene Award, *Ministry & Liturgy Magazine* Visual Art Awards, 1998-99

GUILD SOURCEBOOKS: *Architect's 11, 15*

Michael D. Bigger   P. 175

M.D. Bigger, Sculptor
2226 27th Avenue South
Minneapolis, MN 55406
TEL/FAX   612-722-7628
E-mail: **mbigger@lynxus.com**
Web: **www.michaelbigger.com**

Michael Bigger's sculpture ranges in scale from maquette to monumental. Experienced with all materials, Bigger prefers to work with welded steel. His style is generally non-representational, with conceptual roots in his education in architecture. Commissioned work is welcome.

COLLECTIONS: Vassar College; University of Maine, Augusta; San Antonio Museum of Art; Grupo Villacero, Monterrey, Mexico; Oakland Museum of Art, Oakland, CA; Atlantic Richfield Collection, Los Angeles, CA; Joy of Cooking Corporation, Cincinnati, OH; Wiregrass Museum of Art, Dothan, AL

Leslie C. Birleson   P. 207

422 Cross Street
Woodland, CA 95695
TEL/FAX   530-668-4275

For 27 years, Birleson has created numerous large- and small-scale sculptural installations for both public and private international collections. Birleson's works are internally illuminated sculptures of aluminum, polycarbonate and silk. The works are equally effective in daytime or nighttime.

For the last eight years, he has been exploring the transparency of materials and the sense of movement between painting, sculpture and light. The lighting for all sculptures is a low-wattage, energy-efficient compact fluorescent and dimmable lighting element.

Prices range from $10000 to $500000.

Sharron Bliss   P. 266

Sharron Bliss Fine Arts
559 Monarch Ridge Drive
Walnut Creek, CA 94596
TEL   925-944-6366
FAX   925-274-9312
E-mail: **Blissarts@msn.com**

Using environmentally friendly materials, Sharron Bliss works on paper and publishes limited-edition prints. After daily meditation, she creates work that includes healing abstract and representational images from nature. A colorist, her broad palette range is contemporary and emotionally moving.

A portfolio of images is available upon request.

COMMISSIONS: Grace Hills Country Club, Nagoya, Japan; Ritz-Carlton Hotel, St. Thomas; Nordstrom, Seattle, WA; Informix, Menlo Park, CA; Cisco, San Jose, CA; Mills Peninsula Hospital, San Mateo, CA; David and Lucile Packard Foundation; Xerox, Rochester, NY

Rita Blitt   PP. 176-177

Rita Blitt, Inc.
8900 State Line
Leawood, KS 66206
TEL   913-381-3840
FAX   913-381-5624
E-mail: **rita@ritablitt.com**
Web: **www.ritablitt.com**

Rita Blitt's *Passionate Gesture* sculpture series I through XI echoes the title of the recently published *Rita Blitt: The Passionate Gesture* as well as the dancing brushstrokes of her paintings.

This series, cast in bronze, began as ribbons of acrylic that Blitt heated, shaped and recombined in dancing positions. She now envisions creating them life-size or larger.

Blitt, who recently was honored as the first artist to exhibit in the new Brandeis University Women's Center in Waltham, MA, has exhibited and installed monumental sculpture up to 60 feet tall in the United States and abroad.

Her sculpture has been referred to as a link between nature, humans and architecture.

PUBLICATIONS: *Rita Blitt: The Passionate Gesture*, 2000, also available as a limited-edition book and sculpture

Barney Boller P. 139

Boller Studios
PO Box 903
2032 Route 213
Rifton, NY 12471
TEL 845-658-8351
FAX 845-658-3144
E-mail: **barneyboller@hotmail.com**
Web: **www.barneyboller.com**

Barney Boller, an artist living in the Catskill Mountains of upstate New York, is well known for his distinctive and highly polished bronze wildlife sculpture. His work covers a wide range of animal subjects — from North American to African — and can be found in private and public collections worldwide.

COMMISSIONS: Nemacolin Woodlands Resort, 84 Lumber Company

COLLECTIONS: Glasgow Museum of Art, Glasgow, Scotland; Bennington Center for the Arts, Bennington, VT

PUBLICATIONS: *Wildlife Journal, Wildlife Art Magazine, U.S. Art Magazine*

Eric Boyer P. 140

683 East Putney Brook Road
Westminster West, VT 05346
TEL/FAX 802-257-2027
E-mail: **eboyer@sover.net**
Web: **www.boyermesh.com**

Eric Boyer creates original sculpture in woven steel wire mesh. The work juxtaposes the sensuality and spirituality of classical nude sculptures with an exciting industrial material.

Formed by hand, these sculptures nurture a unique relationship to light — now transparent, now opaque. Boyer's work, which can be designed for wall hanging or freestanding, has been exhibited nationally and collected internationally since 1989. Commissions are accepted.

GUILD SOURCEBOOKS: *Designer's 11, 13, 15*

David B. Brackett P. 350

404 Penn Street
New Bethlehem, PA 16242
TEL 814-275-1846
E-mail: **dbrackett@clarion.edu**

David Brackett masterfully combines screen-printed cotton webbing with intricately dyed and handwoven cloth. Painted, woven and photographic images are derived through a background in science and an exploration of the formation of pattern in nature. These fabric collages are machine-stitched to form a durable surface rich in pattern, texture and color.

EXHIBITIONS & AWARDS: Lancaster Museum of Art, Lancaster, PA, 2000; Buncher Family Foundation Award, Carnegie Museum of Art, 1995; Chautauqua International; Crafts National; second prize, fifth National Fiber Arts Competition, 1992

PUBLICATIONS: *Fiberarts Design Book Six; Fiberarts Design Book Five;* "The Hidden Image," *Fiberarts Magazine,* 1993; "Unfolding Morphology," *Surface Design Journal,* 1991

Kathy Bradford P. 58

North Star Art Glass, Inc.
142 Wichita
Lyons, CO 80540
TEL/FAX 303-823-6511
E-mail: **kathybradford@webtv.net**
Web: **www.kathybradford.com**

Found on the third floor of the Russian Tearoom in New York City is the Bear Ballroom. Here, Kathy Bradford has sandcarved 10 large half-inch-thick glass panels of Russian performing circus bears. The inset of the bear shown in this book demonstrates the carving techniques Bradford is known for.

The 8' x 21' x 6" multi-layered glass wall (also shown) highlights Bradford's artistry in her detailed sandcarving of natural images.

RECENT PROJECTS: Glendale, AZ, Percent for the Arts; Vilar Center for the Arts, Beaver Creek, CO; Russian Tearoom, New York, NY

COMMISSIONS: Russian Tearoom, New York, NY; Good Samaritan Hospital, Chicago, IL; Glendale, AZ, Percent for the Arts

GUILD SOURCEBOOKS: *Architect's 12, 13, 14, 15*

Bramante Studio P. 234

20 Queen Street North
Kitchener, ON N2H 2G8
Canada
TEL 800-295-6902
TEL 519-570-2908
FAX 519-570-2706
E-mail: **info@bramante.com**
Web: **www.bramante.com**

Bramante Studio consists of a group of artists that follow the ideals of the Arts and Crafts Movement. They apply these philosophies to fabric art installations, bronze and resin sculptures and carved and etched glass. Over the last several years, the studio has completed several thousand large-scale installations for clients throughout North America.

To view specific commissions, please view the studio's website at www.bramante.com.

Jeanine Briggs P. 178

PO Box 475441
San Francisco, CA 94123
TEL 415-567-4662
E-mail: **artlinks@pacbell.net**

Jeanine Briggs creates wall and freestanding sculptures; some pieces function as screens, light filters, architectural curtains or space dividers. Environmental concerns influence her construction and materials, which include discarded wood, metal, fiber, cardboard, plastic and ceramics. She brings her sensibilities as a painter to her three-dimensional work, often treating sculptural elements as brushstrokes. She works in a range of sizes and styles and welcomes site-specific projects.

EXHIBITIONS & AWARDS: Artist in residence, San Francisco disposal and recycling facility, October 1999 to January 2000

GUILD SOURCEBOOKS: *Designer's 15*

Barbara Brotherton — P. 324

Barbro Designs
98 Windsor Avenue
San Rafael, CA 94901
TEL   415-485-0242
FAX   415-256-1763
E-mail: **barbro38@hotmail.com**
Web: **www.barbrodesigns.com**

Utilizing materials such as wood, poured stone, metal leaf and patinas, mixed-media artist Barbara Brotherton creates wall pieces that reflect her deep appreciation of Mediterranean and Far Eastern design. This layering process evokes "crusty building surfaces," and can be seen as a representation of natural processes like sedimentation, erosion, entropy and the cycle of birth, death and rebirth.

Her work is widely represented in private and corporate collections. Slides and pricing available upon request. Site-specific commissions are welcomed.

RECENT PROJECTS: *Pathways,* rotunda, U.S. Ambassador's residence, Nicosia, Cyprus

COMMISSIONS: Sheraton Hotel, Newport Beach, CA; St. Vincent Hospital, Indianapolis, IN

GUILD SOURCEBOOKS: *Designer's 10, 12, 14*

Bob Brown — P. 267

Bob Brown Studio
2725 Terry Lake Road
Fort Collins, CO 80524
TEL/FAX   970-224-5473
E-mail: **bobbrown-artist@att.net**

Bob Brown's colorful paintings highlight an area by bringing the bright outdoors inside. The thick texture created with durable acrylic paint and a painting knife provides an intriguing surface. His subjects are representational and mostly landscapes.

Unframed paintings range from 16" x 20" to 36" x 48". Commissions are considered; a brochure is available.

COLLECTIONS: McGraw-Hill Companies, New York, NY; Prince Albert, Monte Carlo, Monaco

EXHIBITIONS & AWARDS: Galleries and public spaces in the United States, Monaco and France

GUILD SOURCEBOOKS: *Designer's 14, 15*

Laura Militzer Bryant — P. 351

2595 30th Avenue North
St. Petersburg, FL 33713
TEL   727-327-3100
FAX   727-321-1905
E-mail: **knitlb@ix.netcom.com**

Florida artist Laura Bryant painstakingly creates richly layered and detailed complex double weaves of wool, rayon, nylon and Lurex. All threads are hand painted and dyed by Bryant with high-quality lightfast dyes. Enhanced by patinated copper backing or floating on a wall, these landscape-inspired geometric images provide an enticing environment for home or office.

COLLECTIONS: City of St. Petersburg, FL; Xerox Corporation, Rochester, NY; Seton Hall University, NJ

EXHIBITIONS & AWARDS: Florida Individual Artist Fellowship, 1994-95; National Endowment for the Arts Visual Artist Fellowship, 1990-91

GUILD SOURCEBOOKS: *Designer's 10, 11, 12, 13, 14, 15*

Fran Bull — P. 268

PO Box 707
Closter, NJ 07624
TEL   201-767-3726
FAX   201-767-7733
E-mail: **franbull@juno.com**

Fran Bull uses every type of acrylic paint to create her opulent abstract works. Metallics and iridescents suggest a range of moods, themes, states of mind and places real or imagined.

RECENT PROJECTS: *Taller Barbará,* an ongoing series of etchings produced in the studio where Miró made his large prints, Barcelona, Spain

COLLECTIONS: Yale University, New Haven, CT; Johnson & Johnson, New Brunswick, NJ; Baltimore Museum of Art, Baltimore, MD; Museum of Modern Art, New York, NY; National Museum of Women in the Arts, Washington, DC

PUBLICATIONS: *Architectural Digest,* April 1981; ink drawings, *Mordant Rhymes*; *Photorealism,* 1980

GUILD SOURCEBOOKS: *Designer's 15*

Myra Burg — PP. 172, 352

6180 West Jefferson, Suite Y
Los Angeles, CA 90016
TEL   310-399-5040
FAX   310-399-0623
E-mail. **myra@myraburg.com**
Web: **www.myraburg.com**

Myra Burg produces innovative site-specific art, enjoying unusual or complicated site parameters. Completed works, custom *Quiet Oboes* and architectural installations such as rolling, pivot and ark doors are also available. Sizes range from tabletop to airplane hangar for freestanding, wall-mounted and aerial constructions.

Since 1976, Burg has produced installations for private collections and public spaces, domestic and abroad. An award winner in both careers, art and architecture, her work is considered of investment quality. Collaborations are welcome.

COLLECTIONS: Benefactors of the Los Angeles County Museum of Art; County of San Luis Obispo; Kennedy Library; Holiday Inns; Apple Computer; Caribe Hilton, Puerto Rico; Universal Studios Japan

GUILD SOURCEBOOKS: *Architect's 14, 15; Designer's 10, 13, 14, 15*

Riis Burwell — P. 179

Riis Burwell Studio
3815 Calistoga Road
Santa Rosa, CA 95404
TEL/FAX   707-538-2676
E-mail: **Riisburwell@aol.com**

Riis Burwell's sculpture reflects his interest in the relationship between order and chaos in nature. His pieces express the constant transition between growth and decay. Burwell works with metals because of their duality of character — strong, yet flexible; rusted and rough, or smooth and gleaming.

COMMISSIONS: Williams Corporation, OK; Valley Lab, CO; Jones Spacelink, CO

EXHIBITIONS & AWARDS: "Contemporary Constructivism," Los Angeles County Museum; Olive Grove Sculpture Gallery, Rutherford, CA; Sandy Carson Gallery, Denver, CO

GUILD SOURCEBOOKS: *Architect's 13, 14, 15*

ARTIST INFORMATION

Bridget Busutil   P. 269

Busutil Impressions, LLC
120 Ralph McGill Boulevard, Studio 906
Atlanta, GA 30308
TEL   404-875-9155
FAX   404-875-9750
E-mail: bmbart@attglobal.net

Bridget Busutil works with oil, acrylics and encaustics on canvas or board. As a landscape artist, she is particularly attracted to trees — their forms, shapes, branches, textures and differences in leaves fascinate her. She is sensitive to their mythical significance, and is very concerned by the danger the current polluted environment represents for them.

RECENT PROJECTS: The Windsor Condominiums, Atlanta, GA

COMMISSIONS: Hilton, Aruba, Caribbean; Banque Nationale de Paris, Basel, Switzerland

EXHIBITIONS & AWARDS: Award recipient, Piccolo Spoleto Festival, Charleston, SC, 2000; award recipient, Low Country Arts and Cultural Council's Juried Visual Arts Exhibition, Charleston, SC, 1997; Decorative Art Exhibition, Paris, France, 1978

Steven Carpenter   P. 270

Valley Art Group
15220 North 63rd Street
Oak Park Heights, MN 55082
TEL   888-470-7303 (Toll free)
TEL   651-430-0617
FAX   651-439-4593
Web: www.valleyartgroup.com

Steven Carpenter's landscapes are easily recognizable because of their vibrant colors — he intensifies the natural color of our surrounding landscape. To achieve his desired coloration while maintaining the freedom to draw, Carpenter frequently works in pastel. His works are created in the studio and are a combination of reality and imagination.

COLLECTIONS: University of Minnesota, Minneapolis, MN; University of Wisconsin, Madison, WI; Honeywell, Minneapolis, MN; 3M, St. Paul, MN; Federal Reserve Bank, Minneapolis, MN; IBM, Minneapolis, MN; American Express, Minneapolis, MN

Warren Carther   P. 59

Carther Studio Inc.
80 George Avenue
Winnipeg, MB R3B 0K1
Canada
TEL   204-956-1615
FAX   204-942-1434
E-mail: warren@cartherstudio.com
Web: www.cartherstudio.com

Glass artist Warren Carther explores light in varied and unusual ways, manipulating the quality of light as it is filtered through the complex layers of his work. His respect and understanding of the structural capabilities of glass combined with his interest in working sculpturally within the architectural environment lead him to produce unique work which crosses the boundaries between architecture and art, two dimensions and three. Innovative techniques in structure, abrasive blast carving, laminations and color application distinguish his often large-scale work. Numerous commissions and publications throughout the world have earned him an international reputation.

COMMISSIONS: Canadian Embassy, Tokyo, Japan; Swire Group, Hong Kong; Charles De Gaulle Airport, Paris, France; Anchorage International Airport, AK

Jill Casty   PP. 129, 152

Jill Casty Design
494 Alvarado Street, Suite D
Monterey, CA 93940
TEL   831-649-0923
FAX   831-649-0713
E-mail: jillcdesign@hotmail.com
Web: www.jillcastydesign.com

Jill Casty's exuberant, graceful art, while inventive and personal, is always sensitive to a site's spirit and spaces as well as to the vision of client and architect. Her aerial pieces — from joyful atrium mobiles to innovative, large-scale hanging art programs — and her festive abstract standing sculptures (up to 30 feet high) employ diverse materials such as metals, acrylics and glass.

RECENT PROJECTS: City of Montclair, CA; SuperMall of the Great Northwest, Auburn, WA; Northwest Plaza, St. Louis, MO

GUILD SOURCEBOOKS: *Architect's 10, 11, 12, 13, 14, 15*

L.T. Cherokee   P. 180

40 Prospect Avenue
Northport, NY 11768
TEL   631-261-3342

L.T. Cherokee has been expressing his vision of form for more than 20 years. His works in bronze, stone and wood are represented at galleries internationally and are widely held in private collections.

Cherokee is most renowned for his ability to breathe a gamut of emotions into the medium and for the subsequent impact on the living environment, bringing fluidity and substance together into graceful, lyrical forms. Many pieces can be scaled to site-specific requirements, integrating well into a variety of spaces. He prefers close collaboration with architects and designers to achieve optimal impact. Brochures are available upon request.

City Glass Specialty, Inc.   P. 60

Richard Hollman
2124 South Calhoun Street
Fort Wayne, IN 46802
TEL   219-744-3301
FAX   219-744-2522

City Glass Specialty is a family-owned business that has been in operation since 1944. City Glass operates as a glazing contractor, tailoring to the needs of the commercial and residential sectors. The art glass studio is a multi-faceted studio featuring commissioned work as well as restoration. The studio offers stained, leaded, engraved, molded, beveled, etched and faceted glass. These forms of art glass have been commissioned and installed in various types of architectural styles and applications.

Clay Architectural Murals LLC — P. 35

Juliet Ehrlich
505 Macon Avenue
Louisville, KY 40207
TEL   502-721-7805

Juliet Ehrlich's clay bas-relief murals are at once both painting and fired sculpture. Her commissions — private, public and corporate — exhibit technical excellence and a stunning diversity. Site-specifically designed, they often require historical, anthropological or corporate research. Collaborations are welcome.

RECENT PROJECTS: "Lynette Jennings," Discovery Channel, 1999-2000; *Abril*, corporate boardroom, Sao Paolo, Brazil, 11' x 3'; *Rousseau's Jungle Scene*, private residence, 6' x 4'

COMMISSIONS: U.S. embassies in New Guinea and Singapore

COLLECTIONS: Maker's Mark, Louisville, KY; Whip-Mix, Louisville, KY

PUBLICATIONS: *Art & Antiques* magazine, December 1999

Jeremy R. Cline — P. 181

Incline Glass
768 Delano Avenue
San Francisco, CA 94112
TEL   415-469-8312
FAX   415-469-8463
E-mail: **jc@jeremycline.com**
Web: **www.jeremycline.com**

Jeremy Cline's glasswork reflects not only his love for the medium but also his fine craftsmanship and an ongoing endeavor to better his working processes. A glass artist since 1987, Cline opened his own studio in 1992. Taking cues from the glass itself, as well as from antiquity and contemporary sources, Cline's personal work examines the vessel as an art form.

The *Birds of Paradise* series (shown in this book) illustrates Cline's ability to transform the medium of glass into an object of inherent movement and flexibility. Each piece incorporates a sensitive color palette with a simple undulating form to create an ever-changing expression of the vessel as organic, suggesting both flower and bird.

In addition to the *Birds of Paradise* series, Cline creates a broad range of work, including fine stemware, custom lighting and solid sculpture. He continues to expand his abilities and methodology in pursuit of excellence in glass.

Jonathan Clowes Sculpture — P. 128

Jonathan J. Clowes
Evelyn J. Clowes
PO Box 274
Acworth, NH 03601
TEL/FAX   603-835-6441
E-mail: **jonathanclowes@top.monad.net**

Power and elegance mark the Clowes' sculptural work. Organic shapes and flowing curves speak of serene seas, soft winds and gracious gestures. Strong lines in wood — balanced with rich colors in metal, blown glass and other materials — create graceful forms in motion.

This husband-and-wife team has over 25 years of experience sculpting for residential, corporate, liturgical and public spaces.

COMMISSIONS: *M.S. Explorer of the Seas*, Royal Caribbean International, Oslo, Norway, 2000; Hilton Hotel International, Tokyo, Japan, 1998; *M.S. Rhapsody of the Seas*, Royal Caribbean Cruise Lines, Oslo, Norway, 1996; Indianapolis Museum of Art, Indianapolis, IN, 1995; Monadnock Paper Inc., Bennington, NH, 1994; Manchester District Courthouse, Manchester, NH, 1993; Antioch New England Graduate School, Keene, NH, 1992; Visalia Convention Center, Visalia, CA, 1992

Gretchen Lee Coles — P. 325

The Great Circle Press
PO Box 456
Glen Ellyn, IL 60138-0456

Cartographer and sculptor Gretchen Lee Coles constructs one-of-a-kind, three-dimensional maps using various appropriate materials such as paper, fabric, wood and ceramic. Her maps express the physical and ephemeral spirit of a place and range from geographic realism to playful abstraction. With more than 20 years of professional experience, Coles honors traditional map making by welcoming teamwork in designing unique maps of real places. Please contact the Great Circle Press for a map list and prices.

EXHIBITIONS & AWARDS: Elmhurst Art Museum, Elmhurst, IL, 2001; Purchase Prize, College of DuPage, Glen Ellyn, IL, 1997

GUILD SOURCEBOOKS: *Designer's 14, 15*

Conrad Schmitt Studios, Inc. — PP. 61, 240

2405 South 162nd Street
New Berlin, WI 53151
TEL   800-969-3033
FAX   262-786-9036
E-mail: **css1889@aol.com**
Web: **www.conradschmitt.com**

Conrad Schmitt Studios creates art for buildings of architectural, historic and religious significance. One of the oldest and largest glass studios in the United States, the company's patented Leptat® etched glass as well as its stained glass creation and restoration work can be seen throughout the country. Since 1889, the studios have provided interior decorative services that also include artwork such as statuary, sculpture, murals and mosaics.

COMMISSIONS: The Egyptian Theater, Boise, ID; University of Notre Dame Main Building, South Bend, IN; Cathedral of St. Paul, Birmingham, AL; Wisconsin Conservatory of Music, Milwaukee, WI; Cathedral of St. Mary, Lafayette, IN; St. Elizabeth Ann Seton Catholic Church, Keller, TX

PUBLICATIONS: *Stained Glass, Inland Architect, Midwest Express Magazine*

Jeffrey Cooper — P. 208

Designer of Sculptural Furnishings in Wood
135 McDonough Street
Portsmouth, NH 03801
TEL/FAX   603-436-7945
E-mail: **jcooper@cooperwoodsculptor.com**
Web: **www.cooperwoodsculptor.com**

High-quality, handcrafted public art is a wonderful way to cherish life and the beautiful things in our world. This is Jeffrey Cooper's philosophy and his passion. His sculpture, especially when placed in settings for children, teaches these lessons of life and beauty to our next generation. By integrating the basics of furniture making techniques with his distinct vision, unique sculptural style and detailed marquetry decorations, he will bring joy and delight to your public spaces.

COMMISSIONS: Jan Kaminis Platt Library, Tampa, FL; Children's Museum of Lowell, MA; York Hospital, York, ME; Texas Children's Hospital, Houston, TX; Newport Hospital, Newport, RI

ARTIST INFORMATION

Robert L. Cooper   P. 247

Cooper Woodworking
PO Box 278
302 South Second Street
Grimes, IA 50111
TEL 515-986-2222
FAX 515-986-9393
E-mail: cooperia@netins.net
Web: www.cooperwoodworking.com

Robert Cooper produces limited-edition and custom-made furniture. He creates his pieces by combining modern design theories with skilled woodworking. His mastery of faux dyeing techniques conserves rare exotic woods.

Cooper recently introduced the debut of his "bobby line" of furniture, pieces that emphasize sophistication and playfulness. The art adorns commercial and residential environments alike.

Cooper's Festival Gallery in West Des Moines, IA, was voted Best New Gallery of the year 2000.

COMMISSIONS: President George W. Bush, Elizabeth Dole

PUBLICATIONS: *Visual Merchandising and Store Design, Modern Salon, Identity Magazine, Who's Who of America*

GUILD SOURCEBOOKS: *Designer's 15*

Pamela Cosper   P. 271

4439 Rolling Pine Drive
West Bloomfield, MI 48323
TEL 248-366-9569
E-mail: pamelacosper@hotmail.com
Web: gallery.passion4art.com/members/cosper

Pamela Cosper has traveled extensively, and her paintings are influenced by a wide variety of architectural, cultural, historical and natural designs. She enjoys the challenge of expressing the personality and interests of her clients in her work.

Cosper's many styles and talents enable her to work well with decorators, architects and individuals to create the look and the feeling they want in a painting. She accepts commission work for projects of any size.

RECENT PROJECTS: 8' x 8' painting commissioned for private residence

Robin Cowley   P. 353

2451 Potomac Street
Oakland, CA 94602-3032
TEL 510-530-1134
FAX 510-482-9465
E-mail: art@robincowley.com
Web: www.robincowley.com

A colorist with a sense of whimsy, Robin Cowley creates abstract fabric fantasies with an upbeat attitude. Constructed using layers of fabric and thread, building on simplicity of color and richness of texture, these wall pieces are suitable for a variety of residential and corporate settings.

COLLECTIONS: U.S. Embassy, Armenia; Circuit City headquarters, Richmond, VA; Summit Medical Center, Oakland, CA

EXHIBITIONS & AWARDS: Contract Design Center, San Francisco, CA, 2000; Zoller Gallery, University Park, PA, 1999; San Francisco Art Commission Gallery, San Francisco, CA, 1998; American Museum of Quilts and Textiles, San Jose, CA, 1997

PUBLICATIONS: *Fiberarts Design Book 6, Surface Design Journal*

GUILD SOURCEBOOKS: *Designer's 11, 12, 13, 14, 15*

William C. Culbertson   P. 209

WCC Design Studios
32 Warren Avenue
North Smithfield, RI 02896
TEL/FAX 401-766-6256
E-mail: wcculbertson@home.com
Web: www.sculpturelab.com

Over the past 20 years, William C. Culbertson has completed numerous public and private commissions worldwide. He has extensive experience working with architects, engineers and designers from initial concept to project completion. Having worked in a variety of media and styles, the artist can work successfully with clients to meet and exceed their sculptural needs.

COMMISSIONS: Children's Television Workshop; Walt Disney Company; Jim Henson Productions; Nickelodeon; Dallas Area Rapid Transit; Rhode Island State Council on the Arts; City of Tampa, FL; City of Providence, RI; Rock Cliff Mansion, Newport, RI; "This Old House," WGBH-TV program; Yu-Zi Paradise, Guilin, People's Republic of China; Hopi Hari, Sao Paulo, Brazil

Phil Daniel   P. 62

Phil Daniel Architectural Stained Glass
321 2nd Avenue North
Minneapolis, MN 55401
TEL 612-332-2525
E-mail: 321studio@prodigy.net
Web: www.phildaniel.com

Phil Daniel combines the traditional aspects and techniques of stained glass with a unique, contemporary vision. His clean, delicate lines are highly complemented by the use of the finest handblown glass. The result is a stunning centerpiece of architectural design that uses light and style to stimulate any space.

COMMISSIONS: Sarah Susanka

EXHIBITIONS & AWARDS: International Market Square, Minneapolis, MN, 2000; Robert Thompson Gallery, Minneapolis, MN, 1999

PUBLICATIONS: *Parade*, 2000; *Minnesota Monthly*, 1999

GUILD SOURCEBOOKS: *Architect's 14*

David M Bowman Studio   P. 318

David M Bowman
PO Box 738
Berkeley, CA 94701
TEL 510-845-1072
E-mail: David@DavidMBowmanStudio.com
Web: www.DavidMBowmanStudio.com

David Bowman designs strong abstract compositions in patinaed brass for residential and public spaces. These wall pieces appear massive, but are actually quite light and can be hung on any type of wall. The patinaed surfaces are durable and weather well out of doors.

Designs can be scaled to fit an intimate corner or to fill an entire wall. Bowman welcomes the opportunity to design wall pieces for specific spaces.

GUILD SOURCEBOOKS: *Designer's 8, 11, 13, 14*

David Wilson Design   P. 63

David Wilson
202 Darby Road
South New Berlin, NY 13843-2212
TEL 607-334-3015
FAX 607-334-7065
E-mail: mail@davidwilsondesign.com
Web: www.davidwilsondesign.com

Renowned for his successful collaborations with architects on large-scale works for both public and private buildings, David Wilson pursues the goal of designing glass that adds to and enriches architecture. Emphasizing the importance of harmony in the built environment, his designs are the result of reducing forms to their simplest solution.

COMMISSIONS: St. Annes Catholic Church, Barrington, IL, 2000; Corning Incorporated, New York, NY, 2000; Stamford Courthouse, Stamford, CT, 2000; Plainfield Station, Plainfield, NJ, 2000

GUILD SOURCEBOOKS: *THE GUILD 1, 2, 3, 4, 5; Architect's 6, 7, 8, 9, 11, 13, 14, 15*

Alonzo Davis   P. 326

2080 Peabody Avenue
Memphis, TN 38104
TEL 901-276-9070
FAX 901-276-0660
E-mail: artalonzo@aol.com
Web: www.alonzodavis.com

Alonzo Davis' *Power Poles* and *Bundles* are paintings in the round on bamboo that take on a sculptural form. He enhances them with color and a variety of other materials, including wax, copper, canvas with burned patterns, and leather.

Varying in length from four to eight feet, the bamboo works can function individually or in a grouping as a bundle or installation. They can be propped against a wall or suspended. The viewer will find manipulated symbols from ethnic and spiritual sources in these unique pole compositions.

Ann L. Deluty   P. 141

12 Randolph Street
Belmont, MA 02478
TEL/FAX 617-484-0069
E-mail: anndel@aol.com
Web: www.ann-deluty.ws

Ann L. Deluty strives to express the essence of natural objects in stone and wood. Her work ranges from abstract to extremely realistic. Her mastery of textures and carving techniques gives an air of realism to any object.

A graduate of the School of the Museum of Fine Arts, she is also known for her portraits of people and pets in bronze, clay and cold-cast bronze.

Deluty has numerous works in private collections, and commissions are welcome. Because of the variety of colors available in alabaster, she can carve to match any color scheme.

Louis DeMartino   PP. 22-23

Louis DeMartino Architectural Sculptor
Box 391370
Anza, CA 92539
TEL 909-763-1315
FAX 909-763-2360
E-mail: louis@louisdemartino.com
Web: www.louisdemartino.com

Louis DeMartino sculpts original architectural elements such as doors, gates, windows, fountains and fences in bronze and stainless steel. His studio, foundry and staff of artisans are located in a mountain valley above Palm Springs. He has lived in New York, Italy and the South Pacific, and works on commissions all over the world.

COMMISSIONS: City of San Francisco, CA; Pacific Telephone; City of Duluth, MN; City of La Quinta, CA; City of Ohara, Japan; City of Los Angeles, CA; United States Olympic Swimming, Colorado Springs, CO; Malcolm Forbes, New York, NY; Lladro, Spain; Frank Sinatra, Palm Springs, CA

Louis DeMartino   PP. 22-23

Louis DeMartino Architectural Sculptor
Box 391370
Anza, CA 92539
TEL 909-763-1315
FAX 909-763-2360
E-mail: louis@louisdemartino.com
Web: www.louisdemartino.com

Louis DeMartino sculpts original architectural elements as functional works of art. His studio, foundry and staff of artisans are located in a mountain valley above Palm Springs. He has lived in New York, Italy and French Polynesia, and he works on commissions all over the world.

As a sculptor, he prefers to highlight architectural elements without distracting from the overall design. He seeks to interpret the location and to take into account the client and architect's visions. He works in bronze, stainless steel, granite, marble and concrete on elements such as doors, gates, fountains, windows, fireplaces, railings, balustrades and fences.

Karl Dempwolf   P. 272

Dempwolf Studio
3962 Witzel Drive
Sherman Oaks, CA 91423
TEL/FAX 818-788-0173
E-mail: dempwolf@pacbell.net
Web: www.netmonet.com

Each of Karl Dempwolf's works starts on location, *en plein aire*. He makes small studies, usually on wood panels, and then translates them to larger works in his studio. Artists such as Hassam, Frieseke, Irvine, Wendt and Rose have all played a part in shaping Dempwolf's painting methods. His mission is not to copy the landscape, but to translate it, with a goal of inspiring and uplifting the viewer.

COLLECTIONS: The National Park Foundation, WA; The McGraw-Hill Publishing Company, New York, NY

EXHIBITIONS & AWARDS: Spring Salon, California Art Club, 2000; 90th Gold Medal Exhibition, Pasadena, CA; "Historic California Wineries Past and Present: Paintings of Living Legends," The Craftsman's Guild and California Heritage Gallery, San Francisco, CA, 2000

PUBLICATIONS: *Art from the Parks,* 1999

ARTIST INFORMATION

Fredric B. DeVantier   P. 235

Fredric B. DeVantier Designer-Metalsmith
PO Box 376
2965 Franklin Street
Sanborn, NY 14132
TEL   716-731-9467
FAX   716-731-2272

The work of Fredric B. DeVantier is hand-wrought and constructed using traditional metal-working methods. His classic and elegant designs are inspired by the natural world, geometry, or the properties of metal. His materials include silver and other nonferrous metals; he also incorporates wood and semiprecious stones into his work.

COMMISSIONS: Trinity Lutheran Church, Wellsboro, PA, 1999

EXHIBITIONS & AWARDS: "Artisans in Silver: Enduring Traditions Through the Next Millennium," National Ornamental Metal Museum, Memphis, TN, 1999

GUILD SOURCEBOOKS: *Architect's 13*

Donna Durbin   P. 355

Donna Durbin, Artist
2711 Main Street #227
Houston, TX 77002
TEL   713-880-3005
FAX   713-880-1720
E-mail: **donnadurbinart@earthlink.net**

Donna Durbin's mixed-media tapestries are created by layering colors of paint, printing, textiles, textures, stitching and collage. Capturing an essence and energy, they add life and warmth to interiors.

In business since 1989, Durbin works with art consultants, architects and designers to create commissioned artwork for hotels, corporate collections and private residences. Portfolio samples and pricing are available upon request.

COMMISSIONS: DoubleTree Hotel, Plano, TX, 2001; Baylor College of Medicine, Houston, TX, 2000; Giarrusso & Associates; Hilton Hotel, Aruba

COLLECTIONS: Exxon, Houston, TX; American Airlines/The Sabre Group, Fort Worth, TX; BASF Corporation, NJ; Ardis Bartle

Jerome R. Durr   P. 65

206 Marcellus Street
Syracuse, NY 13204
TEL   315-428-1322
FAX   315-478-1767
E-mail: **jrdurrøart@aol.com**

Jerome Durr has been designing, fabricating and installing architectural glass artworks using the techniques of painting, etching, carving, slumping, fusing and leading since 1973.

COMMISSIONS: National Baseball Hall of Fame, Cooperstown, NY; Carlisle Corporation, Syracuse, NY; Blair Academy, Blairstown, NJ; Christian Dior Retail, various sites

EXHIBITIONS & AWARDS: Best of Show, Atlanta Art Glass Guild; Best of Show, Cooperstown Art Open

PUBLICATIONS: *Custom Home*, 2000; *Upstate Living Magazine*, 1997

GUILD SOURCEBOOKS: *THE GUILD 4, 5; Architect's 6, 7, 8, 9, 10, 14, 15; Designer's 6*

Richard Erdman   PP. 182, 192

Erdman Studios
3188 South Brownell Road
Williston, VT 05495
TEL   802-660-8727
FAX   802-865-9720
E-mail: **rerdman@together.net**
Web: **www.RichardErdman.com**

Richard Erdman creates abstract stone and bronze sculpture of intimate and monumental size. His art is known for its vitality, energy and technical mastery, seemingly defying the materials from which it is formed. His work is located in museum, public and private collections in 27 countries worldwide.

RECENT PROJECTS: Conrad International Hotel, Singapore; EastWest Institute, New York, Prague and Moscow

COMMISSIONS: King Faisal Foundation, Saudi Arabia; PepsiCo Sculpture Gardens, Purchase, NY; Royal Caribbean Lines, Norway; Four Seasons Park, Singapore; Bankers Trust Co., New York, NY

COLLECTIONS: Minneapolis Institute of Arts, MN; Aldrich Museum of Art, CT; Princeton University, NJ; Museum of Fine Arts, Boston, MA

Feral Design   P. 249

Serge Feral
1732 Ninth Street
Berkeley, CA 94710
TEL/FAX   510-524-7913
E-mail: **sergeferal@yahoo.com**
Web: **sfdesign.8m.com**

French artist Serge Feral conjures lamps from objects in the rough, delighting in the texture of metal, the color of rust, the grain of cement. Composed primarily of automobile parts like leaf springs and side mirrors, his pieces juxtapose metals — colored, sandblasted, rusted and chromed — with cement of varying textures. The body of the lamp itself is often the electrical conduit.

COMMISSIONS: Private homes and businesses in San Francisco, CA; Paris, France; and Nice, France

Catherine K. Ferrell   P. 142

Art Equities, Inc.
12546 N. Highway A1A
Vero Beach, FL 32963-9411
TEL   561-589-1552
FAX   561-589-9425
E-mail: **tcferrell@aol.com**

"Full of life," "joyful" and "wonderful to live and work with" are collectors' words to describe the work of Catherine Ferrell. One dental office is set around a courtyard featuring a sculpture that patients greatly enjoy.

Ferrell's undergraduate degree and master's degree were in fine art. She majored in sculpture, a lifelong passion and joy. She has worked in Italy on commissions for collectors there, and enjoys the interaction and ideas exchanged with the client. Her work is found in museum collections and galleries in the U.S. and abroad.

COMMISSIONS: Dr. Paul Gingras, home and office, Palm Beach, FL; architect Gunther Schultz Franke, Osnabruch, Germany

COLLECTIONS: Norton Gallery of Art, West Palm Beach, FL; Asbury College, Wilmore, KY; Thompson Library, University of Michigan, Flint, MI; Cornell Museum of Art and History, Delray Beach, FL

Bruce Paul Fink — P. 24

90 Pole Bridge Road
Woodstock, CT 06281
TEL 860-974-0130
E-mail: bpfink@artmetal.com
Web: www.artmetal.com/bpfink

As a designer and sculptor, Bruce Paul Fink has produced over 890 unique sculptures with his private studio/foundry. His internationally collected works are created from a wide variety of media.

Additional examples of the artist's sculptures and technical discussions of his work can be found at www.artmetal.com (or located under "bpfink" through any search engine).

The projects shown in this book were created from requests by private home owners for architectural work in site-specific locations.

Rob Fisher — P. 127

Rob Fisher Sculpture
228 North Allegheny Street
Bellefonte, PA 16823
TEL 814-355-1458
FAX 814-353-9060
E-mail: glenunion@aol.com
Web: www.sculpture.org

Rob Fisher produces monumental sculpture using stainless steel and aluminum. *Weather or Not* represents a century of weather fluctuations through varying lengths of chain. *Patterns of Nature* suggests clouds, mist, birds and forests.

COMMISSIONS: Arrivals Hall, Philadelphia International Airport, PA; The Penn Stater Conference Center Hotel, PA; The Habitat Company, IL; Grounds for Sculpture, NJ; Jackson National Life, MI; Banco Popular, VI; Philip Services Corporation, Canada; NationsBank, GA; Osaka Hilton International, Japan; Kingdom of Saudi Arabia

GUILD SOURCEBOOKS: *Architect's 9, 11, 12, 13, 14, 15*

Bill FitzGibbons — P. 210

PO Box 460852
San Antonio, TX 78246
TEL 210-366-3678
FAX 210-366-2273
E-mail: b1409@aol.com
Web: www.billfitzgibbons.com

San Antonio artist Bill FitzGibbons creates public art that is site specific and user friendly. FitzGibbons has also been on several design teams, allowing him to participate in the overall architectural design from the very beginning of a project.

COMMISSIONS: University of Houston at Victoria, Victoria, TX; San Antonio International Airport, San Antonio, TX; Convention Center, Providence, RI; Milles Sculpture Garden, Stockholm, Sweden; Hampshire Sculpture Trust, Winchester, U.K.; Fairbanks Youth Facility, Fairbanks, AK; Spring Hill Elementary School, Anchorage, AK

PUBLICATIONS: *Art In America, Sculpture Magazine, Art News, Public Art Review, Artist Newsletter* (U.K.), *The New York Times*

Barbara Fletcher — P. 342

Paper Dimensions
17 Powerhouse Street #318
Boston, MA 02127
TEL 617-268-8644
FAX 978-670-5290
E-mail: paper3d@hotmail.com
Web: www.paperdimensions.com

Barbara Fletcher creates cast paper pieces that take many forms. Her work ranges from low-relief narrative panels to three-dimensional sculpture as well as a line of sculptural lighting (see *The Designer's Sourcebook 15*).

Fletcher's durable paper castings are painted with acrylic and lightfast dyes; they are suitable for hanging framed or unframed. Flora and fauna have been her preferred themes, but non-representational subjects are also welcome.

COMMISSIONS: Charleton Hospital Maternity Ward, Fall River, MA; Captain Fishbones Restaurant, Quincy, MA

GUILD SOURCEBOOKS: *THE GUILD 1, 5; Designer's 6, 7, 14, 15*

Steve Fontanini — P. 25

Steve Fontanini Architectural
& Ornamental Blacksmithing
PO Box 2298
11400 South Hoback Junction Road
Jackson, WY 83001
TEL 307-733-7668
FAX 307-734-8816
E-mail: sfontani@wyoming.com

The confluence of the Snake and Hoback rivers is where Steve Fontanini and company produce metalwork of all kinds. Stair railings, gates and chandeliers are made to your design, or they will be happy to design to fit your needs. Projects are built by forging hot metal and joining the pieces with traditional methods such as rivets, collars and mortise-and-tenon joints. Fontanini's work is found throughout the United States.

Marilyn Forth — PP. 356-357

416 David Drive
North Syracuse, NY 13212
TEL 315-458-3786
FAX 315-458-4828

Marilyn Forth paints with fiber-reactive dyes. She uses the ancient technique of hot wax flowing through a *tjanting* tool to create the intricate drawings of white lines. The wax is ultimately removed. The paintings are resistant to the effects of light.

Forth has taught fiber art at Syracuse University, and has created artwork for corporate and residential clients. Photos of completed commissions are sent to the client for final approval prior to shipping.

RECENT PROJECTS: State Bank of Chittenango grant to educate students on the life of a professional artist

Marilyn Forth — PP. 356-357

416 David Drive
North Syracuse, NY 13212
TEL 315-458-3786
FAX 315-458-4828

COMMISSIONS: Kaiser Permanente Medical Center, Anaheim, CA; St. Vincent's Medical Center, Erie, PA; Susan and Evan Kutch, Commack, NY; commissions through Glass Growers Gallery, Erie, PA

COLLECTIONS: Pat and Diane Croce, owners of the Philadelphia 76ers NBA team; St. Vincent's Medical Center, Erie, PA

EXHIBITIONS & AWARDS: Finger Lakes Show, Rochester Memorial Art Gallery, Rochester, NY; Everson Museum, Syracuse, NY; featured artist, Rochester Memorial Art Gallery Sales Gallery, Rochester, NY

PUBLICATIONS: *The Ultimate T-Shirt Book; Women's Artist Date Book,* 1998

GUILD SOURCEBOOKS: *Designer's 6, 7, 8, 10, 11, 12, 13, 14*

Norman Foster — P. 273

418 Orange Avenue
Sand City, CA 93955
TEL 831-394-9259
TEL 831-624-9629

PO Box 223172
Carmel, CA 93922

Norman Foster directly applies pigments to his own formula of waxes and oils, blending them to create the expressive hues found in his finished paintings. Using a large variety of brushes and other tools, he works directly on board and linen canvas.

COLLECTIONS: First National Bank of South Texas, San Antonio; private collections in Texas, California, New York, Brussels and London

EXHIBITIONS & AWARDS: *Who's Who in the Southwest, Who's Who in Interior Design, Who's Who in the Pacific Rim, Who's Who in the World*

PUBLICATIONS: *Grasslands; Art Now Gallery Guide Southwest,* November 1995; *Art Now Gallery Guide West Coast,* February 1993; *Visions Art Quarterly,* Fall 1993

Douglas Olmsted Freeman — P. 211

Doug Freeman Sculpture Studio
310 North 2nd Street
Minneapolis, MN 55401
TEL 612-339-7150
FAX 612-339-5201
E-mail: **dfree@twincities.infi.net**
Web: **www.freemanstudio.com**

Doug Freeman works sensitively with individuals and communities to create public art that becomes part of a neighborhood — an enduring symbol and a place for people. His figurative sculptures are cast in bronze. The fountains' palettes may also include stainless steel, concrete, glass, stone and a touch of gold leaf.

COMMISSIONS: *The Cincinnati Flying Pigs, The Fountain of the Wind, The Seven Lucky Gods of Japan*

GUILD SOURCEBOOKS: *Architect's 10, 11, 12*

G. Byron Peck/City Arts — P. 113

G. Byron Peck
1857 Lamont Street NW
Washington, DC 20010
TEL/FAX 202-331-1966
E-mail: **byronpeck@hotmail.com**
Web: **www.peckstudios.com**
Web: **www.cityartsdc.org**

Peck Studios has been creating murals, trompe l'oeil and fine artwork for a variety of clients and projects for more than 20 years.

The studio's portfolio of projects is available for review at your request and convenience.

RECENT PROJECTS: Nine-story trompe l'oeil mural, City of Knoxville, TN; ceiling mural for music room, McLean, VA; 60-foot mural for Metro Center subway station, Washington, DC

COLLECTIONS: The Kennedy Center for the Performing Arts; The Smithsonian; American embassies in Crete, Chile and Guyana; Georgetown Park; more than 90 others here and abroad

PUBLICATIONS: *Metropolitan Home; Interior Design; The New York Times; The Washington Post*

GUILD SOURCEBOOKS: *Architect's 6, 7, 8, 9, 10, 11, 12, 13, 14, 15*

Stephanie Gassman — P. 212

2135 Central Parkway
Cincinnati, OH 45214
TEL 513-241-1557
FAX 513-984-3943
E-mail: **stephanie_gassman@fuse.net**

Stephanie Gassman creates commissioned wall reliefs for public, corporate and residential environments around the United States. She enjoys historical research and the challenge of using a variety of materials to make an original statement. Her diverse portfolio reflects her ability to handle large as well as small projects, logos and established color schemes, while maintaining a contemporary, visual excitement.

A commission list, slides and pricing are available upon request.

GUILD SOURCEBOOKS: *Designer's 13, 14, 15*

Wolfgang Gersch — P. 114

Meta Art Studios
71 Encantado Loop
Santa Fe, NM 87505
TEL 505-466-2100
FAX 505-466-2020
E-mail: **art@metaartstudios.com**
Web: **www.metaartstudios.com**

Wolfgang Gersch has created more than 400 murals in the United States. Famous in his repertoire are his impressive interiors of large skies and landscapes which grace the walls of many prestigious institutions. He has been painting for over 30 years in a great variety of expressions and themes. Trompe l'oeil, architectural murals or three-dimensional illusions are masterfully executed. Faux finishes, surface effects, glazes, marbleizing and stone textures are sensitive, rich and complex; they give any space a fine ambience.

Gersch has worked with many interior designers, architects, contractors, professionals and corporate clients. He offers the flexibility and speed of computer-generated mural designs and presentations. Digital mural printing is available — please inquire for more information.

The majority of Gersch's mural art projects range from $1500 to $15000. For more examples of his work, visit the artist's website.

Lois Key Giffen — P. 183

1600 79th Street Ocean
Marathon, FL 33050
TEL/FAX 305-743-3546
E-mail: bobgiffen@aol.com

Lois Key Giffen has lived and worked on five continents, and her paintings and sculpture are collected worldwide. Inspired by the beauty of the Florida Keys, she creates an atmosphere of serenity and joy. Her kinetic works are designed to aid in meditation. She works in clay, stone, bronze, copper and steel, as well as painting in oils and acrylics. Her recent work emphasizes the playful aspect of art.

COMMISSIONS: Steel wall decoration for Mikosukee Indian Hotel, Miami, FL

COLLECTIONS: Various collections in Australia, Austria, Cyprus, Great Britain, Ireland, East and West Malaysia, Malta, Sweden and the United States

EXHIBITIONS & AWARDS: Two-person exhibition, Key West, FL; solo exhibitions in Benghazi, Libya; Tripoli, Libya; Sale, Australia; Kota Kinabalu, Borneo (East Malaysia); Kuala Lumpur, Malaysia; London, England

GUILD SOURCEBOOKS: *Architect's 13, 14; Designer's 12, 15*

Joan Giordano — P. 327

Joan Giordano Studios
136 Grand Street
New York, NY 10013
TEL 212-431-6244
TEL 212-481-7761
FAX 212-481-3128
E-mail: jaggior@aol.com

Fusing handmade paper with scraggly and scorched cable, copper and wax, Joan Giordano continues to investigate the most intimate textures of paper — to understand and wheedle out the hidden secrets of this infinitely malleable material.

Internationally acclaimed, Giordano's wall sculptures are the focal point of collections worldwide. Her unique sculptures can be adapted to accommodate an unlimited number of design and architectural challenges.

Commissions and site-specific projects are welcome. Contact the artist for more information and prices.

Glassic Art — PP. 66-67

Leslie Rankin
7809 Holly Knoll Avenue
Las Vegas, NV 89129
TEL 888-834-1639 (Toll free)
TEL 702-658-7588
FAX 702-658-7342
E-mail: glassicart@glassicart.com
Web: www.glassicart.com

True connoisseurs, collectors, curators and the most discriminating buyers appreciate the outstanding quality of Glassic Art's creations — unique glass products developed from 23 years of experience. The studio offers completion within deadlines, service beyond compare and unique one-of-a-kind pieces that have been receiving rave reviews from investors and viewers for years.

The "glassic art" created at the studio is a multi-dimensional medium in glass made by sandblasting, painting, welding, fusion, kiln-formed glass, metal and bonding techniques. From fine art to functional, Glassic Art's pieces are used for murals; bars and countertops; staircases; room dividers; entries; freeform sculptures; and floor, shower and swimming pool tiles. The possibilities for projects are limitless.

Glassic Art — PP. 66-67

Leslie Rankin
7809 Holly Knoll Avenue
Las Vegas, NV 89129
TEL 888-834-1639 (Toll free)
TEL 702-658-7588
FAX 702-658-7342
E-mail: glassicart@glassicart.com
Web: www.glassicart.com

The true connoisseur will appreciate the workmanship of Glassic Art's unique glass products. With exemplary service, the studio's exclusive pieces receive rave reviews by investors, critics and viewers.

The "glassic art" created at the studio is a multi-dimensional medium utilizing sandblasting, painting, welding, fusion, kiln-formed glass, metal and bonding techniques. Glassic Art's pieces have become murals; bar and countertops; staircases; room dividers; entries; sculptures; and floor, shower and swimming pool tiles.

RECENT PROJECTS: "Modern Masters," Home and Garden Television, Fall 2000

COMMISSIONS: Celebrity and private residences; various casino/resorts, including the Mirage, Rio and Bellagio

GUILD SOURCEBOOKS: *Architect's 12, 15*

Gordon Huether + Partners — P. 72

Gordon Huether
101 South Coombs Street, Suite X
Napa, CA 94559
TEL 707-255-5954
FAX 707-255-5991
E-mail: mail@gordonhuether.com
Web: www.gordonhuether.com

The Gordon Huether + Partners studio (formerly Architectural Glass Design, Inc.) brings more than 23 years of experience in creating large-scale, site-specific art installations to public projects, private enterprises and private residences worldwide. With a strong background in glass art, the studio has expanded its artistic palette in the last few years to include integration with other media, such as steel, acrylic, resin, fiber optics, water and neon. The studio's goal remains the successful integration of art into architecture.

Cali Gorevic — P. 299

377 Lane Gate Road
Cold Spring, NY 10516
TEL 845-265-4625
FAX 845-265-4620
E-mail: calig@mindspring.com
Web: www.caligorevic.com

"I am drawn to mysterious places — forest landscapes where fairy tales can happen. For me, the art of photography is in the darkroom — there, I draw from my memory and imagination as I use various techniques to convey the enhanced reality that I experience in the forests."

Cali Gorevic

Cali Gorevic's dramatic black-and-white photographs emphasize the beauty and mystery of nature. They are primarily 2.25" format or infrared silver prints in limited editions. Many of the most popular images are available as giclée prints, also in editions.

Gorevic's work has been exhibited nationally and internationally. She has won numerous awards and her photographs have been purchased by private and corporate buyers.

Gorevic is also a sculptor. Her photographs and sculpture can be viewed on her website, www.caligorevic.com.

ARTIST INFORMATION

Graphics in Wool   P. 354

Anna Vojik
49 South Washington
Hinsdale, IL 60521
TEL   630-887-8281
FAX   708-447-5867
E-mail: **interarts@aol.com**

Graphics in Wool's exquisitely detailed works are handwoven by highly skilled artisans who ingeniously recreate original artwork in tapestry. Each piece is produced entirely by hand in much the same way it was in 3000 B.C.

Graphics in Wool has established a reputation for superb craftsmanship and a remarkable range of creative designs. Tapestry complements and is completed by its environment. In that regard, the studio has a great respect for spaces.

Commission inquiries are welcomed; completed pieces are also available. Visuals and pricing are available upon request.

EXHIBITIONS & AWARDS: ADEX award (first place, wall decor), *Design Journal,* Santa Monica, CA, 1999

GUILD SOURCEBOOKS: *Designer's 15*

George Mossman Greenamyer   P. 213

Careswell Sculpture and Ironworks
994 Careswell Street
Marshfield, MA 02050-5637
TEL/FAX   781-834-9688
E-mail: **burbank@thecia.net**

George Mossman Greenamyer's recent public sculptures are kinetic — either motor or wind driven. The narrative behind the work can be either historical or contemporary, but they are always colorful, humorous and very accessible to the viewer. He heads a team that provides physical and narrative site analysis, design, drafting, engineering, in-house fabrication, installation, documentation and project management.

COMMISSIONS: New Jersey Department of Labor, Trenton, NJ; Laumeier Sculpture Park, St. Louis, MO; Atlantic City International Airport, NJ; One Parkway, Philadelphia, PA; Charlotte/Douglas International Airport, NC

GUILD SOURCEBOOKS: *Architect's 13, 14, 15*

Rich Griendling   P. 130

Griendling Designs
700 Walnut Creek Road
Elizabethtown, KY 42701
TEL   270-737-4875
E-mail: **griendlingdesign@kvnet.org**
Web: **www.griendlingdesigns.com**

Sculptor Rich Griendling's artworks capture the grace and beauty of the human form and celebrate the power of the human spirit. Best known for his suspended white plaster sculptures, Griendling creates site-specific works in a variety of mediums, including bronze. All sculptures are engineered to withstand the rigors of public art.

COMMISSIONS: Coca-Cola Bottling Company, Kentucky Fried Chicken, Alabama Music Hall of Fame, Alabama Sports Hall of Fame, University of Kentucky Children's Hospital, Tennessee State Museum, John Hardin High School Performing Arts Center, First Federal Savings Bank

COLLECTIONS: Evansville Museum of Arts and Sciences, Hospital Corporation of America, Hilliard Lyons Inc.

Elizabeth Guarisco   P. 143

The Horse in Bronze
21257 Foxcroft Road
Middleburg, VA 20117
TEL   540-554-8897
TEL   540-554-4829

For centuries, the horse has captivated man and his imagination. The horse in bronze has lent a sense of grace, dignity and elegance to rooms throughout history — from Ancient Greece and Rome to the Renaissance, from the Impressionist period to modern times. Emperors, kings and presidents, lords and ladies, scholars and commoners have all been inspired by the powerful energy of an equine bronze.

Guarisco's bronzes accurately capture the natural beauty and powerful inner spirit of the horse. She also uses the equine image as an ideal means to explore form and to mirror human emotion. Her work is in important collections throughout the world.

A color catalog is available.

Niki Gulley   P. 274

7439 Brentcove Circle
Dallas, TX 75214
TEL   214-803-5812
FAX   214-823-8866
E-mail: **niki@nikigulley.com**
Web: **www.nikigulley.com**

Niki Gulley paints vibrant landscapes and florals using pastels on a sanded surface. This medium allows her to imitate the velvety lush feel of nature while capturing the bold colors of light. Gulley's impressionistic interpretations are created out of a feeling of true joy, which she translates onto the canvas for the viewer to share.

COMMISSIONS: Nayna Networks, SHORE Community Services, White Rock Montessori

EXHIBITIONS & AWARDS: Texas Artists Museum; exhibitions in Colorado, Louisiana, Connecticut, New Mexico, Nebraska and Texas

Mark Eric Gulsrud   PP. 68-69

Architectural Glass/Sculpture
3309 Tahoma Place West
Tacoma, WA 98466
TEL   253-566-1720
FAX   253-565-5981

Primarily site specific, Mark Eric Gulsrud's commission work can be found internationally, including public, private, corporate and liturgical settings. He works in a variety of media, including custom handblown leaded glass; sandcarved, laminated and cast glass; handmade ceramic; stone; and carved wood.

Encouraging professional collaboration, the artist is personally involved in all phases of design, fabrication and installation. He is primarily concerned with the harmonious integration of artwork and its environment.

GUILD SOURCEBOOKS: *THE GUILD 3, 4; Architect's 7, 8, 9, 10, 11, 12, 13, 14, 15*

Mark Eric Gulsrud   PP. 68-69

Architectural Glass/Sculpture
3309 Tahoma Place West
Tacoma, WA 98466
TEL 253-566-1720
FAX 253-565-5981

Primarily site specific, Mark Eric Gulsrud's commission work can be found internationally, including public, private, corporate and liturgical settings. He works in a variety of media, including custom handblown leaded glass; sandcarved, laminated and cast glass; handmade ceramic; stone; and carved wood.

Encouraging professional collaboration, the artist is personally involved in all phases of design, fabrication and installation. He is primarily concerned with the harmonious integration of artwork and its environment.

GUILD SOURCEBOOKS: *THE GUILD 3, 4; Architect's 7, 8, 9, 10, 11, 12, 13, 14, 15*

Henry Halem   PP. 70-71

Halem Studios
429 Carthage Avenue
Kent, OH 44240
TEL 330-673-8632
FAX 330-677-2488
E-mail: hhalem@glassnotes.com
Web: www.glassnotes.com

Henry Halem uses diverse techniques that employ glass as his primary means of expression. One can find his installations as large colorful fused and cast window treatments, glass wall treatments, door lites, room dividers and large cast glass interior or exterior panels. Halem's ability to work with architects and designers puts him in the forefront of his field. His recent installation for Ohio University retrofitted colorful fused glass panels into an existing window and entrance for the student union. Halem is also available for consultation on your next glass project.

COMMISSIONS: Rapid Transit Authority, Cleveland, OH; Ferro Corporation corporate headquarters; Ohio University, Ironton, OH; numerous private home commissions

Hammerton   PP. 250-251

2149 South 3140 West
Salt Lake City, UT 84119-1264
TEL 801-973-8095
FAX 801-973-0234
E-mail: info@hammerton.com
Web: www.hammerton.com

Hammerton is a five-year-old company that has experienced phenomenal growth. The wrought iron decor company has built its reputation on creative designs backed by the superb craftsmanship of its own artisans and sculptors.

Hammerton has a line of over 200 catalog items, but about 20% of its productions are custom pieces — either designed by the client or by Hammerton's own designers.

The company's creations grace the homes of numerous celebrities and prominent citizens worldwide, but its products are found mostly in the homes of discriminating people who just enjoy the beauty and quality of Hammerton accessories.

Joan Rothchild Hardin   P. 36

Joan Rothchild Hardin Ceramics
393 West Broadway #4
New York, NY 10012
TEL 212-966-9433
TEL/FAX 212-431-9196 (Studio)
E-mail: joan@hardintiles.com
Web: www.hardintiles.com

Award-winning artist Joan Rothchild Hardin paints abstract and representational designs with layers of ceramic glazes on commercial tile blanks. Her art tiles can be installed or hung as paintings, adding a jewel-like richness to residential, corporate and public projects. Custom commissions are welcomed.

COMMISSIONS: West Village Veterinary Hospital, New York, NY, 2000

COLLECTIONS: Private residences throughout the United States

PUBLICATIONS: *Decorative Art Tiles*, 2001

GUILD SOURCEBOOKS: *Designer's 14, 15*

Tim Harding   P. 358

402 North Main Street
Stillwater, MN 55082
TEL 651 351-0383
FAX 651-351-1051
Web: www.timharding.com

Harding's impressionistic *Water* series wall pieces are done in layered, stitched and cut silks and are characterized by vibrant, lustrous colors and richly faceted textures. These large-scale, semi-abstract images deal with the distortion of light reflected and refracted by water. Influenced by color field painters, Harding's work incorporates shimmering, luminescent surfaces with subtle illusions of depth and motion.

COMMISSIONS: Mayo Clinic; MCI; SeaWorld; Kaiser Permanente; Neutrogena; Cargill; Nokia; Banner Aerospace; GMAC; Hyatt Regency Hotels; Lawson Software; Minneapolis Institute of Arts; St. Paul Companies; Westlaw; Cooper-Hewitt Museum; U.S. Embassy, Bangkok

Brower Hatcher   PP. 184, 222

c/o Exhibit A
210 West Exchange Street
Providence, RI 02903
TEL 401-455-3990
FAX 401-455-3910

Brower Hatcher forms an optical field by integrating glass, stone and ceramic elements into a three-dimensional matrix of stainless steel rods and wire.

RECENT PROJECTS: Laumeier Sculpture Park, St. Louis, MO; Northwest Airlines, Minneapolis, MN; Fidelity Investments, Smithfield, RI; pedestrian bridge, Columbus State Community College, Columbus, OH; Grounds for Sculpture, Hamilton, NJ

COMMISSIONS: Columbus State Community College, Columbus, OH, 2000; Northwest Airlines, Minneapolis, MN, 2000; Fidelity Investments, Smithfield, RI, 2000; Department of Cultural Affairs, City of New York, NY, 1995; Metropolitan Life Insurance, Houston, TX, 1994; Brigham Young University, Provo, UT, 1994; St. Paul Companies, St. Paul, MN, 1994; City of Philadelphia, PA, 1990; Walker Art Center, Minneapolis, MN, 1988

ARTIST INFORMATION

Yoshi Hayashi P. 275

255 Kansas Street #330
San Francisco, CA 94103
TEL/FAX 415-552-0755
E-mail: yoshihayashi@att.net

Hayashi's designs range from very traditional 17th-century Japanese lacquer art themes that are delicate with intricate detail to those that are boldly geometric and contemporary. By skillfully applying metallic leaf and bronzing powders, he adds illumination and contrast to the network of color, pattern and texture. His original designs include screens, wall panels and decorative objects.

COMMISSIONS: Private residence, Hawaii, 2000; Disney Ambassador Hotel, Maihama, Tokyo, Japan, 1999; Ocean Princess, Santa Monica, CA, 1999

GUILD SOURCEBOOKS: *THE GUILD 3, 4, 5; Designer's 6, 7, 8, 9, 10, 11, 12, 13, 14, 15*

Steve Heimann P. 276

196 Stefanic Avenue
Elmwood Park, NJ 07407
TEL 201-797-5434
E-mail: steve@steveheimann.com
Web: www.steveheimann.com

Like icons in their simplicity, Heimann's works employ few elements. He creates images which seek to engage the viewer into a feeling of resonance, much the way religious icons seek to elicit that response in believers.

Heimann's distinctive style is featured in corporate collections and extends to an international audience through numerous commissions for postage stamps. Countries that have commissioned stamps include the British Virgin Islands, Grenada, Sierra Leone, Uganda, Tanzania, Dominica and Antigua/Barbuda. In 1999, seven paintings were featured in "Extreme Homes," a production of the Home & Garden Network.

A catalog is available.

GUILD SOURCEBOOKS: *Designer's 15*

Helaman Ferguson, Sculptor P. 185

Helaman Ferguson
10512 Pilla Terra Court
Laurel, MD 20723-5728
TEL 301-604-4270
FAX 301-776-0499
E-mail: helamanf@helasculpt.com
Web: www.helasculpt.com

Helaman Ferguson's sculpture celebrates science and mathematics in granite, marble and bronze.

COLLECTIONS: University of St. Thomas, St. Paul, MN; American Center for Physics, MD; Smith College, Northampton, MA; National Council of Teachers of Mathematics, VA; Mathematical Sciences Research Institute, University of California at Berkeley; Clay Mathematics Institute, Cambridge, MA; Center for Communications Research, San Diego, CA; Mathematical Association of America, Washington, DC; American Mathematical Society, RI; Weisman Art Museum, University of Minnesota

Laurel Herter P. 73

Laurel Herter Design
PO Box 1291
132 Bridge Street
Bluffton, SC 29910
TEL 843-757-6580
FAX 843-757-6581
E-mail: herter@hargray.com

Laurel Herter Design incorporates innovative and traditional methods of glass crafting, providing architectural commissions for commercial, liturgical and residential environments.

For the past 25 years, the studio has drawn on natural forms to enhance the geometric and linear expressions of architecture. Collaboration with designers, architects, builders and skilled glass craftspeople throughout the country assures the highest level of detail and quality.

Techniques include carved, sandblasted, stained and leaded, cast and slumped, jeweled, beveled and brilliant-cut work.

Karen Heyl P. 37

907 Sonia Place
Escondido, CA 92026
TEL 760-489-7106
E-mail: Heylstone2@aol.com

1310 Pendleton Street, Suite 101
Cincinnati, OH 45210-2198
TEL 513-421-9791

Karen Heyl's award-winning limestone mural relief sculpture combines Old World stone carving techniques with contemporary design, lending itself to a variety of architectural applications, monumental and small. Using varied textural surfaces, Heyl creates aesthetic sophistication with simplified sensual forms.

Collaborating with architects, art consultants and interior and landscape designers, she has received commissions from hospitals, corporations, universities, parks, churches, cities and private collectors. Her works have gained regional and national recognition. Pricing upon request.

GUILD SOURCEBOOKS: *Architect's 9, 12, 13, 14, 15*

Tom Holdman P. 75

Glass Elegance by Holdman Studios
10790 North 6000 West
Highland, UT 84003
TEL 801-756-0737
E-mail: tom@holdman.com
Web: www.holdman.com

Holdman Studios has been creating glass art of elegance and style since 1988. Works are located in community centers, churches, public libraries and residential properties. The studio's pieces have been found in many magazines and newspapers, including *USA Today*.

From Holdman's vivid imagination come designs that range from traditional painted to Art Deco to contemporary glass. Commissions have included glass curtains, murals and large outdoor skylights, among others.

To view more of Holdman's creations, visit his website.

Claudia Hollister — PP. 38-39

PMB 158
333 S. State Street, Suite V
Lake Oswego, OR 97034-3691
TEL   503-636-6684
FAX   503-226-0429

Utilizing hand-built colored porcelain, Claudia Hollister creates site-specific architectural wall pieces for public, corporate and residential environments. Highly textured and richly colored, Hollister sets her work apart by combining the intricate techniques of inlaying, embossing and hand carving three-dimensional elements on tiles.

COMMISSIONS: Beth-El Zedick Synagogue, Indianapolis, IN; Kelsey Seybold Medical Center, Houston, TX; Anderson Consulting, Houston, TX; Longmont United Hospital, Longmont, CO; General Instrument, Horsham, PA; Marriott Hotel, Denver, CO; Parkway Veterinary Clinic, Lake Oswego, OR

COLLECTIONS: The White House, Washington, DC

GUILD SOURCEBOOKS: *Designer's 8, 11, 13, 14, 15*

Robert Holmes — P. 144

PO Box 244
270 Pilot's Reach
The Sea Ranch, CA 95497
TEL   800-700-9022
TEL/FAX   707-575-0776
E-mail: **info@rhsculptor.com**
Web: **www.robertholmessculpture.com**

Robert Holmes is represented in fine art galleries internationally. His semi-abstract, figurative cast bronze sculpture (small to monumental in scale) are in collections throughout the world. To ensure quality, Holmes established his own foundry, Bronze + Inc., in Sebastopol, CA.

Please contact the artist for more information.

GUILD SOURCEBOOKS: *Architect's 7, 8, 9, 10, 11, 12, 13, 14, 15*

Erling Hope — P. 236

Hope Liturgical Works
1411-B Sag/Bridge Turnpike
Sag Harbor, NY 11963
TEL/FAX   631-725-4294
E-mail: **hopelitwrk@aol.com**

Versed in a wide range of materials and techniques, Erling Hope uses a multidisciplinary approach to explore the influence of objects, images and the built environment on faith and the contemporary liturgical experience.

Hope serves as director of the Society for the Arts, Religion and Contemporary Culture in New York City, and as artist in residence for the Institute for Theology and the Arts at Andover Newton Theological School in Boston. He exhibits widely and is in numerous private and liturgical collections.

GUILD SOURCEBOOKS: *Architect's 13*

Bill Hopen — P. 237

Hopen Studio Inc.
266 North Hill
Sutton, WV 26601
TEL   800-872-8578
TEL   304-765-5611
E-mail: **hopen@access.mountain.net**
Web: **www.aagg.com/hopen**

Bill Hopen's ability to listen and intuitively understand what a congregation wishes to express is his true strength; expressing that spiritual essence within a sculptural form is what makes his work so special, so radiant. Scores of churches throughout the U.S. have commissioned Hopen to work with their liturgical designers and architects to create meaningful and beautiful works that fuse with the spirit, color and composition of their worship space.

"I take what is in your heart and I put it in my heart ... then, I sculpt."
Bill Hopen

GUILD SOURCEBOOKS: *Architect's 9, 10, 11, 12, 13, 15*

Mark Hopkins — P. 145

Mark Hopkins Sculpture Inc.
21 Shorter Industrial Boulevard
Rome, GA 30165
TEL   800-678-6564
FAX   706-235-2814
Web: **www.markhopkinssculpture.com**

From children, wildlife, western subjects and more, Mark Hopkins is known for his work's diversity and his unique ability to capture the essence of any theme he sculpts. "Bronze in motion" is a trademarked term often used to describe Hopkins' beautiful and flowing style.

RECENT PROJECTS: Alabama Sports Hall of Fame, Chicago Bulls, City of Atlanta, Coca-Cola Corporation, Merrill Lynch

PUBLICATIONS: *Southwest Art, Wildlife Art, Traditional Building*

Paul Housberg — P. 74

Glass Project, Inc.
875 North Main Road
Jamestown, RI 02835
TEL   401-560-0880
Web. **www.glassproject.com**

Paul Housberg creates site-specific works in glass. Central to his work is the use of light, color and texture to shape and define a space. Housberg is a graduate of the Rhode Island School of Design and a Fulbright Scholar in architectural glass.

The artist welcomes inquiries regarding any planned or contemplated project.

RECENT PROJECTS: William J. Nealon Federal Building, Scranton, PA; BankRI, Providence, RI; Peninsula Hotel, Chicago, IL; Pfizer Inc., Groton, CT; Dreyfus Corporation, New York, NY

PUBLICATIONS: *Stained Glass Quarterly,* 2000; *The Art of Glass: Integrating Architecture and Glass,* 1998; *Glass Art Magazine,* 1996

GUILD SOURCEBOOKS: *Architect's 6, 7, 8, 9, 10, 11, 13, 15*

ARTIST INFORMATION

Bruce Howdle — P. 40

225 Commerce Street
Mineral Point, WI 53565
TEL 608-987-3590
E-mail: bhowdle@chorus.net
Web: www.brucehowdle.cjb.net
Web: www.artstop.com

Bruce Howdle has been a ceramic sculptor since 1976. He has produced work ranging from thrown forms up to 6 feet in height to 30-foot relief murals utilizing 9 tons of clay.

He fires with a sodium process that melts the clay surface, preserving the integrity of the media and creating a very durable piece.

His work is suitable for freestanding or installed wall locations; pieces are in large public institutions, banks, corporations, private offices and homes. Prices range from $1500 to $150000. Howdle collaborates closely with his clients and provides detailed drawings of his proposed projects.

GUILD SOURCEBOOKS: *Architect's 7, 9, 10, 11, 12, 13, 14, 15*

Jon Barlow Hudson — P. 214

Hudson Sculpture Ltd.
PO Box 710
325 North Walnut Street
Yellow Springs, OH 45387
TEL/FAX 937-767-7766
E-mail: 102024.40@compuserve.com

Jon Barlow Hudson creates architectural-scale sculpture in a wide range of media, including stainless steel, granite, marble, bronze, painted steel, water and light. Large-scale projects are installed throughout the U.S.; he has 15 projects installed in 10 other countries. Scale, material and locations are not obstacles for him — the more challenging the project, the better.

RECENT PROJECTS: Open Air Sculpture Park, Aswan, Egypt; Mairie, Ville du Pradet, Var, France

COMMISSIONS: Executive Jet, Columbus, OH, 2000; Medical College of Ohio, Toledo, OH, Percent for Art Program, 1998

EXHIBITIONS & AWARDS: Ludwig Vogelstein Foundation, 1996; Partners of the Americas, USIA/Brazil, 1992; Lusk Memorial Fellowship, I.I.E./Italy, 1982-83

GUILD SOURCEBOOKS: *Architect's 7*

Patricia B. Ingersoll — P. 277

Tish Ingersoll
915 Spring Garden Street
Philadelphia, PA 19123
TEL 215-236-1350
FAX 215-236-2631
E-mail: Tishing@aol.com

Patricia Ingersoll's paintings and handmade sculpture embody the concerns she has explored and continues to investigate: the forces of nature — the symbiotic relationship of trees and vines, the interdependence of trees and rocks. Her skills as a painter have allowed her to enter a subconscious place of mystery and complexity where colors and forms are the vehicle for her spiritual journey.

RECENT PROJECTS: Independence Foundation Grant Exhibition, Nexus Foundation for Today's Art, Philadelphia, PA, May 2001; "Wallpower," Fleisher Art Memorial, Philadelphia, PA, 2000; Fleisher Challenge Exhibit, Fleisher Art Memorial, Philadelphia, PA, 1999

COMMISSIONS: City of Philadelphia, PA; six murals, City of Philadelphia Department of Recreation Mural Arts Program; Radnor Corporation, Radnor, PA; numerous private commissions

Ione — P. 328

2222 Avenue of the Stars, Suite 2302
Los Angeles, CA 90067
TEL 310-556-4382
FAX 310-556-1664
E-mail: icitrin@aol.com
Web: www.jolaf.com/Ione

Ione uses only one name, but a variety of styles to soothe her imagination. A native of Chicago, she is a former television star and commercial voice-over artist. She now wins awards and sells her creativity through her hands. Ione works from her soul, wanting to fill the world with love and beauty.

Please contact the artist for prices. Slides and photographs are available upon request.

EXHIBITIONS & AWARDS: Gold medal winner, Nielson Bainbridge-Armstrong Art Show; grand winner, *Art Calendar* magazine Crabbie contest

Victor Issa — P. 146

Victor Issa Studios
3950 North County Road 27
Loveland, CO 80538
TEL 970-663-4805
FAX 970-962-6780
E-mail: info@victorissa.com
Web: www.victorissa.com

"Creating living bronze®," "classical beauty," "incredible sensitivity," "wonderfully expressive," "engaging" and "interactive" are some of the descriptions of Victor Issa's work. His 15-year career includes many public and private commissions across the country. Issa's work is internationally collected, with public and private placements across the U.S.

COMMISSIONS: Private placements; City of San Dimas; PCAHS, Denver, CO; SDA Headquarters, MD

GUILD SOURCEBOOKS: *Architect's 13, 14*

Michael Jacobsen — P. 186

FineheArtSculpture
2300 37th Street
Bellingham, WA 98226
TEL 360-671-3494
E-mail: mjacobsen@telcomplus.net
Web: www.fineheartsculpture.com

"Dramatic" and "inspiring" are terms that best describe the abstract and representational sculptures of Michael Jacobsen. His clean artistic images radiate a powerful presence, attract the viewer at a visceral level and are long remembered. His elegant and sensual forms soften the corporate foyer or highlight the landscaped environment.

Jacobsen has years of experience working with architects and designers on private and public projects while meeting tight schedules on budget.

GUILD SOURCEBOOKS: *Architect's 15*

Caroline Jasper   P. 278

Caroline Jasper Studio
1113 Andreas Drive
Bel Air, MD 21015
TEL   410-838-4111
FAX   410-838-4445
E-mail: jasperinc@mindspring.com
Web: www.carolinejasper.com

"It's always about the light."

Caroline Jasper

Red is colorist Caroline Jasper's trademark. Her painterly landscape, water and architectural oils, each begun on red canvas, record her attraction to sunlight's luminous effects.

She welcomes inquiries.

COLLECTIONS: McGraw-Hill Publishers, private and corporate collections nationwide

EXHIBITIONS & AWARDS: Cover Award, *North Light Magazine*, 1999

PUBLICATIONS: *Water Soluble Oils* by Sean Dye, 2001; *Beautiful Things*, 2000

GUILD SOURCEBOOKS: *Designer's 15*

John Charles Gordon Studios, Inc.   P. 131

4-B Pine Street
Avondale, GA 30002
TEL   404-294-8080
FAX   404-294-4442
E-mail: jcgstudios@mindspring.com
Web: www.johncharlesgordon.com

Since its beginning in Los Angeles, John Charles Gordon Studios has produced art products for corporate offices, lobbies, concourses, reception/pre-function areas, restaurants, casinos and other public spaces.

The studio provides custom design and fabrication of themed feature items as well as large-scale wall and aerial sculptures, murals, bas-relief resin casting and unique decorative objects, providing solutions to budget, mechanical and developmental issues.

Gregory Johnson   P. 215

Graphic Designs & Associates, Inc.
9220 Mainsail Drive
Gainesville, GA 30506
TEL   888-887-4499 (Toll free)
TEL   770-887-1561
E-mail: gjhotmetal@email.msn.com
Web: www.sculpture.org

Whether suggesting "the presence of the missing soldier," or inviting children to sit in the *Storyteller's Circle of Rocks,* Gregory Johnson's original bronze sculptures prompt physical participation or mental contemplation, adding an interactive element to any architectural setting. He expertly captures intriguing and intimate details to preserve precious heritage and memories that endure for generations.

Nationally recognized, he has designed five awe-inspiring war memorials and has also sculpted striking portrait busts of dignitaries, celebrities and the common man. His commemorative subjects are featured in government, public and private collections throughout the United States and the world.

Barry Woods Johnston   P. 147

SculptureWorks, Inc.
2423 Pickwick Road
Baltimore, MD 21207
TEL   410-448-1945
FAX   410-448-2663
E-mail: sculptureworks@sculptorjohnston
    .com

Barry Woods Johnston's sculptures have won awards and commissions for 25 years. Energy, movement and drama radiate from Johnston's imaginative works. Educated in architecture, he mastered the figure at the Pennsylvania Academy, National Academy of Design, and in Florence, Italy. Life-size pieces begin at $25000.

COMMISSIONS: Washington National Cathedral; the Lafayette Center, Washington, DC; City Hall, Hampton, VA; the Women's Hospital, Evanston, IL; People's Republic of China

COLLECTIONS: The Vatican, Georgetown University, James Michener Museum of Art

GUILD SOURCEBOOKS: *Architect's: 13, 14, 15*

Judy B. Dales, Quiltmaker   P. 359

Judy B. Dales
2254 Craftsbury Road
Greensboro, VT 05841
E-mail: jubda@aol.com
Web: www.judydales.com

Judy B. Dales uses fluid lines, undulating shapes and complex color to produce works of richness, depth and movement. These pieced and quilted hangings stimulate the imagination and bring warmth to any environment.

COMMISSIONS: Children's Inn, National Institute of Health, Bethesda, MD, 1994; Morris Museum of Arts and Sciences, Convent Station, NJ, 1988

COLLECTIONS: White House Craft Collection, Washington, DC; Newark Museum, Newark, NJ

EXHIBITIONS & AWARDS: "100 Best Quilts of the 20th Century," Houston, TX, 2000; New Jersey fellowship grant, 1989, 1984

PUBLICATIONS: *Curves In Motion* by Judy B. Dales, 1999

Juliearts.com   PP. 300-301

Julie Betts Testwuide
482 Underhill Avenue
Yorktown Heights, NY 10598
TEL   914-962-5096
FAX   914-962-9655
E-mail: jbt@juliearts.com
Web: www.juliearts.com

Julie Betts Testwuide is well known for her evocative images that are a mixture of photography and painting. She creates works of art that are delicately detailed and saturated with the light and mood reminiscent of an impressionist painting. Whether the scene has been captured in the United States or Europe, her images are timeless and focus on simple beauty.

Testwuide has won numerous awards and her work has been widely published. She exhibits in galleries in France, New York, Massachusetts, Atlanta and Vail, CO. Her artwork is included in many private and public collections.

A selection of her artwork can be viewed and purchased on her website, www.juliearts.com.

COMMISSIONS: Marriott Hotel, Tampa, FL, 2000; Savannah Golf Club, Savannah, GA, 2000

ARTIST INFORMATION

Jurs Architectural Glass   P. 76

Shelley Jurs
4167 Wilshire Boulevard
Oakland, CA 94602
TEL 800-679-9772
FAX 510-531-6173
E-mail: jursag@sirius.com
Web: www.art-glass-doors.com

Shelley Jurs' architectural glass pieces range from stunning craftsman-style doors to enormous, artistically designed window walls and skylights that break out of the borders of symmetry.

Since 1978, she has worked closely with clients and their design teams to provide spectacular finished works of art glass for private, corporate, public and religious environments.

In the 1970s, Jurs' extensive work with glass included studying at the California College of Arts and Crafts, apprenticing at Willets Stained Glass Studios in Pennsylvania and assisting acclaimed glass artist Ludwig Schaffrath in Germany.

Juanita Y. Kauffman   P. 238

148 Monmouth Street
Hightstown, NJ 08520
TEL 609-448-5335
E-mail: velvetoverground@earthlink.net
Web: www.JYKart.com

Juanita Y. Kauffman's paintings on silk incorporate abstracted natural, celestial and human forms. They can be suspended in space or framed as wall art. Commissions have included large gothic and smaller modern settings. Kauffman also creates artwear and stained glass designs.

RECENT PROJECTS: Four 25-foot paintings, Princeton University Chapel, NJ; installation of two 25-foot paintings for inaugural service, Union Theological Seminary, Riverside Church, New York, NY; holiday installation for Interchurch Center Chapel, New York, NY

Peter Kaufman   P. 252

Peter Kaufman Studio
120 South Main Street
Port Chester, NY 10573
TEL 914-934-0964
FAX 914-934-1054
E-mail: pkstudio@earthlink.net

Peter Kaufman uses the finest materials and meticulous craftsmanship to create furniture and cabinetry of uncompromising quality and integrity. Whether the designs are based on a client's vision or on his own, Kaufman takes great care in selecting the materials and the techniques to make that vision a reality. He believes that a job well done and a satisfied customer are parts of his profit, and he feels fortunate to be able to use his skills to create work that will last for generations.

Commissions are welcomed, please contact the artist for information.

Gary Kazanjian   P. 77

Kazanjian Architectural Glass
423 Pier Avenue
Hermosa Beach, CA 90254
TEL/FAX 310-374-7798
E-mail: kazanjianstudio@hotmail.com

Gary Kazanjian's work is about clean, elegant images that are strong, yet not overpowering. He uses a large amount of clear, textured glass that provides detail and obscurity (if desired) as well as a visual feast. Various lead widths are employed to support the intent of the design. The architectural context and the clients' wishes are joined with his knowledge, experience and vision to provide the inspiration for a project.

RECENT PROJECTS: Ner-Tamid Synagogue, Rancho Palas Verdes, CA; restaurant design, Neiman Marcus, Plano, TX

COMMISSIONS: Westec Security, chairman's office, Japan, 1998; Hollywood Digital Offices, Santa Monica, CA, 1997

GUILD SOURCEBOOKS: *Architect's 14, 15*

Guy Kemper   PP. 78-79

Kemper Studio
190 North Broadway
Lexington, KY 40507
TEL/FAX 859-254-3507
E-mail: kemperstudio@juno.com

Guy Kemper transforms lightspaces with designs that reflect the room's spirit, the client's desires and the architect's recommendations. He strives for a design of harmonious essentials that will outlast fashion. He guarantees his work for his lifetime.

RECENT PROJECTS: St. Joseph East Hospital, Lexington, KY, 2000; Bellarmine University Chapel, Louisville, KY, 2000; Greater Orlando International Airport, 2000

COMMISSIONS: Woodford County High School, Versailles, KY, 1998; Lexington Public Library, 1997; Jewish Hospital, Louisville, KY, 1995; O'Brien residence, Fort Lauderdale, FL, 1995; Engman residence, Seattle, WA, 1994

Guy Kemper   PP. 78-79

Kemper Studio
190 North Broadway
Lexington, KY 40507
TEL/FAX 859-254-3507
E-mail: kemperstudio@juno.com

COLLECTIONS: Sheikh Maktoum al-Maktoum, king of Dubai; Gainsborough Stud Management, Berkshire, England; Radford Acupuncture Clinic, Perthshire, Scotland

EXHIBITIONS & AWARDS: Owensboro Museum of Fine Art, Owensboro, KY, 1997; Macon and Company Fine Art, Atlanta, GA, 1995; Deuxième Salon International du Vitrail, Chartres and Nîmes, France, 1989

PUBLICATIONS: *Beautiful Things*, 2000; *USAir Magazine*, 1995; *Albenaa*, architecture magazine, Saudi Arabia, 1993; *The New York Times*, 1992; *Travel and Leisure*, 1991; *Deuxième Salon International du Vitrail*, France

GUILD SOURCEBOOKS: *Architect's 9, 10, 11, 14, 15*

Ellen Mears Kennedy P. 343

9210 Midwood Road
Silver Spring, MD 20910
TEL 301-587-4782
FAX 301-587-7223
E-mail: emearskenn@aol.com
Web: www.guild.com

Ellen Mears Kennedy's artwork is constructed of hundreds of double-sided papers, all handmade in her studio from pigmented pulp. Each paper has a left and right side that displays a unique shade. When the paper is folded, one color shows on the left side and a second color shows on the right.

As viewers walk past each construction, the colors subtly change as they see alternating sides of the design — the hues shift, growing darker or lighter, depending on the observers' positions. The design is always in motion. The geometry of intersecting color patterns is softened by the texture of each paper's deckled edge and made fluid by the viewers' movements.

John Kennedy P. 148

996 Tuxedo Circle
Palm Springs, CA 92262
TEL 760-320-9205
FAX 760-320-9516
E-mail: JKsKarma@aol.com
Web: www.kennedysculpture.com

Born in Burma of Scottish parents, John Kennedy was educated in India and England. He now resides in Palm Springs, CA. His work is represented by several prestigious galleries in the United States, Germany, England, Switzerland and Hong Kong, and is in many private and corporate collections.

COMMISSIONS: Oxford Museum, England; International Red Cross, Switzerland; Barbara Sinatra Children's Center, CA; Kansas Health Foundation, KS; City of Brea, Public Art Program, CA; Sun Bus Headquarters, CA; Performing Arts Council, Annenberg Theater, Palm Springs, CA; Palm Springs International Film Festival, Palm Springs, CA; Public Library, Palm Desert, CA

GUILD SOURCEBOOKS: *Architect's 9, 11, 12, 13, 14; Designer's 7, 8*

Stephen Knapp P. 80

74 Commodore Road
Worcester, MA 01602-2792
TEL 508-757-2507
FAX 508-797-3228
E-mail: sk@stephenknapp.com
Web: www.stephenknapp.com

For 30 years, Stephen Knapp has collaborated with designers and architects on integrated architectural commissions for private, corporate and public projects here and abroad. He is the author of *The Art of Glass* (Rockford Publishers, 1998), "A Guide to Architectural Art Glass" in *Architectural Record* (May 1995), and "Architectural Art Glass" in *Glass Magazine* (May 1995).

Knapp works with kiln-formed, cast and dichroic glass; steel; wood and stone to create glass walls, doors, windows, screens, atrium pieces, sculpture, lighting and furniture.

COMMISSIONS: Worcester Medical Center, Worcester, MA; The Sam Nunn Federal Center, Atlanta, GA; Kilroy Airport Center, Long Beach, CA; Fox Chase Cancer Institute, Philadelphia, PA; CNA Insurance Companies, Chicago, IL; Dana Farber Cancer Institute, Boston, MA; Sprint, Washington, DC; *Splendour of the Seas*, Royal Caribbean Cruise Lines; Harnischfeger Industries, Milwaukee, WI; private residences

Ellen Kochansky PP. 330-331

EKO
1237 Mile Creek Road
Pickens, SC 29671
TEL 864-868-9749
FAX 864-868-4250
E-mail: ekochansky@aol.com

In 20 years of public and private commissions, Kochansky has extended the quilter's concerns of color and technique into philosophical issues of community and environment. Current two- and three-dimensional mixed-media works combine distance impact with close-up interest. Still suggesting quilts, they may involve contributed materials from individuals or members of the sponsoring group, creating a dynamic commitment. Cities, churches, businesses, hospitals, libraries and families can commemorate an anniversary or event using prepared request letters. The process can also generate self-funding and publicity opportunities for the sponsor.

COMMISSIONS: Hines Interests, IBM, Emory University

COLLECTIONS: Many private and museum collections, including the White House Collection

Karl P. Koenig P. 302

DT Enterprises
6435 Nabor Road NW
Albuquerque, NM 87107
TEL 505-344-4429
FAX 505-344-8570
E-mail: kpkoe@swcp.com

Karl P. Koenig works toward a pictorialist, 19th-century quality in his gumoil photographic prints. The prints draw from that period, as well as from the impressionists; when they are successful, they evoke emotional recollection.

His work is contact printed on cotton rag paper in sizes up to 22" x 30".

RECENT PROJECTS: *Hier ist kein warum*, 80 gumoil images of concentration camp residue featuring 10 camps in 6 countries

COLLECTIONS: University of New Mexico Art Museum; Museum of New Mexico, Santa Fe; Capitol Art Collection, state capitol building, Santa Fe; Instituto de Artes Graficas de Oaxaca (Foto Centro Manuel Bravo)

PUBLICATIONS: *Gumoil Photographic Printing* by Karl P. Koenig, 1999; *Photowork; View Camera; Camera Arts; Photo Techniques; Camera and Darkroom*

Joan Kopchik P. 344

1335 Stephen Way
Southampton, PA 18966-4349
TEL 215-322-1862
FAX 215-322-5031
E-mail: jkopchik@voicenet.com

Joan Kopchik casts wet sheets of handmade paper into plaster forms to create sculptural wall pieces. She incorporates mixed-media elements into her designs to develop a rich, complex, personal iconography. Multiple layers of pigments protect the work, making it suitable for hanging without framing.

COLLECTIONS: The Pew Charitable Trust, Philadelphia, PA; First Union Bank, Philadelphia, PA; Kaiser Permanente, Baltimore, MD

PUBLICATIONS: *Juried Portfolio: Old Ways, New Views: Photographic Processes on Handmade Paper*, 1999

GUILD SOURCEBOOKS: *Designer's 6, 7, 8, 11, 15*

Tuck Langland P. 149

Tuck Langland, Sculptor
12632 Anderson Road
Granger, IN 46530
TEL/FAX 219-272-2708
E-mail: **tuckandjan@aol.com**
Web: **www.iusb.edu/~hlanglan/Gallery1.html**

Specializing in figurative bronze sculptures for gardens and public spaces, smaller indoor figures and desk-size corporate awards, Langland's work is available from his catalog or by commission. He is a Fellow in the National Sculpture Society and a member of the National Academy of Art.

COMMISSIONS: Indiana University, City of Mishawaka, First Source Bank

COLLECTIONS: Lincoln National, Meijer Sculpture Garden, Smithsonian Collections, Midwest Museum of American Art, Minnesota Museum of American Art

PUBLICATIONS: *From Clay to Bronze* by Tuck Langland

GUILD SOURCEBOOKS: *Architect's 8, 9, 10, 11, 12, 13, 14*

Lauren Camp, Fiber Artist P. 360

Lauren Camp
25 Theresa Lane
Santa Fe, NM 87505
TEL 505-474-7943
E-mail: **lauren@laurencamp.com**
Web: **www.laurencamp.com**

Lauren Camp creates original fiber works with the soul of jazz and the joy of color. She works intuitively, combining texture and pattern to design vibrant abstract studies. Exceptional handwork, glorious hand-dyed and digitally printed fabric, and dense machine quilting define her signature style. Her award-winning pieces have been exhibited nationally and in Europe.

COLLECTIONS: Vista Grande Community Center, Sandia Park, NM; Sheriff's Substation & Communications Center, Albuquerque, NM

GUILD SOURCEBOOKS: *Designer's 15*

Duncan Laurie P. 81

Duncan Laurie Architectural Glass & Design
PO Box 78
Jamestown, RI 02835
TEL 401-423-3992
FAX 401-423-3711
E-mail: **ditl@edgenet.net**

Duncan Laurie Architectural Glass & Design executes and designs site-specific glass commissions using a variety of techniques, including sandblasting, etching, thermal spray metal coatings and custom laminates.

The studio's proprietary designs, blending carved glass and metal surfaces together, work especially well as aerial topographies. High-resolution satellite images are available for most locations.

These treatments appeal to clients seeking a global or regional distinction to their interiors, whether agricultural, industrial or urban.

COMMISSIONS: Citigroup Corporate Center, Capital Cities ABC, Electra Records, Estée Lauder, Lincoln Square

J. Kenneth Leap P. 239

The Painted Window
12 Washington Avenue
Runnemede, NJ 08078
TEL 856-939-5813
FAX 856-939-5934
E-mail: **jkennethleap@excite.com**
Web: **www.jkennethleap.com**

J. Kenneth Leap brings a painter's eye to the field of architectural stained glass. His images are created by the meticulous application of layers of kiln-fired, vitreous pigments over mouth-blown colored glass.

RECENT PROJECTS: The Joyce Skipper Memorial (pictured), 10' x 15' altar window depicting the text of Isaiah 40:31, interfaith chapel at a nursing home in Burlington, NJ; 14 lancet windows showing the progression of the seasons for the same building

Marlene Lenker P. 279

28 Northview Terrace
Cedar Grove, NJ 07009
TEL 973-239-8671

Lenker Fine Arts
13 Crosstrees Hill Road
Essex, CT 06426
TEL 860-767-2098 (Studio)
E-mail: **lenkerart@prodigy.net**
Web: **www.guild.com**

Marlene Lenker is a mixed-media layerist and colorist, painting on canvas and paper in transparent and opaque layers. Her brushstrokes and marks are unique, intuitive expressions of energy and spirit. Her monotypes and collages are evocative abstract layers of mixed media.

COLLECTIONS: American Airlines, Lever Bros., Arthur Young, PepsiCo, Kidder Peabody, Union Carbide, Pfizer, Warner-Lambert, Vista Hotels, Horcht, CIBA, Merrill Lynch, Hoffman-LaRoche

PUBLICATIONS: *Bridging Time and Space*, 1999; *Layering*, 1991; *Who's Who in America; Who's Who of American Artists; Who's Who of Women Artists; Who's Who of World Women*

GUILD SOURCEBOOKS: *Designer's 10, 12, 13, 15*

LepoWorks, Inc. P. 216

David Lepo
Robert Lepo
4640 Allentown Road
Lima, OH 45807
TEL 419-339-5370
E-mail: **dlepo@woh.rr.com**
Web: **www.lepoworks.com**

LepoWorks is a family of artists who use their individual talents to create work that reveals the studio's one-of-a-kind philosophy.

For 30 years, LepoWorks has designed private, public and corporate art to match the clientele's particular aesthetic preferences. The studio enhances interior and exterior architectural elements and spaces, offering artistic solutions meeting budget and deadline demands. LepoWorks expresses its diversity through a multitude of materials used in traditional and contemporary styles.

GUILD SOURCEBOOKS: *Architect's 8, 9, 10, 11, 12, 13*

Alan LeQuire P. 150

Alan LeQuire, Sculptor
1222 Fourth Avenue North
Nashville, TN 37208
TEL/FAX **615-242-5408**
E-mail: **lequire@mindspring.com**
Web: **www.alanlequire.com**

Alan LeQuire is a figurative sculptor who has become well known in his native Southeast for his public commissions and sensitive portraiture. LeQuire works in virtually all sculpture materials, both direct carving and casting in his own foundry. He has completed a number of architectural, collaborative and site-specific projects since he began accepting commissions in 1981.

RECENT PROJECTS: *75th Anniversary Suffrage Memorial,* three life-size bronze figures, Knoxville, TN; *Musica,* monumental figurative sculpture, City of Nashville's Music Row; portrait group, three life-size bronze figures, Columbia/HCA, Nashville, TN; Nashville Public Library doors, 24 relief panels in bronze, Nashville, TN; *Jack Daniels,* life-size bronze portrait, Jack Daniels Distillery, Lynchburg, TN; *Teacher and Student,* life-size bronze portrait, Montgomery Bell Academy, Nashville, TN

Verena Levine P. 361

Verena Levine Pictorial Quilts
4305 37th Street NW
Washington, DC 20008
TEL **202-537-0916**
E-mail: **verenalevi@cs.com**
Web: **www.verenalevine.com**

Verena Levine's quilts depict scenes of contemporary urban and rural American life. For 20 years, she has produced original works of all sizes — including large installations — for corporate and residential spaces in the U.S. and abroad.

Machine-pieced and appliquéd from many different fabrics, her quilts are sturdy and easy to install. The time from a contract to the completed work averages 6 to 12 weeks.

Slides, pricing and scheduling upon request. Completed works are also available.

Linda M. Leviton P. 319

Linda Leviton Sculpture
1011 Colony Way
Columbus, OH 43235
TEL **614-433-7486**
FAX **614-433-0806**
E-mail: **lindaleviton@columbus.rr.com**

Linda Leviton is a sculptor who works mainly with copper and brass. Using patina and oil paint, she applies color to metal, creating sculptural paintings that hang on the wall. Etching textures in copper, folding, hammering, layering and bending create dimensional effects that cannot be found in traditional painting. These works can be constructed in sections to fill spaces that require large lightweight artwork.

She has completed commissions for a number of religious institutions, state governments and private collectors. Commission work is priced per square foot.

Please contact the artist for a page of slides that demonstrates other metal techniques and designs.

GUILD SOURCEBOOKS: *Designer's 15*

Mark J. Levy P. 82

Mark Levy Studio
PO Box 4722
Chatsworth, CA 91304
TEL **818-595-1195**
FAX **818-595-1166**
E-mail: **mlstudio@earthlink.net**
Web: **www.marklevystudio.com**

As an architect, Mark Levy's artistic vision is in harmony with the space his work occupies. An open design dialog with his clients exceeds everyone's expectations. Employing flat, fused, slumped and carved glass enables him to achieve any effect required. Uncommon attention to detail is his hallmark.

An 80-page book has just been published on his award-winning works by Wardell Publications. Specially designed crating and shipping systems ensure the safe and on-time delivery of his works worldwide.

COMMISSIONS: La Quinta City Hall, La Quinta, CA; Studio City Branch of the Los Angeles, CA, Public Library; The Walt Disney Company; Winterthur Museum; Eastman Kodak; Hilton Hotels; Herb Alpert; Dudley Moore; Priscilla Presley

Norma Lewis P. 187

Norma Lewis Studios
30500 Aurora del Mar
Carmel, CA 93923
TEL **831-625-1046**
FAX **831-625-5733**
E-mail: **norma@dlewis.com**

Norma Lewis' works are non-representational, although they often suggest life forms. They embody integrity of material, grace of weight and balance and simplicity of form. She doesn't force the dialog, but waits for the shapes to introduce themselves. She then embraces and builds on what they suggest.

Working primarily in bronze, Lewis' sculptures are in collections worldwide, including the United States, Canada, Hong Kong, Germany, Saudi Arabia and Venezuela. Her prices range from $1000 for pedestal art to $75000 for monumental works.

GUILD SOURCEBOOKS: *Architect's 13, 14, 15; Designer's 14, 15*

Jacques Lieberman Editions P. 329

Jacques Lieberman
170 Mercer Street 3W
New York, NY 10012-3263
TEL **212-219-0939**
FAX **212-925-8545**
E-mail: **jalie@mindspring.com**
Web: **www.jacqueslieberman.com**

Jacques Lieberman creates all of his images with computer software. The output is printed on rag paper for limited-edition signed prints, on tiles for wall installations and on fabric for studio-created wearable art.

RECENT PROJECTS: New collection of 60 studio-printed textile scarves

COLLECTIONS: Numerous collections in Argentina, Belgium, Brazil, Canada, Equador, France, Japan, Honduras, Israel, Italy, Mexico, the Philippines, Singapore, Spain, Italy and the U.S.

EXHIBITIONS & AWARDS: The National Academy; Artexpo; National Art Center; Cooper Gallery; Vasarely Center; Aames Gallery; American Craft Council shows

PUBLICATIONS: *New York Arts Journal, Arts Magazine, Art Business News, Indulge Magazine*

GUILD SOURCEBOOKS: *Designer's 11, 15*

Kerin Lifland   PP. 108, 115

Kerin Lifland Design
2015 5th Avenue
Los Angeles, CA 90018
TEL/FAX 323-733-3172
E-mail: kjslifland@mediaone.net
Web: www.kerinlifland.com

Kerin Lifland has been building one-of-a-kind freestanding furniture for over 12 years. Recently, he had the opportunity to more directly combine his woodworking skills with his drawing and painting background to design and produce the paneled study pictured in this book.

The Italian Renaissance-inspired room features six large panels of trompe l'oeil marquetry, with thematic still lifes representing music and travel as well as four carved clamshell motifs. In addition, 200 linear feet of corkscrew design inlay strips frame the panels and outline the room.

PUBLICATIONS: *Metropolitan Home, Furniture Studio One*

GUILD SOURCEBOOKS: *Designer's 13*

Liturgical Environments Company   P. 83

Jerry Krauski
10814W County Highway B
Hayward, WI 54843
TEL 800-449-8554
TEL 715-462-3097
FAX 715-462-3481
E-mail: artglass@win.bright.net
Web: www.liturgicalenvironments.com

Jerry Krauski's studio has created architectural glass for more than 38 years. Faceted, leaded and carved glass are his media of expression.

Krauski's life goal has been to use his artistic talent to satisfy the needs and desires of the faith community. His vast experience spans from traditional art glass (symbols, figures and Byzantine icons) to contemporary art glass styles.

Each of the artist's commissions is custom designed to ensure harmony with the client's space.

GUILD SOURCEBOOKS: *Architect's 8, 9*

Lightspann Illumination Design, Inc.   P. 253

Christina Spann
2855 Mandela Parkway, Suite 11
Oakland, CA 94603
TEL 510-663-9500
FAX 510-663-9550
E-mail: cspan@lightspann.com
Web: www.lightspann.com

Lightspann Illumination Design designs and fabricates custom artistic lighting fixtures. The studio specializes in design for residential, hospitality and commercial applications, using quality materials and state-of-the-art specifications.

COMMISSIONS: Postrio Restaurant, Las Vegas, NV; River Bend Hotel, Uruguay; Charleston Performing Arts Center, Charleston, SC

COLLECTIONS: University of Arizona, Cheesecake Factory corporate collection

EXHIBITIONS & AWARDS: Decorative Lighting – Hospitality Award, ASID, 2000; Best New Sconce – Residential Award, ADEX, 1999

PUBLICATIONS: "Best Residential Lighting," San Francisco Chronicle, 2000; *Residential Lighting* by Randall Whitehead, 1999

GUILD SOURCEBOOKS: *Designer's 10, 11, 13*

Joyce P. Lopez   PP. 306, 363

Joyce Lopez Studio
1147 West Ohio Street #304
Chicago, IL 60622-5874
TEL 312-243-5033
FAX 312-243-7566
E-mail: JoyceLopez@aol.com

Joyce Lopez maintains studios in Tanzania and Chicago. She works with a variety of photographic techniques, including Polaroid transfers, straight photography and archival digital photographs. Subjects include objects, landscapes, people, architecture and animals.

COMMISSIONS: Nokia Corporation, City of Chicago, Sony Corporation, State of Washington, Health South

EXHIBITIONS & AWARDS: One Off Gallery, Nairobi; Albuquerque Museum; Wood Street Gallery, Chicago; Tucson Museum; "From Lausanne to Beijing — International Tapestry Exhibition 2000," Beijing, China

PUBLICATIONS: Book covers for Pearson Education and Harper Collins

GUILD SOURCEBOOKS: *THE GUILD 1, 2, 3, 4, 5; Architect's 8, 11, 13, 15; Designer's 6, 7, 8, 9, 10, 11, 12, 13, 14, 15*

Linda Filby-Fisher Quilt Artist   P. 362

Linda Filby-Fisher
6401 West 67th Street
Overland Park, KS 66202
TEL 913-722-2608
Web: www.guild.com
Web: www.saqa.com

Linda Filby-Fisher's art quilts, with their international fabrics, text, colors, embellishments and textures, are created using traditional and unique processes. The results are works of detailed design and visual impact.

Each piece, often double sided, includes an embroidered legend grounding the quilt in history and meaning.

The artist's work can be found nationally in exhibits, collections and publications. She welcomes commissions. Slides and resume are available upon request.

GUILD SOURCEBOOKS: *Designer's 15*

Joyce P. Lopez   PP. 306, 363

Joyce Lopez Studio
1147 West Ohio Street #304
Chicago, IL 60622-5874
TEL 312-243-5033
FAX 312-243-7566
E-mail: JoyceLopez@aol.com

Joyce Lopez meticulously creates her sculpture out of chromed steel tubes and French thread. With over 300 colors to choose from, color specifications are always met. Her stunning sculptures enrich corporate, public and private interiors.

RECENT PROJECTS: Nokia Collection, Dallas, TX

COMMISSIONS: City of Chicago, 2000; Health South, Birmingham, AL, 1997; State of Washington, 1995

COLLECTIONS: Sony Corporation, IL; Jim Beam Brands, IL; Bank of America, Chicago, IL

EXHIBITIONS & AWARDS: San Diego Art Institute, 2000; Beijing International Tapestry Exhibition, China, 2000; Fort Wayne Art Museum, IN, 2000; Albuquerque Museum, NM, 1999

PUBLICATIONS: Cover image, Pearson Education mathematics book; cover image, four mathematics books, Harper Collins

Luminous Artworks P. 334

Candice Gawne
558 Shepard Street
San Pedro, CA 90731
TEL 310-521-9024
FAX 310-521-9034
E-mail: cgawne@earthlink.net
Web: www.luminousartworks.com
Web: www.rainbowdoorway.com

Using neon backlighting, glass, Plexiglas, paint, wood and steel, artist Candice Gawne has combined her talents as a painter and light sculptor to create colorful, three-dimensional wall and freestanding sculptures. These site-specific luminous artworks, which can also be animated, enhance our public, corporate and private lives, day and night.

COMMISSIONS: Cabrillo Marine Aquarium, Los Angeles, CA; Il Forno Restaurant, Tokyo, Japan

COLLECTIONS: Frederick Weisman Foundation of Art, Penny Marshall, Robin Williams

EXHIBITIONS & AWARDS: "Neon/Nature," Oceanside Museum; "Elements," Los Angeles Municipal Gallery; "Traveling Light," Seto, Japan

PUBLICATIONS: *Contemporary Neon* by Rudy Stern, *Feng Shui* by Carol King, *Liquid Fire* by Michael Webb

Elizabeth MacDonald PP. 42-43, 248

Box 186
Bridgewater, CT 06752
TEL 860-354-0594
FAX 860-350-4052
Web: www.garden-art.com/sculpture/macdonald/elizabeth.html

Elizabeth MacDonald produces tile paintings that suggest the patinas of age. These compositions are suitable for either in- or out-of-doors and take the form of freestanding columns, wall panels or architectural installations.

COMMISSIONS: Conrad International Hotel, Hong Kong; St. Luke's Hospital, Denver, CO; Department of Environmental Protection, Hartford, CT (Percent for Art); Milliken, Spartanburg, SC; University of Maryland Medical Center; Chubb and Sons; Pitney Bowes; the Aetna Life Insurance Company; IBM

EXHIBITIONS & AWARDS: The Works Gallery, Philadelphia, PA, 2000; Bachelier-Cordonsky, Kent, CT, 2000; State of Connecticut Governor's Arts Award, 1999

GUILD SOURCEBOOKS: *THE GUILD 1, 2, 3, 4, 5; Architect's 6, 7, 8, 9, 10, 11, 12, 13, 14, 15; Designer's: 6, 8, 9, 10, 11, 12, 13, 14, 15*

Elizabeth MacDonald PP. 42-43, 248

Box 186
Bridgewater, CT 06752
TEL 860-354-0594
FAX 860-350-4052
Web: www.garden-art.com/sculpture/macdonald/elizabeth.html

Through clay, Elizabeth MacDonald expresses her connection to the natural world. Each work speaks to the process of change, whether through the appearance of age or the spontaneity of gesture.

Lured by color and texture, ancient in feeling, she often expresses these qualities through the use of fragmentation. Small surface elements draw the viewer into a larger context, where hundreds of parts interact to form a whole.

Organized as a grid, torn and textured squares compose a rhythmic pattern which balances the energy of the organic. In her work, marks of color and texture are created by pressing powdered pigments into thin, textured stoneware.

Ellen Mandelbaum P. 84

Ellen Mandelbaum Glass Art
39-49 46 Street
Long Island City, NY 11104-1407
TEL/FAX 718-361-8154

Since 1971, Ellen Mandelbaum has created original architectural art celebrating the beauty of glass, sometimes combining architectural leaded glass with glass painting fired for permanence.

"Her approach to brush and paint expresses to me all that painterly implies."
Andrew Moor, *Architectural Glass Art,* 1997

RECENT PROJECTS: 18' x 30' art glass window, South Carolina Aquarium, Charleston, Eskew + Architects; 28 windows, Marian Woods, church for five orders of nuns, Hartsdale, NY

EXHIBITIONS & AWARDS: AIA Award of Excellence for Religious Art, Adath Jeshurun Synagogue, MN, architects: Finegold and Alexander, 1997; *Who's Who in American Art*

GUILD SOURCEBOOKS: *The Guild 1, 2, 3, 5; Architect's 6, 8, 9, 11, 12, 13, 14, 15*

Anne Marchand PP. 122, 280-281

Marchand Studio
1413 17th Street NW
Washington, DC 20036-6402
TEL 202-265-5882 (Extension 2)
FAX 202-265-0232
E-mail: foster99@ix.netcom.com
Web: www.annemarchand.com

Anne Marchand's cityscapes are brilliant complements to private collections as well as corporate environments. Known as an accomplished colorist, Marchand uses vibrant hues to echo the richness, poetry and energy of urban landscapes. Architecture, geometry, musical rhythms and striking vistas are hallmarks of Marchand's enchanting works.

COMMISSIONS: Allfirst, MD; Centerstage Productions, VA; Blom & Dorn Gallery, New York, NY; private residences

COLLECTIONS: AT&T Broadband, Alabama Power Company, HealthSouth, IBM, Kennedy Center, US Trust

GUILD SOURCEBOOKS: *Designer's 13, 14, 15*

Anne Marchand PP. 122, 280-281

Marchand Studio
1413 17th Street NW
Washington, DC 20036-6402
TEL 202-265-5882 (Extension 2)
FAX 202-265-0232
E-mail: foster99@ix.netcom.com
Web: www.annemarchand.com

Anne Marchand's abstract paintings resonate with the movement of universal energies. Marchand, an accomplished colorist, is recognized for her lyrical and musical compositions. Her colorful rhythms and melodies are emphasized by bold linear accents. Through her layering technique, she paints a rich tapestry of textured surface and vibrant hues.

COMMISSIONS: Allfirst, MD; Blom & Dorn Gallery, New York, NY; Centerstage Productions, VA; private residences; Richards, Spears, Kibbe & Orbe, Washington, DC

COLLECTIONS: AT&T Broadband, Alabama Power Company, HealthSouth, IBM, Kennedy Center, US Trust

GUILD SOURCEBOOKS: *Designer's 13, 14, 15*

ARTIST INFORMATION

Charlene Marsh
PP. 364-365

Charlene Marsh Studio
4013 Lanam Ridge Road
Nashville, IN 47448
TEL   812-988-4497
FAX   812-988-6522
E-mail: ArtistChar@aol.com
Web: www.charlenemarsh.com

Masterful use of color sets Charlene Marsh's work apart. Gold thread, hand-dyed wool, silk and cotton are tufted and sculpted onto a cotton backing to give her work an intricate three-dimensional relief effect. These stunning artworks have attracted the attention of jurors, curators and collectors throughout the country.

RECENT PROJECTS: The White House, Washington, DC; Knoy Hall, Purdue University, West Lafayette, IN; Minnetrista Cultural Center, Muncie, IN

COLLECTIONS: Indianapolis Museum of Art; Harrison Steel Castings Company, Attica, IN; Indiana Orthopaedics and Sports Medicine, IN; Evansville Museum of Arts & Science, IN

EXHIBITIONS: National Women's Museum of Art, Washington, DC, 1999-2000

GUILD SOURCEBOOKS: *Architect's 15*

Mollie Massie
PP. 26-27

Myers Massie Studio, Inc.
PO Box 30073
8602 Granville Street
Vancouver, BC V6P 6S3
Canada
TEL   604-266-5009
FAX   604-266-8431
E-mail: mollie@myersmassiestudio.com
Web: www.myersmassiestudio.com

Thousands of years after the first rock carvings were made, Vancouver artist Mollie Massie uses this ancient imagery to tell her clients' life histories, or "stories," in steel. Massie works with architects, interior designers and individual clients to create unique, functional "art to live with." Her metalwork, cut by hand with an oxy-acetylene torch from weathering steel, ranges from fireplace screens, tools, gates and chandeliers to tables, chairs and custom drawer pulls. She tells her clients, "the sky's the limit — if you can imagine it, I can most likely create it for you."

COMMISSIONS: Private homes; Grouse Mountain; Four Seasons Resorts

PUBLICATIONS: *Home Magazine, Log Home Living, Log Home Design Ideas, Canadian House & Home, Style At Home, Metropolitan Home, Architectural Digest, Better Homes & Gardens*

Franz Mayer of Munich, Inc.
PP. 44, 85

5 Tudor City Place #701
New York, NY 10017
TEL   212-661-1694

Seidlstr. 25
D-80335 Munich, Germany
TEL   011-49-89-595484
FAX   011-49-89-593446
E-mail: info@mayer-of-munich.com
Web: www.mayer-of-munich.com

Franz Mayer of Munich's business for 154 years has been art and architecture. The studio specializes in both artistic mosaic and architectural glass. Founded in 1847, it is to this day one of the foremost studios in these fields. The studio's work in the new and exciting technique of "floatglass painting" allows new and unknown possibilities in architectural art.

Franz Mayer of Munich, Inc., are craftsmen in the traditional European sense rather than artists. The studio is put to the service of independent artists and designers, who supervise the design work and direct the craftsmen in the realization of their artistic vision.

See more work by Franz Mayer of Munich, Inc., in the Architectural Glass section of this book.

Franz Mayer of Munich, Inc.
PP. 44, 85

5 Tudor City Place #701
New York, NY 10017
TEL   212-661-1694

Seidlstr. 25
D-80335 Munich, Germany
TEL   011-49-89-595484
FAX   011-49-89-593446
E-mail: info@mayer-of-munich.com
Web: www.mayer-of-munich.com

Franz Mayer of Munich's business for 154 years has been art and architecture. The studio specializes in both artistic mosaic and architectural glass. Founded in 1847, it is to this day one of the foremost studios in these fields. The studio's work in new and exciting mosaic and glass techniques allows new and unknown possibilities in architectural art.

Franz Mayer of Munich, Inc., are craftsmen in the traditional European sense rather than artists. The studio is put to the service of independent artists and designers, who supervise the design work and direct the craftsmen in the realization of their artistic vision.

See more work by Franz Mayer of Munich, Inc., in the Architectural Ceramics, Mosaics & Wall Reliefs section of this book.

R.W. McBride
P. 153

R.W. McBride Studio
80 North Roop Street
Susanville, CA 96130
TEL   530-257-3985
FAX   530-257-7999
E-mail: thebid@thegrid.net

Ron McBride's love for nature has driven him to become an accomplished wildlife sculptor. Working with hand-forged metal, chiseled stone and other elements, McBride brings his sculptures to life with texture and metal dye finishes.

By incorporating both hot and cold forging in his fabricated sculptures, McBride creates one-of-a-kind interior and exterior pieces for private, corporate and public commissions. A professional artist for more than 30 years, McBride knows the importance of quality, price and timely delivery.

He has developed the skills and understanding to work well in collaborative efforts. Sculptures range from pedestal to monumental.

GUILD SOURCEBOOKS: *Architect's 14*

E. Joseph McCarthy
P. 45

Custom Tile Studio
76 Hope Street, Suite B2
Greenfield, MA 01301-3515
TEL   413-772-8816
FAX   413-772-8811
E-mail: cts@crocker.com
Web: www.crocker.com/~cts

E. Joseph McCarthy and his staff have been designing and executing fine ceramic tile environments for over 20 years.

Specializing in large-scale murals, they custom design each piece to fit into the decor and configurations of a specific location.

COMMISSIONS: Savannah Hotel, Barbados; Celebrity Cruise Lines, FL; Merck and Company, NJ; Edsel B. Ford Center, MI; Valley Children's Hospital, CA; Kahalan Madarin Orient Hotel, HI

GUILD SOURCEBOOKS: *Architect's 9, 10, 12, 13, 15; Designer's 7, 11, 13, 14, 15*

Susan McGehee   P. 321

Metallic Strands
540 23rd Street
Manhattan Beach, CA 90266
TEL 310-545-4112
FAX 310-546-7152
E-mail: metlstrnds@aol.com
Web: www.metalstrands.com

Susan McGehee weaves wires and metals into striking forms. Applying traditional weaving techniques to nontraditional materials, she uses her computer-linked loom to create contemporary hangings that seem to float on the wall. These lightweight, easily installed and maintained pieces complement both residential and commercial settings.

COMMISSIONS: Hughes Communications Satellite Services, Inc., El Segundo, CA; Nokia, Burlingame, MA; Stevie Wonder, Los Angeles, CA; TriStar Imports, St. Louis, MO

PUBLICATIONS: *Design in Wire* by Barbara McGuire; *Sunset Magazine*

GUILD SOURCEBOOKS: *Designer's 12, 13, 14, 15*

McMow Art Glass, Inc.   P. 241

Shanon and Phil Materio
701 North Dixie Highway
Lake Worth, FL 33460
TEL 561-585-9011
FAX 561-586-2292
E-mail: mcmow@mcmow.com
Web: www.mcmow.com

McMow Art Glass offers the best in stained and beveled art glass as well as beautiful designs in carved, etched and faceted glass. McMow works closely with church committees, architects and builders to reflect the spiritual journey of all congregations. McMow ships its work throughout the U.S. and Europe.

RECENT PROJECTS: Memorial Presbyterian, West Palm Beach, FL; Church of the Epiphany, Pt. Orange, FL; Congregation Israel, Flint, MI

COMMISSIONS: Westin Stonebriar Hotel and Conference Center, Frisco, TX; Gianni Versace estate, South Beach, FL

PUBLICATIONS: *South Florida Design Resources,* 1999; *The World & I,* 1998; *Windows of Distinction,* 1995; *Vogue,* 1994

GUILD SOURCEBOOKS: *Architect's 8, 9, 14*

Trena McNabb   PP. 218, 286

McNabb Studio, Inc.
PO Box 327
Bethania, NC 27010
TEL 336-924-6053
FAX 336-924-4854
E-mail: trena@tmcnabb.com
Web: www.tmcnabb.com

Trena McNabb's distinctive style is a curious and elegant synthesis of realism and imagination. Her colorful images tell specific stories, and the geometric shapes are superimposed with an unusual and harmonious concept of beauty. Her multilayered montages of realistically rendered, brightly lit and thematically related scenes and brilliantly colored images entice viewers to look beyond the obvious.

COMMISSIONS: Charlotte/Mecklenburg Public Art Commission, Fannie Mae Mortgage, Hahnemann University Hospital, Japan Tobacco, KinderCare ChildCare, McGraw-Hill Publishing, Kaiser Permanente Hospital, PDS Engineering, Wingate Hotel

GUILD SOURCEBOOKS: *Architect's 6, 7, 8, 9, 10, 11, 12, 13, 14; Designer's 8, 9, 10, 11, 12, 13, 14*

Barbara McQueeney   P. 366

McQueeney Designs
2415 Converse
Dallas, TX 75207
TEL 214-630-4955
FAX 214-630-1023
E-mail: barbara@mcqueeneydesigns.com
Web: www.mcqueeneydesigns.com

Barbara McQueeney's textiles are an exploration of making simple shapes into complex cloth. Circles, squares and triangles are found repeatedly throughout her art. Use of these universal symbols, which have occurred in every culture throughout history, lends an ancient and everlasting quality to her work.

While many of her pieces reflect an ethnic influence, she remains fluid in her ability to interpret the parameters of each individual project. Portfolio available upon request.

GUILD SOURCEBOOKS: *Designer's 13, 14, 15*

Meamar   PP. 116-117

37338 Fowler Street
Newark, CA 94560
TEL 510-435-4152
Web: www.meamar.com

For Meamar, each work is as individual as the client. He goes to great lengths to reveal the appropriate feeling for the piece, transforming any interior environment with a magical depth. The results are breathtaking.

Meamar's expertise is the result of years of study under the masters in Italy as well as personal experience. He also works in other mediums, including modern sculpture and relief.

COMMISSIONS: Disney Co., Los Angeles, CA; E-Trade mansion, San Francisco Bay area

PUBLICATIONS: *Sunset Magazine*

Meamar   PP. 116-117

37338 Fowler Street
Newark, CA 94560
TEL 510-435-4152
Web: www.meamar.com

Transforming a blank wall into serene scenery is Meamar's speciality. Whether the wall consists of a little space over a mantel or a large area in a living room, Meamar magically transforms the space.

The fresco shown in this book demonstrates how he creates a tranquil setting with the combination of natural and manmade materials. Using icons like a peacock, he creates a mood to identify with the personalities of his clients.

John Medwedeff   P. 217

Medwedeff Forge & Design
695 Future Lane
Murphysboro, IL 62966
TEL **618-687-4304**
FAX **618-687-5220**
E-mail: **jmedwedeff@aol.com**

Working in steel and bronze, Medwedeff produces monumental public sculpture, fountains, architectural ironwork, lighting and furniture. Master craftsmanship, knowledge of design history and aesthetic considerations result in work that integrates the conceptual and planned function of the object or sculpture on time and within budget.

COMMISSIONS: Jed Johnson & Associates, New York, NY; Robert A.M. Stern Architects, New York, NY; State of Illinois; Memphis Arts Council; John Deere

PUBLICATIONS: *Direct Metal Sculpture* and *The Contemporary Blacksmith* by Dona Meilach; *Fabricator; House & Garden; British Blacksmith; Metalsmith*

Meltdown Glass Art & Design LLC   PP. 86, 157

BJ Katz
PO Box 2110
Tempe, AZ 85280
TEL **800-845-6221**
FAX **480-633-3344**
E-mail: **MeltdownAZ@aol.com**
Web: **www.meltdownglass.com**
Web: **www.bjkatz.com**

Since 1994, Meltdown Glass Art & Design has served the architectural and design community. Meltdown creates site-specific architectural kiln-cast glass for commercial, residential, public and liturgical projects. Works include sculptures, murals, room dividers, art screens, door and window inserts, tabletops and much more — innovative glass limited only by your imagination.

COMMISSIONS: Sheraton Hotels; American Express Corporation; Metropolitan Chicago Healthcare Council

EXHIBITIONS & AWARDS: Southwest Region of the Construction Specifications Institute Regional Craftsmanship Award, 2000

PUBLICATIONS: *Phoenix Home & Garden,* August 2000; *Interior Design,* May 2000; *Interiors,* May 2000; *Arizona Republic,* July 1999

Meltdown Glass Art & Design LLC   PP. 86, 157

BJ Katz
PO Box 2110
Tempe, AZ 85280
TEL **800-845-6221**
FAX **480-633-3344**
E-mail: **MeltdownAZ@aol.com**
Web: **www.meltdownglass.com**
Web: **www.bjkatz.com**

Glass artist BJ Katz has developed a technique on the cutting-edge of kiln-fired glass technology combining glass casting, draping and painting. Each torso metaphorically explores the uniqueness of human existence by drawing attention to the juxtaposition of the inner emotional psychological world and surface appearance.

COLLECTIONS: American Express Corporation, Phoenix, AZ; Yellow-eyed Penguin Conservatory Educational Center, New Zealand; International Cat Museum, Amsterdam, Holland; numerous private collections

EXHIBITIONS & AWARDS: Regional Craftsmanship Award, Southwest Region of the Construction Specifications Institute, 2000

George Thomas Mendel   P. 303

PO Box 13605
Pittsburgh, PA 15243
TEL **412-563-7918**
Web: **www.photo-now.com**
Web: **www.guild.com**

George Thomas Mendel, a location/freelance and fine art photographer, has been working with the medium for more than 20 years. In this time he has produced a variety of portfolios, which include architecture, waterscapes and humanitarian projects.

Primarily working in black and white as an art form, limited-edition prints are produced by way of traditional fiber-based gelatin silver (cold or warm tone per request).

His creative use of light and composition is matched by his master craftsmanship in the darkroom, producing the highest level of quality and archival stability. Project portfolios are available for view on his website gallery, and commissioned project and documentation services are available by request.

PUBLICATIONS: *Beautiful Things,* 2000

GUILD SOURCEBOOKS: *Designer's 15*

Mia Tyson, Inc.   P. 254

Mia Tyson
2449 Pawpaw Drive
Rock Hill, SC 29730
TEL/FAX **803-789-3225**
E-mail: **mia@miatyson.com**
Web: **www.miatyson.com**

Mia Tyson's work aims to express a gaiety in movement as well as a fleshy tension in the surface. These elements allow the outer structure to reveal its intent of female spirituality, producing a continuity of form and outline.

After creating the form out of specially prepared porcelain slabs, Tyson applies a thin coat of black slip to the surface. She then carves her designs directly into the underlying white porcelain clay body. Once the original etched drawing is complete, the piece undergoes a carefully executed firing process that produces the distinctive black-and-white finish that has become her signature.

EXHIBITIONS & AWARDS: *NICHE* award winner, handbuilt ceramics, Philadelphia, PA, 1999; first place clay award, ACC Southeast Exhibition, Gatlinburg, TN, 1998; Spoleto Art Exhibition award, Charleston, SC, 1998; Charlotte Douglas Airport; Treegrate Design Award

PUBLICATIONS: *New Art International*

Michael Davis Stained Glass Inc.   P. 87

Michael Davis
240 West 102nd Street #61
New York, NY 10025
TEL/FAX **212-865-2403**
E-mail: **Mdstained@aol.com**

Each Michael Davis stained glass commission is a unique stew created from reaction and interaction with the client and space. A broad palate of techniques and aesthetics, including hot glass, fused glass, painted and fired vitreous paints, sandblasting, plating, and historic and contemporary design are brought to each project.

RECENT PROJECTS: Sliding doors separating living room from music room, Landau residence, Mountain Lakes, NJ, 2000

COMMISSIONS: Wilkens residence, New York, NY; Robins residence, San Francisco, CA; Albert residence, Bolton, VT; Tonic Restaurant, New York, NY; St. Mary's Church, Brooklyn, NY

PUBLICATIONS: *Stained Glass Design Sourcebook* by Lynette Wrigley, 1996; *American Craft* magazine, 1989; "Best Bets," *New York* magazine, 1987

Bj. Michaelis P. 151

Bj. Michaelis Enterprises
9616 Yorkridge Court
Miamisburg, OH 45342-5208
TEL **937-436-1688**
E-mail: **bjlm@worldnet.att.net**
Web: **www.artplaces.com**
Web: **www.geocities.com/bj_Michaelis/index.html**

Michaelis' clay and bronze sculptures reach the emotions of many. She seeks to provide fine art with a heart to private homes, public areas and business facilities. She has worked for years doing one-of-a-kind life-size child portrait busts and sculptures for proud parents and grandparents. Michaelis now happily offers limited-edition bronze sculptures.

The artist welcomes contact and discussion concerning any of her limited-edition bronze sculptures.

COMMISSIONS: City of Englewood, OH; Bethany Lutheran Village, Dayton, OH; Epiphany Lutheran Church, Dayton, OH

GUILD SOURCEBOOKS: *Architect's 15*

Peter W. Michel P. 219

Peter W. Michel, Sculptor
36 Kellogg Street
Clinton, NY 13323
TEL **315-853-8146**
FAX **315-859-1480**
E-mail: **peter@petermichel.com**
Web: **www.petermichel.com**

Peter Michel's sculptures celebrate relationships, self, community and the spirit of playfulness. The brightly colored work is scaled from intimate wall and tabletop pieces to monumental outdoor public art. His current work is created using CAD software and computer-controlled water jet or laser-cutting methods to cut wood, aluminum or steel. Pieces are then painted by hand or powder coated.

EXHIBITIONS & AWARDS: Pier Walk, Chicago, 2000; Pier Walk, Chicago, 1999; Chesterwood Museum, Stockbridge, MA, 1994

Marlene Miller P. 41

MillerClay Designs
114 Walnut
Washington, IL 61571
TEL **309-444-8608**
E-mail: **millerclay@att.net**

Marlene Miller has exhibited as a figurative ceramic sculptor nationally since 1978, and internationally since 1992. Her wall relief and freestanding sculpture — ranging in scale from monumental to intimate — evoke human presence, dignity and warmth. She achieves rich variations of texture and color in stoneware suitable for interior and outdoor installations.

Miller welcomes collaborations with architects and interior designers on residential and commercial projects.

PUBLICATIONS: *Ceramics Monthly,* April 2000; *Ceramics Monthly,* cover and feature article, November 1996

Pat Musick P. 333

CAMUS, Inc.
PO Box 919
#2 Pack McClain Road
Huntsville, AR 72740
TEL **501-559-2966**
FAX **501-559-2828**
E-mail: **camus@madisoncounty.net**
Web: **www.camusart.com**

Pat Musick uses stone, steel, wood, canvas and glass in her work. Tensions between these disparate elements produce eloquent arguments for the relationships of culture and nature, man and the earth, forever linked.

RECENT PROJECTS: Irving Arts Center, TX; Chattanooga State Community College, TN; Ozarks Woodland Sculpture Garden, AR

COMMISSIONS: Promus Hotels, Memphis, TN; Staffmark, Fayetteville, AR; Little Rock Baptist Hospital, AR

COLLECTIONS: Arkansas Arts Center, Little Rock, AR; Albrecht-Kemper Museum, St. Joseph, MO; Springfield Museum, MO; Huntsville Museum, AL; Walton Arts Center, Fayetteville, AR

James C. Myford P. 188

320 Cranberry Road
Grove City, PA 16127
TEL/FAX **724-458-9672**

James C. Myford's cast and fabricated aluminum sculptures, though often outwardly abstract, are closely linked to nature and reality. The energy and vitality expressed in his compositions reflect a subtle inner strength and spirit that expand and interact gracefully with space.

Myford's sculptures are found in corporate, museum, university, public and private collections throughout the United States. His works are also in collections in Japan, Sweden, Venezuela, Australia and Brazil.

COMMISSIONS: Tracewell Systems, Columbus, OH, 2000; Aluminum Company of America, Pittsburgh, PA, 2000; Soffer Organization, Pittsburgh, PA, 1999; Medical College of Wisconsin, Milwaukee, WI, 1999

GUILD SOURCEBOOKS: *Architect's 9, 10, 11, 12, 13, 14, 15*

Stephanie L. Nadolski P. 282

Nadolski Fine Art & Design
680 Americana Drive #12
Annapolis, MD 21403-3171
TEL **410-263-8492**
FAX **410-263-8497**
E-mail: **stephn@artlover.com**
Web: **www.sln-artworks.com**

Stephanie Nadolski's recent works integrate handmade papers and found objects with paintings and monotypes. Her facility with color, sensitivity to texture and exploitation of the unpredictable run consistently through her works in all media.

COMMISSIONS: Unique Coupon, IL; Le Club, Galveston, TX; ACA Corporation, IL; Ann Grant, IL; Michael Murray, IL

COLLECTIONS: Museum of Art of the American West, University of Mississippi, Arthur Anderson, Wausau Insurance

PUBLICATIONS: *Seafood Leader,* September 1997; *Chicago Art Review,* 1989; cover image, *Tide Teamwork,* 1989

ARTIST INFORMATION

James C. Nagle   P. 189

James C. Nagle Fine Art
1136 E. Commonwealth Place
Chandler, AZ 85225
TEL **480-963-8195**
FAX **480-857-3188 (Call first)**
E-mail: **extraice@msn.com**
Web: **www.jcnaglefineart.com**

Since the mid-1970s, James Nagle has worked as an artist, creating paintings and sculpture in a variety of mediums that are part of collections worldwide. His work brings the ideas of colloquial language into our sensory world, addressing the ironies of being human.

The demand for Nagle's work increases each year as people begin to see him as a kind of inner-terrestrial explorer.

Commissions are welcomed.

Prices are available upon request.

Marlies Merk Najaka   P. 283

241 Central Park West
New York, NY 10024
TEL **212-580-0058**
E-mail: **najaka@att.net**
Web: **www.watercolorart.com**

Marlies Merk Najaka's watercolor paintings are reproduced as giclée prints. The giclée process permits custom sizes and the ability to print on heavy watercolor paper or canvas. Each print is signed and has a certificate of authenticity.

Please visit the artist's website for more information and to view additional work.

EXHIBITIONS & AWARDS: American Watercolor Society, 2001; finalist, *American Artist* magazine competition, 2001; National Academy Museum Biennial, 2000; traveling exhibition, American Watercolor Society, 1999; signature member, National Watercolor Society, 1999

PUBLICATIONS: *Splash 6: The Magic of Texture*, 2000; *Splash 5: The Best of Watercolor*, 1998

GUILD SOURCEBOOKS: *Designer's 14, 15*

National Sculptors' Guild   PP. 154-155

2683 North Taft Avenue
Loveland, CO 80538
TEL **970-667-2015**
FAX **970-667-2068**
E-mail: **nsg@frii.com**
Web: **www.columbinensg.com**

The National Sculptors' Guild specializes in limited-edition and site-specific sculptures in bronze, stone and stainless steel. Life-size to monumental works by Guild members have been placed in private, public, corporate and museum collections throughout the world.

Sculptors: Gary Alsum, Kathleen Caricof, Tim Cherry, Dee Clements, Jane DeDecker, Carol Gold, Bruce Gueswel, Denny Haskew, Tuck Langland, Mark Leichliter, Herb Mignery, Gino Miles, Leo E. Osborne, Rosetta, Sandy Scott, Sharles, Shirley Thomson-Smith, Kent Ullberg, C.T. Whitehouse

GUILD SOURCEBOOKS: *Architect's 9, 10, 11, 12, 14, 15*

National Sculptors' Guild   PP. 154-155

2683 North Taft Avenue
Loveland, CO 80538
TEL **970-667-2015**
FAX **970-667-2068**
E-mail: **nsg@frii.com**
Web: **www.columbinensg.com**

Founded in 1992 by six sculptors and Executive Director John Kinkade, the National Sculptors' Guild is a growing organization of 19 nationally renowned artists.

The Guild works in a design-team approach with individuals, corporations, museums and public art commissions on local, regional and national monument installations. This team approach has recently earned an esteemed Orchid Award from the American Institute of Architects.

Visit the Guild's website for more details and visuals.

NeoGraphique   PP. 304-305

Roy Ritola
100 Ebbtide Avenue #520
Sausalito, CA 94965
TEL **415-332-8611**
FAX **415-332-8607**
E-mail: **info@neographique.com**
Web: **www.neographique.com**

Roy Ritola is a trained professional graphic designer. His artwork is created through the lens of a camera (both traditional and digital) and is usually quite graphic, if not abstract, in style. While often mistaken for paintings, his images are not retouched and are reproduced as limited-edition giclée prints. His most recent works are still life floral studies produced at his studio in Sausalito, CA.

Ritola's limited-edition prints have been collected by numerous corporate organizations as well as private collectors.

PUBLICATIONS: *Photo Graphis Annual*, 1991; *Leica Magazine*

New World Productions   P. 118

Skip Dyrda
1938 Adams Lane, Suite 206
Sarasota, FL 34236
TEL/FAX **941-366-5520**
E-mail: **painterskip@emurals.com**
Web: **www.emurals.com**

New World Productions is owned and operated by Skip Dyrda, whose artistic knowledge and creativity can be found on furniture, *objets d'art*, walls, ceilings and just about any surface you can imagine. His eye for detail and originality are especially evident in his area of specialty, trompe l'oeil.

Dyrda's commissions can be found around the world from St. Armand's Circle to Buenos Aires.

RECENT PROJECTS: The Crisp Building mural, Sarasota, FL, 62' x 92'

EXHIBITIONS & AWARDS: "Best mural in town," The Crisp Building, Sarasota, FL, *Weekly Planet* readers award; "Best of public art in Sarasota 2000," *Sarasota Herald Tribune*

GUILD SOURCEBOOKS: *Architect's 15*

Bruce A. Niemi   P. 220

Sculpture by Niemi
13300 116th Street
Kenosha, WI 53142
TEL   262-857-3456
FAX   262-857-4567
E-mail: sculpture@bruceniemi.com
Web: www.bruceniemi.com

From tabletop to site-specific public art, Bruce Niemi's welded stainless steel and bronze sculptures emanate aesthetics, balance, energy and a structural integrity that reflects the artist's personality.

COMMISSIONS: City Hall, Chicago Heights, IL, 2000; Cary Academy, Cary, NC, 2000

COLLECTIONS: Windway Corporation, Sheboygan, WI

EXHIBITIONS & AWARDS: Sculpture at the Airport, South Bend, IN, 2000-2002; El Paseo Sculpture Exhibition, Palm Desert, CA, 1999-2001; solo exhibition, Shidoni Gallery, Santa Fe, NM, 1999

GUILD SOURCEBOOKS: Architect's 9, 10, 11, 14, 15

Nancy Egol Nikkal   P. 284

22 Dogwood Lane
Tenafly, NJ 07670
TEL   201-568-0159
FAX   201-568-0873
E-mail: nikkal@bellatlantic.net
Web: www.nikkal.com

Nancy Egol Nikkal uses collage, digital and traditional printmaking, drawing and painting to produce imagery that is abstracted, layered and tactile. Her media include acrylic, wax, powdered pigments, inks, glazes, crayon and pencil. Her collage papers are appropriated, handmade and imported. Each piece is painted, textured and torn by hand.

Nikkal's collage paintings and prints have been commissioned as unique digital translations that incorporate painting and collage, available on paper and canvas in custom sizes. A color catalog of her work is available.

COMMISSIONS: Corporate Art West, Bellevue, WA, 2000, 1999

PUBLICATIONS: *Birds in Art*, Leigh Yawkey Woodson Art Museum, 2000, 1998; *Bridging Time & Space: Essays on Layered Art*, 1998

GUILD SOURCEBOOKS: *Designer's 13, 15*

Joel O'Dorisio   P. 191

Lost Angel Glass
79 West Market Street
Corning, NY 14830
TEL/FAX   607-937-3578
E-mail: odo@LostAngelGlass.com
Web: www.LostAngelGlass.com

Joel O'Dorisio casts glass to reflect nature's beauty by combining bark texture with intriguing three-dimensional forms. His sculptures range in size from intimate to architectural. The artist is adept at applying his design sense in realizing each client's unique vision.

COMMISSIONS: Lucent Technologies, 2001; Ohio State University, 1996 to the present; Museum of American Glass, Milville, NJ, 1996

EXHIBITIONS & AWARDS: *NICHE* Award, cast glass, *NICHE* magazine, 2000; Westmorland County Museum of Art, Greensburg, PA, 2000

Joan Osborn-Dunkle   P. 285

Gallery on Fifth Annex
950 Third Avenue North
Naples, FL 34102
TEL   941-435-7377
FAX   941-435-0164
E-mail: joan818@aol.com
Web: www.art-smart.com

Joan Osborn-Dunkle's artwork is intuitive — concerned with the magic of transformation, reflecting her curiosity of "what if," and involving a sense of freedom and unpredictability.

Along with acrylic and oil pigments, the materials she uses include paper of various thicknesses, parts of old paintings, scraps of metal, wood and powdered pigments. Her collage paintings create connections to music, numerals and the written word, with found objects unifying the material world with a very personal world — giving her work a sense of mystery.

PUBLICATIONS: *Basic Watercolor Painting* by Judith Campbell-Reed; *Painters Wild Workshop* by Lynn L. Loscutoff

GUILD SOURCEBOOKS: *Designer's 14*

Matthew O'Shea   P. 307

Matthew O'Shea Photography
4814 Washington Boulevard
St. Louis, MO 63108
TEL   314-361-8080
FAX   314-361-1245
E-mail: oshea@mail.com

Using a medium format camera that produces a 6 x 7 centimeter negative, Matthew O'Shea captures simple, evocative black-and-white images. The negatives are personally scanned using a Flextight Drum Scanner and toned in Adobe Photoshop.

Besides individual images, O'Shea combines his photographs with various scanned objects, textures and surfaces to create compelling, cubist-like collages.

Finished work is printed by the artist on archival watercolor paper using archival ink as limited-edition giclée prints.

Thomas Alex Osika   P. 193

Taosculptor, Inc.
4 Great Pond Lane
Redding, CT 06896
TEL   203-894-9791
E-mail: taosculptor@earthlink.net

Thomas Alex Osika's sculptures grace numerous collections that also include works by artists such as Picasso, Moore and Noguchi. His work is abstract, but always has strong suggestions of human or natural passages within it. Carvings in wood are used as a basis and template for enlargement into bronze. All bronze sculptures are cast in limited editions of nine or less.

GUILD SOURCEBOOKS: *Architect's 15*

Pante Studio   P. 242

Michael Demetz
Minert 7
Ortisei 39046
Italy
TEL   0039-0471-796514
FAX   0039-0471-797523
E-mail: info@pantestudio.it
Web: www.pantestudio.it

Pante Studio combines the centennial tradition of wood sculpting with the demands of contemporary design. The studio's goal is to unite the profound beliefs of the Christian faith and the creativity of architects and artists, developing statues, ornaments, altars and more starting from the sketchboard. Different woods, bronze, stone and fiberglass are used for liturgical and secular works.

RECENT PROJECTS: St. Frances Catholic Church, Wantagh, NY; Wisconsin Lutheran Seminary, Mequon, WI; St. Conrad Catholic Church, Hohenems, Austria; Plan de Corones Ski Resort, Dolomites, Italy

Rita Paul   P. 46

Art on Tiles
32 Washington Square West
New York, NY 10011
TEL   212-777-9515
FAX   212-505-2399
E-mail: d-rpaul@ix.netcom.com

Rita Paul searches to catch the excitement and beauty of her original artwork (as well as that of other artists) to use in commercial application. Ceramic tiles and glazes afford her work a jewel-like quality and add an extra dimension. She can create a new environment by marrying the perfect image with the appropriate textures and surfaces.

RECENT PROJECTS: Redoing hallways with tile insets in an ongoing job

COMMISSIONS: Cafe Lalo, Manhattan, NY; bathroom mural for private dwelling, New York, NY; nude mural for lounge and nine floral murals on every landing of Washington Square Hotel, New York, NY; murals, paintings and etched glass windows for C3 Restaurant, New York, NY

GUILD SOURCEBOOKS: *Architect's 11, 12, 13, 14; Designer's 10, 13*

Paula Slater Sculpture   P. 161

Paula B. Slater, M.A.
17415 Meadow View Drive
Middletown, CA 95461
TEL/FAX   707-987-2048
E-mail: cpslater@inreach.com
Web: www.PaulaSlater.com

Paula Slater, M.A., is a specialist in finely finished, site-specific sculptures — both life-size and monumental. She combines a masterful command of the human form and expression with an exceptional gift for bringing each exquisite detail to life. Her sculptures exude connectedness and a joy of being in the moment. As well as bronze commissions, Slater is currently sculpting two beautiful Lalique-like acrylic commissions — a nine-foot Art Deco angel and a life-size woman riding horseback. Both private and corporate clients find working with Slater a pleasurable and professional experience.

COMMISSIONS: Atlantis Resort, Bahamas; Desert Dreams, Fountain Hills, AZ; The Sands, Atlantic City, NJ

Carolyn Payne   P. 47

Payne Creations Tile
4829 North Antioch
Kansas City, MO 64119
TEL   800-880-8660
TEL   816-452-8660
FAX   816-452-0070
E-mail: golftile@swbell.net
Web: www.paynecreations.com

Since 1984, Carolyn Payne has used manufactured tile as her canvas. She has a unique style of applying layers of ceramic glaze to achieve richly textured colored art. Her expansive repertoire, designed for interior and exterior applications, includes ceramic murals, signage, fountains, historic landmarks and recognition donor walls. Payne's recent emphasis has been tile for wine cellars and golf course design.

COMMISSIONS: Community Center, North Kansas City, MO; Country Club Plaza, J.C. Nichols Co., Kansas City, MO; Harrah's Casino, East Chicago, IN; Park University, Parkville, MO; University of Kansas, Lawrence, KS; Lehigh University, Bethlehem, PA; Weslyan College, La Quinta Preservation Foundation, Bartlesville, OK

GUILD SOURCEBOOKS: *Designer's 11, 12, 14, 15*

Rob Peacock   P. 255

Rob Peacock Furniture
3 Moulton Ridge Road
Kensington, NH 03833
TEL/FAX   603-772-9523
E-mail: lahlah@mediaone.net

Rob Peacock is a New Hampshire resident. His work is a combination of plant-, fish-, insect- and bird-like forms which create whimsical yet sophisticated furniture and lighting.

Made of solid brass, each piece is formed, fabricated and patinaed with the highest standard of design and craftsmanship. His work is truly unique and punctuates residential, commercial and public spaces with extreme style and intrigue.

Pearl River Glass Studio, Inc.   P. 88

Andrew Cary Young
142 Millsaps Avenue
Jackson, MS 39202
TEL   800-771-3639
FAX   601-969-9315
E-mail: prgs@netdoor.com
Web: www.prgs.com

"To be creative means to be in that state in which truth can come into being."

J. Krishnamurti

Creativity is the most important tool at Pearl River Glass Studio. Serving liturgical, corporate and residential clients since 1975, owner and designer Andrew Young and his staff provide personal and professional service from design through installation. The studio designs original artwork in glass by skillfully incorporating traditional and unconventional techniques, such as restoration, painting, acid etching and carving.

RECENT PROJECTS: St. Francis of Assisi Catholic Church, Madison, MS; University Chapel, University of Mississippi, Oxford, MS

PUBLICATIONS: *Art in Mississippi 1720-1980*, 1998

GUILD SOURCEBOOKS: *Architect's 15*

Peter Colombo
Artistic Mosaics — P. 48

Peter Colombo
600 Huyler Street
South Hackensack, NJ 07606
TEL 201-641-7964
FAX 201-641-5884
E-mail: pcmosaic@worldnet.att.net
Web: www.petercolomboartisticmosaics.com

Peter Colombo is a graduate of the School of Visual Arts in New York City. The artist uses glass, handmade ceramic tile and natural stone to create site-specific mosaics in both public and private environments.

These media combine durability and low maintenance, while allowing full color and flexibility in design and style. The studio offers original or collaborative designs, fabrications from artwork and on-site installations.

GUILD SOURCEBOOKS: *Architect's 9, 10, 11, 12, 13, 14, 15*

Christopher Petrich — PP. 308-309

CoolPhoto.Com
3741 North 29th Street
Tacoma, WA 98407
TEL 253-752-4664
FAX 253-276-0116
E-mail: cpetrich@email.com
Web: www.CoolPhoto.com

Christopher Petrich's pictures possess a beauty, high and light, like the works in silver of the ancient Irish. Within his photographs, a simple line can swell to a great size and a looming mass can disappear in movement. Passion always informs his work, exposing darkness rimmed with humor. His art is fierce and exact and his ideas are cool.

"I force my compositions to resonate, to shudder. My pictures emerge as a moving surface to my eye, like wind on water."

Christopher Petrich

RECENT PROJECTS: *Two days in San Francisco with a No. 2 Folding Cartridge Hawk-Eye Model B; LumenAria: In the Key of Light; CoolPhoto Guide to Puget Sound Lighthouses*

Christopher Petrich — PP. 308-309

CoolPhoto.Com
3741 North 29th Street
Tacoma, WA 98407
TEL 253-752-4664
FAX 253-276-0116
E-mail: cpetrich@email.com
Web: www.CoolPhoto.com

COLLECTIONS: Gordon Bowker, Seattle, WA; Catholic Community Services, Seattle, WA; Kathleen Flynn, AIA, Southport, CT; Franciscan Sisters, Portland, OR; Rick Gottas, Tacoma, WA; James Hauer, San Francisco, CA; James McGowan, Edinborough, Scotland; Phil Raymer, Redmond, WA; Alan Ross, Santa Fe, NM; Tacoma Public Library; Kirk Weller, Portland, OR

EXHIBITIONS & AWARDS: Tahoma Center Gallery, Tacoma, WA, 2000, 1996; GUILD.com, 1999; Borders Books, 1997; American Art Company, Tacoma, WA, 1993; Handforth Gallery, Tacoma, WA, 1993; Canon USA, Los Angeles, CA, 1985; Downtown Gallery, Tacoma, WA, 1984; Sandpiper Gallery, 1984; Grand Prize, Tacoma Art Museum, 1983; Tacoma Art Museum, Annual Photography Exhibit, 1975-83; Silver Image Gallery, 1974

Delmar Pettigrew — P. 159

201 West 21st Street
Kearney, NE 68845
TEL 308-233-5504
E-mail: dpettimar@aol.com
Web: www.marthapettigrew.com

Award-winning sculptor Del Pettigrew has studied with numerous professionals via workshops and has developed a loyal following for his work. Although he is primarily known for his wildlife sculptures, he enjoys creating works based on the human figure as well. "I enjoy portraying the human figure in a somewhat less-than-representational form — the possibilities are infinite," he says. He likes to leave his surfaces "unfettered" for a rather impressionistic feeling.

COLLECTIONS: Galleries in Delray Beach, FL; Scottsdale, AZ; Aspen, CO; and Loveland, CO

EXHIBITIONS & AWARDS: The Spirit of the Great Plains Art Show and Exhibition, Museum of Nebraska Art, Kearney, NE; "The Heritage of Audubon," Museum of Nebraska Art, Kearney, NE; Mountain Oyster Club Art Show and Sale, Tucson, AZ; Scottsdale Celebration of Fine Art, Scottsdale, AZ

Martha Pettigrew — PP. 158, 160

201 West 21st Street
Kearney, NE 68845
TEL 308-233-5504
E-mail: dpettimar@aol.com
Web: www.marthapettigrew.com

Award-winning sculptor Martha Pettigrew has achieved recognition on a national and world level afforded only to the most accomplished artists. Formerly an illustrator for the Nebraska State Museum in Lincoln, NE, she began sculpting in 1990. Since that time, her work has been overwhelmingly accepted by private collectors, museums and many corporate collections.

COMMISSIONS: Life-size running horse, J.P. Morgan Company, New York, NY; one and one-quarter life-size bison, Irvine Company, Irvine, CA; portrait bust of former governor Frank B. Morrison, Museum of Nebraska Art, Kearney, NE; *The Enduring Navajo*, life-size sculpture, Loveland High Plains Art Council, Loveland, CO, for Benson Park Sculpture Garden

Robert Pfitzenmeier — P. 132

Metalmorphosis
111 First Street, Suite 1-3A
Jersey City, NJ 07302
TEL 201-659-7629
FAX 201-659-4203
Web: www.metalmorphosis.org

Pfitz designs his work with a sparseness and delicacy that transcends the limited space it occupies. These geometric abstractions enliven spaces with an elegant, upbeat spirit. Complex kinetics and a wide use of polychromed or anodized color support this atmosphere. Anodized zirconium responds to light, yielding a full spectrum of colors that vary with changing light conditions.

For 25 years, Pfitz has been constructing sculpture and suspended installations for public, private and corporate clients.

David L. Phelps — P. 162

Phelps Sculpture Studio
11621 North Santa Fe Avenue B-12
Oklahoma City, OK 73114
TEL/FAX 405-752-9512
E-mail: davidlphelps@excite.com

David L. Phelps creates monumental commissioned works across the United States. His bronze sculptures are in notable international public and private collections.

Phelps' figurative bronzes, ranging up to three times life-size, appear to emerge from the ground. They are serenely contemplative, and each piece is imbued with a dry, subtle humor.

COMMISSIONS: Bricktown, Oklahoma City, OK, 2000; Rancho Santa Fe, CA, 2000; Aspen, CO, 2000; McCarren International Airport, Las Vegas, NV, 1999

GUILD SOURCEBOOKS: *Architect's 12, 15*

Binh Pho — PP. 256, 262

Wonders of Wood
48W175 Pine Tree Drive
Maple Park, IL 60151
TEL 630-365-5462
FAX 630-365-5837
E-mail: toriale@msn.com
Web: www.wondersofwood.net

Binh Pho is a Chicago-based artist who works primarily with wood. He combines lathe work, sculpting and piercing techniques to create commanding primitive art forms.

COMMISSIONS: Honeywell Corporation, Cupertino, CA; Olympia Network, St. Louis, MO; Frontier Development, Denver, CO; Judy Brook Collection I.F.D.A., San Francisco, CA

COLLECTIONS: The White House, Washington, DC; Honeywell, Cupertino, CA; Union Planters Bank, St. Louis, MO; Hillary R. Clinton, Chappaqua, NY

EXHIBITIONS & AWARDS: Challenge VI 2001, Phillip and Muriel Berman Museum of Art, Collegeville, PA; SOFA 2000, Chicago, IL; Collector of Wood Art 2000 Forum, Charlotte, NC; Best in Wood, Midwest Salutes the Master Art Festival, 1999; Best in Wood, Midwest Salutes the Master Art Festival, 1998

Michael F. Pilla — P. 89

Monarch Studios, Inc.
2242 University Avenue #316
St. Paul, MN 55114
TEL 651-644-7927
FAX 651-649-0456
E-mail: monart7@mr.net
Web: www.mfpilla.com

Michael F. Pilla shares and enlightens the visions his clients feel. As the commission of Saint Ambrose Catholic Church of Woodbury, MN, shows, Michael Pilla's use of symbolic form brings to life a timeless design of spiritual power. The whole of Saint Ambrose is bathed in colored light and connects the ancient and contemporary stained glass traditions, thereby enhancing the worship place. This work was made with blown glass and lead.

Pilla has received recognition as a contemporary stained glass master by HGTV in their "Modern Masters" series currently being shown on cable television.

GUILD SOURCEBOOKS: *THE GUILD 4; Architect's 6, 7, 8, 9, 10, 12, 13, 15*

William Poulson — P. 257

W. Poulson Glass Studio
PO Box 705
Arnold, CA 95223
TEL/FAX 209-795-5365
Web: www.guild.com

William Poulson's unique folding screens and lamps are inspired by the Asian masters of *ukiyo-e* (wood block prints) and *sumie* brush painting. As a third-generation woodworker, Poulson's remarkable craftsmanship is expressed in unsparing attention to detail.

More than 20 years ago, Poulson joined his skills in cabinetry and furniture making with his new-found love for art glass to create stunning functional art that combines the beauty and softness of wood and the brilliance of glass. His numerous public and private art glass commissions incorporate his original designs based on nature themes.

Please call or write for prices.

COMMISSIONS: Calaveras County Library, San Andreas, CA, 1995

EXHIBITIONS & AWARDS: *Tissiack* solo exhibition, Yosemite National Park Visitor Center, 1990

Angelica Pozo — P. 49

Earthen Angel Ceramics
1193 Holmden Avenue
Cleveland, OH 44109-1837
TEL 216-241-6936
FAX 216-861-6566
E-mail: angelicapozo@earthlink.net
Web: www.angelicapozo.com

Angelica Pozo's public art pieces utilize a variety of techniques, an openness for site-related thematic references and an intuitive sense for creating engaging experiences in public spaces. These characteristics vitalize Pozo's work with a signature energy as opposed to a signature look.

COMMISSIONS: Greater Cleveland Regional Transit Authority; University Hospitals of Cleveland, OH; Cleveland State University, OH; Ohio State University, Columbus; Waxner Center for Senior Citizens, Baltimore, MD

COLLECTIONS: American Craft Museum, New York, NY; Progressive Corporation, Cleveland, OH; Advanced Elastomer Systems, Akron, OH

EXHIBITIONS & AWARDS: Individual Artist Fellowship Award, Ohio Arts Council; NEA Regional Visual Arts Fellowship Award, Arts Midwest

Pozycinski Studios — P. 194

Joseph and Georgia Pozycinski
1044 Andrews Road
Sparta, MO 65753
TEL 417-634-3976
FAX 417-634-4111
E-mail: jpgp@pozycinskibronze.com
Web: www.artbronzesculpture.com

Pozycinski Studios has complete capabilities in sand casting, lost-wax casting and fabrication in bronze. Joseph and Georgia Pozycinski's work ranges in size from small collectible bronzes to large-scale sculpture, all done in limited editions. Many corporate, commercial and residential settings are enhanced by their bronze fountains and sculptures.

The Pozycinskis' work has been described as a union of aesthetic sensibilities responsive to a demanding yet elegant, rich and powerful medium.

Pozycinski Studios has a large body of marketing materials including postcards, brochures, slides and an extensive website.

PUBLICATIONS: *Beautiful Things*, 2000

GUILD SOURCEBOOKS: *Architect's 15*

Frances G. Pratt   P. 332

Frances G. Pratt, Sculptor
1010 Memorial Drive #9-A
Cambridge, MA 02138-4855
TEL   617-491-0132
FAX   617-491-6473
E-mail: fgpsculpt@aol.com

Frances G. Pratt's wall sculptures for the private residence or the office, small or large, bring energy and humanity to their environment. Sculptured works can be single pieces, or a group of related pieces, for the interior or exterior. The wall sculptures naturally complement Pratt's garden and public sculptures, featured in earlier GUILD sourcebooks. Prices range between $2000 and $10000.

COMMISSIONS: Neiman Marcus, Northbrook, IL; Verizon Corporation, Framingham, MA; Forest City Management, Cambridge, MA; Connecticut College, New London, CT; Babson College, Wellesley, MA

GUILD SOURCEBOOKS: *Architect's 14, 15*

Presentations Gallery   P. 243
Synagogue Arts & Furnishings

Michael Berkowicz
Bonnie Srolovitz
200 Lexington Avenue #423
New York, NY 10016
TEL   212-481-8181
FAX   212-779-9015
E-mail: SynagFurn@aol.com
Web: www.SynagogueFurnishings.com

Design with respect for tradition — these designers and fabricators offer liturgical furnishings, congregational seating and space planning with specialization in synagogues and Holocaust memorials. Presentations also creates meaningful donor recognition works to enhance fund-raising.

COMMISSIONS: Woodbury Jewish Center, Long Island, NY; Sutton Place Synagogue/ Synagogue to the United Nations, New York, NY; Congregation Micah, Brentwood, TN; Variety Preschoolers Workshop

EXHIBITIONS & AWARDS: Award for Religious Art, IFRAA, 1999, 1995; finalist, Spertus Museum Judaica Prize; permanent collection, Jewish Museum, New York, NY

PUBLICATIONS: *Faith & Form Magazine, The Art of Hanukkah*

John Pugh   P. 119

PO Box 1332
Los Gatos, CA 95031
TEL   408-353-3370
FAX   408-353-1223
Web: www.artofjohnpugh.com

John Pugh's painted images transform flat walls into other "spaces." He has been awarded an array of national public art projects as well as receiving international attention for his trompe l'oeil work. For all murals, indoor or outdoor, large or small, projects may be painted in Pugh's studio on canvas or non-woven media (an outdoor material) and then site-specifically integrated.

For more information, visit his website or ask for a brochure.

GUILD SOURCEBOOKS: *Architect's 7, 8, 9, 11, 12, 13, 14, 15; Designer's 9, 11, 12, 13*

Maya Radoczy   P. 90

Contemporary Art Glass
PO Box 31422
Seattle, WA 98103
TEL   206-527-5022
FAX   206-524-9266
E-mail: Maya@serv.net
Web: www.mayaglass.com

Maya Radoczy is known for creating cast glass collages and bas-relief images for corporate, public and residential projects. She exhibits internationally and is included in numerous collections.

RECENT PROJECTS: "Modern Masters," Home and Garden Television, 1999

COMMISSIONS: REI Flagship Stores, Tokyo, Japan and Denver, CO, 2000; City of Seattle, WA, 1999; Public Library, Bend, OR, 1999; REI-Landmark Building, Seattle, WA, 1996; Washington State Arts Commission, Enterprise School, Federal Way, WA, 1996

EXHIBITIONS & AWARDS: Northwest Women in Glass, Tacoma, WA, 1999; Lois Nieter Gallery, Los Angeles, CA, 1996; Glas Galarie, Frauenau, Germany, 1995

PUBLICATIONS: *American Craft*, April/May 2000; *Art Business News*, 1999

Jane Rankin   P. 163

Jane Rankin Sculpture Studio
PO Box 1297
19335 Greenwood Drive
Monument, CO 80132
TEL   719-488-9223
FAX   719-488-1650 (Call first)
E-mail: jrankin@magpiehill.com

Jane Rankin creates limited-edition figurative sculpture with an emphasis on children and child-related things.

COMMISSIONS: Town Hall, Cary, NC, 1999; Morse Park, Lakewood, CO, 1998

COLLECTIONS: Colorado Springs Fine Art Center, Colorado Springs, CO; Buell Children's Museum, Pueblo, CO; Association of Christian Schools International, Colorado Springs, CO; Lincoln Children's Museum, Lincoln, NE; Creative Artist Agency, Beverly Hills, CA

EXHIBITIONS & AWARDS: American Numismatic Association, Colorado Springs, CO, 1999-2000; Colorado Springs Airport, 1999

GUILD SOURCEBOOKS: *Architect's 14, 15*

Blair Reed   P. 91

Blair Reed Art Glass
4885 Franklin Road
Bloomfield, MI 48302
TEL   248-855-3757
FAX   248-353-0678

For the past 20 years, Blair Reed has made an impressive impact in the design world with his ability to create meaningful and enduring works of art in carved architectural glass. They are full of energy, versatile and blend well in a variety of environments.

Reed has the imagination and skill to respond to your vision or to provide his own vision to fit your needs.

COMMISSIONS: Ford Motors Worldwide Headquarters; 68-foot mural, Henry Ford Hospital; Guardian Industries; SAS Institute

Kia Ricchi · P. 221

Centerline Production, Inc.
4516 Pine Lake Drive
St. Cloud, FL 34769
TEL/FAX 407-891-1422
E-mail: Kia@gdi.net
Web: www.centerlineart.com

Kia Ricchi creates sculpture that is functional and aesthetic. Made from cement and steel, her sculptures enhance pool and garden settings. Her work can also be placed in high-traffic areas such as airports and malls, where it provides public seating.

COMMISSIONS: Hardin Holding, Ft. Lauderdale, FL, 2001; Stainsafe Corporation, Palm Beach, FL, 2000

EXHIBITIONS & AWARDS: Second place, Ann Norton Sculpture Garden, Palm Beach, FL, 2000; Orlando Museum of Art, Orlando, FL, 1999

PUBLICATIONS: *Florida Design*, Winter 2000; *Landscape Architect*, 1999; *Landscape Architecture*, 1999

Henry B. Richardson · P. 190

One Cottage Street
Easthampton, MA 01027
TEL 413-527-1444
E-mail: Henry@henryrichardson.com
Web: www.henryrichardson.com

The sound of breaking glass calls to mind images of destruction. In Henry Richardson's studio, however, broken glass is the element of creation. Richardson uses fractured glass to create sculptures and furniture that are prized for their originality and craftsmanship.

Richardson has worked successfully with architects and designers, and his work can be found in numerous corporate and private settings.

EXHIBITIONS & AWARDS: Holsten Gallery, MA; Wit Gallery, Lenox, MA; Heller Gallery, NY; Longstreth Goldberg Gallery, FL

GUILD SOURCEBOOKS: *Designer's 15*

Kim H. Ritter · P. 367

Gallery Quilts
18727 Point Lookout
Houston, TX 77058
TEL 281-333-3224
FAX 281-333-8581
E-mail: kim@galleryquilts.com
Web: www.galleryquilts.com

Kim H. Ritter creates layered quilted constructions in silk and cotton, incorporating surface treatments such as dyeing, painting and digital and hand-printing processes. Her art quilts and mixed-media installations for unique spaces explore the tension between surface and layer, hidden and revealed.

COLLECTIONS: TAACL, Houston, TX; other museum, private and corporate collections

EXHIBITIONS & AWARDS: "Face Value: Quilts by Kim H. Ritter," Wheelwright Museum of the American Indian, Santa Fe, NM

PUBLICATIONS: *Fiberarts Design Book Six*, 1999; *Quick Quilting* by Kim H. Ritter, 1994

Kevin B. Robb · P. 195

Kevin Robb Studios, LLC
7001 West 35th Avenue
Wheat Ridge, CO 80033
TEL 303-431-4758
FAX 303-425-8802
E-mail: 3d@kevinrobb.com
Web: www.kevinrobb.com

Kevin Robb creates individual contemporary sculptures in stainless steel or bronze as well as limited-edition cast bronze for intimate environments or large-scale public areas. Robb brings a natural curiosity to his work combined with the knowledge gained from an understanding of how positive and negative spaces, shadow and light work together.

RECENT PROJECTS: Pueblo Community College, CO; Frederik Meijer Gardens, Grand Rapids, MI; Marchon Corporate Headquarters, Melville, NY

COMMISSIONS: Premier, Inc., Charlotte, NC; Lake Isle Townhome, East Chester, NY

GUILD SOURCEBOOKS: *Architect's 12, 13, 15*

Priscilla Robinson · P. 346

2811 Hancock Drive
Austin, TX 78731
TEL 512-452-3516
TEL 505-758-2608
FAX 512-452-3516
E-mail: pjr@priscillarobinson.com
Web: www.priscillarobinson.com

Priscilla Robinson creates three-dimensional wall sculptures and heavily textured paintings using organic plant cellulose and space-age synthetics. These unique pieces are designed for specific locations in large corporate lobbies and intimate private residences.

COMMISSIONS: Blue Cross Blue Shield, Shell Oil, Tokyo Electron American Headquarters

COLLECTIONS: American Airlines, Chevron Pipeline

EXHIBITIONS: Holland Paper Biennale; Museum de Corso, Rome

GUILD SOURCEBOOKS: *Designer's 14*

Christina Roe · P. 345

Fantan Studio
1010 Deveggio Lane
Angels Camp, CA 95222
TEL 209-736-1810
FAX 209-736-1811
E-mail: christinaroe@hotmail.com

Having lived in Asia for 27 years, Christina Roe infuses her dimensional wall sculptures with cross-cultural eclecticism. Trained as a fine artist with a background in papier mâché, she now combines that technique with hand-cast recycled paper. She has exhibited and sold her work in the U.S. and internationally.

Her new works include abstract and pictorial imagery as well as compositions that incorporate architectural details and bas-relief ornamentation. Richly colored and textured, her multi-layered relief surfaces are both durable and lightweight. Wires attached to the back enable them to be hung unframed.

Limited-edition multiples of some images are available. Modular units can be combined to create large installations.

Completed work is available and commissions are welcomed. Prices range from $100 to $5000.

Timothy Rose — P. 133

Timothy Rose Mobiles
Building 153, 4th & Waterfront
Mare Island, CA 94592
TEL 707-562-3158
FAX 415-331-5041
E-mail: **troseart@aol.com**
Web: **www.mobilesculpture.com**

California artist Timothy Rose creates articulated mobile sculptures that animate large and small spaces. Custom-made for each site, his mobiles reflect the client's vision coupled with his own joyful aesthetic.

COMMISSIONS: South Carolina Aquarium, Charleston, SC; Children's Ward, Silver Springs, MD; Chula Vista Nature Center, Chula Vista, CA

PUBLICATIONS: *InterActivity: the Fine Art of Making Mobiles*, 2000

Talli Rosner-Kozuch — PP. 310-311

Pho Tal, Inc.
15 North Summit Street
Tenafly, NJ 07670
TEL 201-569-3199
FAX 201-569-3392
E-mail: **tal@photal.com**
Web: **www.photal.com**

Talli Rosner-Kozuch works in black and white, sepia tones, color, platinum prints, lithographs and etchings. Her areas of expertise include large-format photography. The images range in size and vary in style from architectural portraiture and documentary to landscape and still life. Using signature techniques, she achieves a unique blend of minimalism and sensuality in her work.

RECENT PROJECTS: Series from flowers shot with candlelight at night; *Days of the Dead*, documentary from two visits to Mexico; documentary shows from two visits to Morocco

COMMISSIONS: Restaurants, hotels, banks, corporations, building entrances, stores, Ethan Allen catalog

GUILD SOURCEBOOKS: *Designer's 14, 15*

Talli Rosner-Kozuch — PP. 310-311

Pho Tal, Inc.
15 North Summit Street
Tenafly, NJ 07670
TEL 201-569-3199
FAX 201-569-3392
E-mail: **tal@photal.com**
Web: **www.photal.com**

Talli Rosner-Kozuch uses light to sculpt portraits and still lifes of flowers, fruits and other natural elements. She uses her images as symbols for themes such as individuals versus a group, life and death, and femininity versus masculinity. Her minimalistic images include subtle hints to the story behind the picture.

COLLECTIONS: The Polaroid Collection, Boston, MA; Twin Lab, Long Island, NY; private collectors in New York, Connecticut, New Jersey, Washington, California, Europe and Israel

PUBLICATIONS: *Photography in New York*, 1998-2001; *Yediot-Achronot* newspaper, 2000; *Focus*, 2000, 1999; *New York Art Magazine*, 2000, 1999; "South Coast Style," *Art on Paper*, 1999; *Elle*, December 1998; six posters, New York Graphic Society; one poster, Scandecor

Daryl Rush — P. 28

Architectural Details by Daryl Rush
PO Box 11640
Piedmont, CA 94611
TEL 510-654-1050
FAX 510-654-1099
E-mail: **therush@pacbell.net**

Daryl Rush comes from a tradition of artist craftsmen. He collaborates with clients, creating sculptural and structural site-specific works. Objects are crafted to provide visual as well as tactile satisfaction, and are said to have "the feel of jewelry." They are embedded in the architecture of a building as a handcrafted connection or highlight. His works are hot forged in bronze, monel or steel and are robust and durable, requiring little or no upkeep. Their beauty is assured for time to come.

Brian F. Russell — P. 196

Brian Russell Designs/Ironwood, LLC
10385 Long Road
Arlington, TN 38002
TEL 901-867-7300
FAX 901-867-7843
E-mail: **anvil@concentric.net**
Web: **www.brianrusselldesigns.com**

Combining cast glass and hot-forged metals gives Brian Russell the ability to create unique statements that convey a sense of the timeless with a strong sculptural aesthetic. Founded in the crafts, Russell's art explores the materials' intrinsic qualities as they relate to emotional responses.

Since 1984, he has collaborated with design professionals on numerous public, private and corporate sculpture projects.

COMMISSIONS: Rhodes College, Memphis, TN, 2000; Ballet Memphis building, Cordova, TN, 1998; Al Pacino, New York, NY, 1995; Limn Company, San Francisco, CA, 1994

PUBLICATIONS: *Contemporary Blacksmithing* by Dona Meilach, 2000

GUILD SOURCEBOOKS: *Architect's 6, 7, 14, 15; Designer's 6, 7*

James Thomas Russell — PP. 198-199

James Russell Sculpture
1930 Lomita Boulevard
Lomita, CA 90717
TEL 310-326-0785
FAX 310-326-1470
E-mail: **james@russellsculpture.com**
Web: **www.russellsculpture.com**

Elegantly crafted and fastidiously polished, James T. Russell's sculptures are ribbons of stainless steel gracefully arching and twirling in space. His professional career is in its fourth decade, including worldwide commissions of innovative and durable sculptures ranging from wall reliefs to gallery editions to fountain settings and monumental towers of gleaming inspiration.

COMMISSIONS: Princess Cruises, Monfalcone, Italy, 2000; City of South San Francisco, CA, 1999; AT Kearney Inc., Chicago, IL, 1999; Motorola Corporation, Beijing, China, 1998

COLLECTIONS: *Architectural Digest*, CA; Riverside Art Museum, Riverside, CA; Caesar's World, Century City, CA

PUBLICATIONS: *Landscape Architect*, 2000; *Focus Santa Fe*, 2000; *Art Calendar*, 1999

GUILD SOURCEBOOKS: *Architect's 7, 8, 12, 13, 14, 15*

ARTIST INFORMATION

James Thomas Russell PP. 198-199

James Russell Sculpture
1930 Lomita Boulevard
Lomita, CA 90717
TEL   310-326-0785
FAX   310-326-1470
E-mail: **james@russellsculpture.com**
Web: **www.russellsculpture.com**

Elegantly crafted and fastidiously polished, James T. Russell's sculptures are ribbons of stainless steel gracefully arching and twirling in space. His professional career is in its fourth decade, including worldwide commissions of innovative and durable sculptures ranging from wall reliefs to gallery editions to fountain settings and monumental towers of gleaming inspiration.

COMMISSIONS: Princess Cruises, Monfalcone, Italy, 2000; City of South San Francisco, CA, 1999; AT Kearney Inc., Chicago, IL, 1999; Motorola Corporation, Beijing, China, 1998

COLLECTIONS: *Architectural Digest,* CA; Riverside Art Museum, Riverside, CA; Caesar's World, Century City, CA

PUBLICATIONS: *Landscape Architect,* 2000; *Focus Santa Fe,* 2000; *Art Calendar,* 1999

GUILD SOURCEBOOKS: *Architect's 7, 8, 12, 13, 14, 15*

Bob Russo P. 287

The Art Commission
6332 North Hampton Drive NE
Atlanta, GA 30328
TEL/FAX   404-252-6394

Bob Russo is a painter of the special places, people and events pertinent to each client and site. His work connects us to each other and to our environment, bringing smiles of recognition and pride.

For more than 30 years, Russo has been creating commissioned paintings and drawings for commercial, government, public and private clients. By combining research and excellent design, workmanship and detail with a touch of storytelling and mystery, his subjects blossom into paintings that are more than background decoration. His is the rare ability to enrich seemingly "common" material with layers of fascination.

GUILD SOURCEBOOKS: *Designer's 15*

Sable Studios P. 134

Paul Sable
2737 Rosedale Avenue
Soquel, CA 95073
TEL   800-233-7309
TEL   831-475-1220 (Studio)
E-mail: **paul@sablestudios.com**
Web: **www.sablestudios.com**

Paul Sable has collaborated successfully with art consultants, architects and designers for over 35 years. His kinetic acrylic mobiles integrate color, light and movement to create a multi-dimensional experience. His custom-designed sculptures harmonize into private, corporate and public spaces.

RECENT PROJECTS: 15' x 15' x 18' mobile for Union City Senior Center, CA; Lucent Technologies, CO

COMMISSIONS: Lucent Technologies, FL and CO; Metro Plaza building, San Jose, CA; Syntex Corporation, Hayward, CA; City Hall, Union City, CA; Metro Life, San Jose, CA; Berklee Performance Center, Boston, MA

COLLECTIONS: Syntex, Quantum, 3 Comm, Loral and Cadence corporations; Lucent Technologies; Avaya Communications

Gary San Pietro P. 312

Gary San Pietro Fine Photography
204 Tookany Creek Parkway
Elkins Park, PA 19027
TEL   215-782-8242
E-mail: **gary@garysanpietro.com**
Web: **www.garysanpietro.com**

For over 20 years, Gary San Pietro's unique sense of abstraction, color and design has produced a wide range of powerful and hypnotic images that communicate the essence of his subject, be it architectural, industrial or natural.

His images enhance the interiors of countless residential and over 100 corporate and institutional spaces, including those of American Express, GE, IBM, Vanguard and the Portuguese Embassy.

A wide range of images and all other associated information is available on the website.

Commissions are welcomed.

RECENT PROJECTS: Dutch tulips; Portuguese, Italian and Mexican landscapes and colored walls

Heath Satow P. 223

Heath Satow Sculpture
TEL   866-432-8411 (Toll free)
E-mail: **heath@publicsculpture.com**
Web: **www.publicsculpture.com**

Designing site-specific sculpture and architectural elements has been Los Angeles artist Heath Satow's focus for over a decade. Using metals in combination with other materials, Satow has created interior and exterior sculptures, mobiles and water features. His unparalleled craftsmanship, reliability and attention to detail make him a favorite among designers and architects.

COMMISSIONS: Raleigh-Durham International Airport, WakeMed Hospital, Whole Foods Inc., ASC Industries, Alien Skin Software, Exploris Museum, First Night International

Helle Scharling-Todd P. 92

Contemporary Glass & Mosaics
3219 Preble Avenue
Ventura, CA 93003
TEL/FAX   805-644-6884
E-mail: **art-glass@dock.net**
Web: **www.glass-mosaics-tiles.com**

Helle Scharling-Todd creates murals, floors, windows and sculptures using leaded glass, sandblasted glass, cast glass, painted glass, mosaics and tiles. Her works use color, forms and lines combined with references to nature, myths and symbols to add a spiritual dimension to functional spaces.

Scharling-Todd's work is found in schools, banks, libraries, malls, churches, public pools and universities worldwide.

COMMISSIONS: Tile mural, Los Angeles Public Works Building; mosaics, Port Hueneme Prueter Library; Chumash Indian Center

EXHIBITIONS & AWARDS: Lead artist, West Side Community Enhancement, Ventura, CA, 2001; Glas Plastiken, Munster, Germany, 1998; Women's Museum, Aarhus, Denmark, 1995

GUILD SOURCEBOOKS: *Architect's 13, 14*

Stephanie Schirm — P. 335

rituals inc.
78 Huron Street
Guelph, ON N1E 5L6
Canada
TEL 519-836-9906
FAX 519-836-5426
E-mail: **sschirm@hotmail.com**

Combining the fundamentals of tapestry, collage and acrylic painting techniques, Stephanie Schirm's fabric creations capture the complexities of spiritual wholeness and enlightenment. Balancing the shock of color with the flow of line and texture, her work is pleasing to the eye and a balm for the soul. Her diverse collection includes pieces commissioned specifically for liturgical use.

Vestment design, tapestries and sanctuary decorations are all available from Schirm's Canadian studio, rituals inc.

COMMISSIONS: Lakeridge Health Chaplaincy, Oshawa, ON, 2000; Our Lady of the Snows, Belleville, IL, 2000; Holy Family Catholic High School, Victoria, MN, 2000; Nell Ramaker, Georgetown, ON, 1998

Susan Sculley — PP. 288-289

4546 North Hermitage #2
Chicago, IL 60640
TEL 773-728-6109
FAX 773-728-9305
E-mail: **sculley@ix.netcom.com**

Susan Sculley works in both oil sticks and pastels to create compositions of color and form that capture the essence of peace and beauty found in the landscape. Working with interior designers, art consultants and galleries, her work is found in both corporate and private settings, whether contemporary or traditional in style.

Commissions are welcome. Pricing, as well as slides and additional visuals, are available upon request.

RECENT PROJECTS: Posters published by Posters International, Toronto, Ontario, Canada

COLLECTIONS: Amoco Corporation, Chicago, IL; Dean Witter, Rockford, IL; Apostolic Church, Chicago, IL; William M. Mercer, Inc., Chicago, IL

PUBLICATIONS: *Beautiful Things,* 2000; *Metropolitan Home,* November/December, 2000; *Where Chicago,* January 1998

GUILD SOURCEBOOKS: *Designer's 15*

John C. Sewell — PP. 224

Vessel Variations
PO Box 820
West Fork, AR 72774
TEL 501-761-3362
FAX 501-761-3275
E-mail: **johncsewell@aol.com**
Web: **www.johnsewell.tripod.com**

John Sewell employs the media of bronze, wood and stone to produce sculpture in graceful and expressive feminine forms. For his bronze sculptures, the original is sculpted from clay, wood or stone and then cast using the lost-wax process. A number are produced as freestanding sculpture, while others are designed for fountain installation. His wood sculptures are carved into unique vessel forms from large solid work pieces, then highly finished and a clear or translucent lacquer applied. Sewell's stone sculptures are produced in much the same way as his work in wood, except that they are solid forms rather than vessels.

RECENT PROJECTS: Benson Park Sculpture Garden, Loveland, CO; Tourist Information Center sculpture garden, Loveland, CO

COLLECTIONS: St. Louis University, St. Louis, MO; Loveland Public Sculpture Collection, Loveland, CO; private collections

Alvin Sher — P. 225

4 North Pine Street
Niantic, CT 06357
TEL/FAX 860-739-7288
E-mail: **alvinisher@netscape.net**
Web: **www.alvinsher.net**

Alvin Sher's sculptures investigate symbolic and environmental issues, utilizing an array of architectural forms such as temples, labyrinths, observatories and solar clocks.

Sher uses techniques such as bronze and iron casting as well as inert gas welding and plasma cutting for stainless steel and aluminum. Computer imaging is used for design and presentation.

The image of the hand is both Sher's signature and a universal symbol with meanings through time ranging from a greeting to our personal extension in space.

His work has been in more than 200 exhibitions, and he has completed commissions and installations in the U.S., Europe and Japan over the past 25 years.

GUILD SOURCEBOOKS: *Architect's 10, 11, 12, 13, 14; Designer's 14*

Michael Shields / Matthew Durbin — P. 93

Creative Stained Glass Studio, Ltd.
221 Corporate Circle, Suite F
Golden, CO 80401
TEL 303-988-0444
FAX 303-988-0213
E-mail: **myksds@aol.com**

Shields, Durbin and their associates create architecturally relevant installations sensitive to diverse environments. Their understanding of glass as an emotionally powerful medium combined with their experience collaborating with architects and design teams results in unique and meaningful community artwork.

RECENT PROJECTS: Sculpture, Children's Hospital, Denver, CO; Grace Lutheran Church, Sandy, UT

COMMISSIONS: Colorado Supreme Court, Denver, CO; Immanuel's Church, Silver Spring, MD; National Mining Hall of Fame Museum, Leadville, CO; Colorado School of Mines, Golden, CO

GUILD SOURCEBOOKS: *Architect's 14*

Gerald Siciliano — P. 165

Studio Design Associates
9 Garfield Place
Brooklyn, NY 11215
TEL/FAX 718-636-4561
E-mail: **gsstudio@concentric.net**
Web: **www.concentric.net/~gsstudio**

Classical figurative and non-representational sculptures, meticulously crafted in elegant and durable materials, are the hallmark of Gerald Siciliano. From the intimate to the monumental, studio and commission-based sculptures are created for discerning collectors, architects, designers and corporations worldwide.

Inquiries via telephone, e-mail or the Internet are welcomed.

COMMISSIONS: American Airlines; American Axle & Manufacturing Company; Bristol-Myers Squibb Co.; The Brooklyn Museum; Canon U.S.A.; Dong Baek Art Center, Pusan, Korea; Generation II USA; The John Templeton Foundation; Kyongnam International Sculpture Symposium; The Mozart Companies; Olympic Park, Pusan, Korea; Sparks Exhibits & Environments Co.; Pusan International Sculpture Symposium

GUILD SOURCEBOOKS: *Architect's 12, 13, 14, 15; Designer's 14, 15*

Susan Singleton   P. 347

AZO Inc.
1101 E. Pike Street
Seattle, WA 98280
TEL 800-344-0390
FAX 360-376-5519
E-mail: **azo@fidalgo.net**
Web: **www.azo.com**

Susan Singleton's work is made from Japanese washi paper that she stitches together, dyes and stencils with metallic, iridescent and subtle colors. Each piece is finished with gold, copper or silver leaf.

Singleton's *Ziggurats* are reflections of a search for order, simplicity, clarity and balance. They are minimal and primitive, yet formal in voice and definitely handmade, with irregular edges, hand-stitching and textural surfaces.

RECENT PROJECTS: Sailfish Point Club, Hutchinson Island, FL, consultant: Dana Bailey; Sprint Federal Headquarters, Washington, DC, Art Resources Inc., MD, consultant: Stacy Sklaver; Nokia, Boston, MA, Art Advisory Boston; Lucent Technology, Morris Plains, NJ, consultant: Susan Cloninger; Chase Manhattan Bank, Houston, TX, consultant: Patty Cwalinski; Hotel Parisi, La Jolla, CA, consultant: Betsy Lane

Jeff G. Smith   PP. 94-95

Architectural Stained Glass, Inc.
PO Box 1126
Fort Davis, TX 79734-1126
TEL 915-426-3311
FAX 915-426-3366
E-mail: **asg@overland.net**
Web: **www.overland.net/~asg**

Jeff Smith has been revitalizing traditional stained glass in refreshing new ways for over 24 years (see *THE GUILD 4* and *The Architect's Sourcebook 6-15*). Architectural Stained Glass, Inc., imbues all of its commissions with a recognizable and unsurpassed level of technical virtuosity and craftsmanship using a palette of the finest materials available.

As elegant and appropriate as Smith's stained glass appears on the surface, it also is always carefully designed to address less apparent needs, including the enhancement or screening of views, solar angle analysis, glare elimination, a dynamic presence in all lighting conditions, spatial separation, circulation definition and creation of privacy.

Jeff G. Smith   PP. 94-95

Architectural Stained Glass, Inc.
PO Box 1126
Fort Davis, TX 79734-1126
TEL 915-426-3311
FAX 915-426-3366
E-mail: **asg@overland.net**
Web: **www.overland.net/~asg**

After 22 great years in Dallas, TX, Architectural Stained Glass, Inc., has relocated to its new facility in the Davis Mountains of west Texas. While still conveniently and centrally located within the continental U.S., Jeff Smith and his studio now work in the scenic tranquility of the Trans-Pecos. Please note the updated contact information listed above.

Questions are welcome. Additional information and pricing are available on request.

COMMISSIONS: Hawthorne Lane Restaurant, San Francisco, CA; St. Matthew Catholic Church, Windham, NH; Quentin N. Burdick Federal Courthouse, Fargo, ND; Washington Hebrew Congregation, Washington, DC; American Airlines Admirals Club, Dallas-Forth Worth, TX; University of Alaska, Fairbanks, AK; Salt Lake (City) Community College Library, Salt Lake City, UT; Wilcox Memorial Hospital Chapel, Lihue, HI

Judy Speezak   P. 368

Speezak Quilt Studio
425 Fifth Avenue
Brooklyn, NY 11215
TEL 718-369-3513
FAX 718-369-7319
E-mail: **speezakquilt@earthlink.net**
Web: **www.speezakquiltstudio.com**

In her latest series, Speezak applies traditional patchwork techniques in a more fluid, informal approach to the creative process. She challenges the conformity of a squared format with an intentional disregard for straight edges and right angles, while remaining true to her meticulous piecing skills. The interplay of colors and shapes reflects her reverence for 20th-century paintings and 19th-century quilts. Private and corporate commissions include wall quilts, bed quilts, throw pillows and *chuppahs* (Jewish wedding canopies). Slides and prices available upon request.

PUBLICATIONS: *Discrete Mathematics,* cover image, 1999; *Quilts: A Living Tradition* by Robert Shaw, 1995

GUILD SOURCEBOOKS: *Designer's 15*

Jacqueline L. Spellens   P. 164

Spellens Sculpture
8939 Wren Circle
Fountain Valley, CA 92708
TEL 714-968-8414
FAX 714-968-4314
E-mail: **jspellart@aol.com**

Jacqueline Spellens' inspiration comes from a global view of the human experience as well as a love of the animals with which we share the planet. Her works exhibit vigor and sensitivity in a variety of media, including terra cotta, marble, alabaster and bronze.

COMMISSIONS: Richardson Leprosarium, Miraj, India, 2000; St. Joseph Hospital, Orange, CA, 1994-2000; Discovery House Founders' Plaque, Junior League of Orange County, Costa Mesa, CA, 1997; Church of St. Luke, El Cajon, CA, 1996; Sheraton, Newport Beach, CA, 1996; St. Jude Medical Center, Orange, CA, 1992-93

COLLECTIONS: Ernst & Whinney, Riverside, CA; Balboa Bay Club, Balboa, CA

Arthur Stern   PP. 96-97

Arthur Stern Studios
1075 Jackson Street
Benicia, CA 94510
TEL/FAX 707-745-8480
E-mail: **arthur@arthurstern.com**
Web: **www.arthurstern.com**

Arthur Stern Studios creates site-specific architectural glass installations, primarily in leaded glass. A specialist in collaboration with other design professionals and clients, the studio currently has installations in 36 states as well as Japan. Commissions range from residential work to large public art projects and churches.

Arthur Stern has been widely published and has won numerous awards, including several American Institute of Architects design awards as well as honors from the The Construction Specifications Institute; the Interfaith Forum on Religion, Art & Architecture; and *Ministry & Liturgy* magazine's BENE Awards.

Arthur Stern   PP. 96-97

Arthur Stern Studios
1075 Jackson Street
Benicia, CA 94510
TEL/FAX 707-745-8480
E-mail: **arthur@arthurstern.com**
Web: **www.arthurstern.com**

Arthur Stern is an award-winning architectural glass artist. The studio offers complete art glass services, beginning with the design process and professional renderings, expert fabrication and following through to installation.

The studio can accommodate projects of any scale. Stern considers himself a designer first and an artist second, and creates each installation with sensitivity to its environment and the project's design criteria. Each project undertaken receives the same thorough attention to detail and fine craftsmanship. Stern also works in other media including wood and glass bas-relief sculpture, mixed-media works on canvas and works on paper.

Jane Sterrett   P. 290

Jane Sterrett Studio
160 Fifth Avenue
New York, NY 10010
TEL 212-929-2566
FAX 212-929-0924
E-mail: **sterjak@ix.netcom.com**
Web: **www.janesterrett.com**

Jane Sterrett's award-winning collage technique combines images from her photographs with mixed media and painterly effects, producing a personal style that is strong in color and tactile values. Her work ranges from traditional sizes to mural scale, and is available as fine digital reproductions printed with archival inks on paper or canvas.

COMMISSIONS: Chase Metrotech Eatery, Brooklyn, NY; Eli Lilly, Indianapolis, IN; Opus Restaurant, Naples, FL; Montefiore Hospital, Bronx, NY

GUILD SOURCEBOOKS: *Designer's 14, 15*

Strong-Cuevas   PP. 200-201

SC Sculpture
PMB #396
459 Columbus Avenue
New York, NY 10024
TEL 212-724-6358
FAX 212-799-1614
Web: **www.sc-sculpture.com**

From fabricated metal to cast bronze and steel, Strong-Cuevas' work is wide ranging. Outdoor projects are her specialty, but she also makes fabricated metal and cast bronze pieces for interior spaces. Communication through space and time and the exploration of outer space and inner consciousness are her main themes. Linking the ideas of the past to those of the future, her symbol is the human face. Like Ballanchine, whose birthday she shares, she is an innovator within a classical tradition. The quality of her sculpture reflects high standards of craftsmanship while the diversity of her work expresses constant creative experimentation.

Strong-Cuevas   PP. 200-201

SC Sculpture
PMB #396
459 Columbus Avenue
New York, NY 10024
TEL 212-724-6358
FAX 212-799-1614
Web: **www.sc-sculpture.com**

COMMISSIONS: Private commission, Park Avenue Terrace, New York, NY, 1997; private commission, Evan Frankel, East Hampton garden, 1982

COLLECTIONS: Bruce Museum, Greenwich, CT; Grounds for Sculpture, Hamilton, NJ

EXHIBITIONS & AWARDS: "Premonitions in Retrospect," solo show, Grounds for Sculpture, Hamilton, NJ, 1999; Bruce Museum, Greenwich, CT, 1985; Guild Hall, East Hampton, NY, 1985

PUBLICATIONS: Oxford University Press *Dictionary of Psychology* by Andrew M. Coleman, cover image, 2001; *Direct Metal Sculpture* by Dona Z. Meilach, 2001; *Contemporary Outdoor Sculpture*, 1999; "In the Service of a Large Idea," *World Sculpture News*, June 1999

Martin Sturman   PP. 258, 320

Martin Sturman Sculptures
416 Cricketfield Court
Westlake Village, CA 91361
TEL 805-381-0032
FAX 805-381-1116
E-mail: **MLSturman@aol.com**
Web: **www.steelsculptures.com**

Martin Sturman creates original contemporary sculptures and furniture in carbon steel or stainless steel. His work is suitable for indoor or outdoor placement.

Stainless steel surfaces are burnished to achieve a beautiful shimmering effect. Carbon steel sculptures are painted with acrylic and coated with polyurethane to preserve color vitality.

Sturman encourages site-specific and collaborative site-specific efforts.

COMMISSIONS: Hyatt Westlake Plaza Hotel, Westlake Village, CA; Tesoro Galleries, Beverly Hills, CA; McGraw-Hill Publishing Company, Columbus, OH

GUILD SOURCEBOOKS: *Architect's 12, 14; Designer's 7, 8, 9, 10, 11, 12, 13, 14, 15*

Naomi Tagini   P. 336

Rollercoaster by Naomi Tagini
1902 Comstock Avenue
Los Angeles, CA 90025
TEL 310-552-1877
FAX 310-552-2679
FAX 310-277-5329
Web: **www.rlrcoastr.com**

Naomi Tagini creates moveable blocks of color for positioning practically anywhere in an environment — down a hallway, up a staircase or around a corner.

She creates her graphic art for the wall using several coats of paint that is brushed, rolled or sprayed on; she frequently applies a crackle finish at the end of her design process. Each completed piece proves that color, texture, clean lines and asymmetry can all be achieved through the versatility of wood.

Tagini's work is created in pieces that are meant to be interchangeable. She wants the owner to have fun with the work — to rearrange it on a whim and participate with it.

Larger format work and custom colors are available.

Taracor Fine Art Consulting P. 166

Taryn Wise
PO Box 20542
Sedona, AZ 86341-0542
TEL **888-470-2511**
FAX **520-284-2038**
E-mail: **twwise@taracor.com**
Web: **www.taracor.com**

Taracor is a fine art consulting firm specializing in art acquisitions and placement. Its goal is to make the process of bringing artwork into a client's environment as thoroughly seamless and integrated as possible.

Taracor offers total business solutions, working directly with both businesses and individuals, interior designers, architects and real estate professionals. The firm works in mixed media, bronze, monumental bronze, paintings, photography and more. Bronze artists Ken Rowe and Bob Piercey encourage site-specific commissions.

Richard Taylor P. 197

Richard Taylor LLC
3007 North Newhall Street
Milwaukee, WI 53211
TEL **414-486-6227**
FAX **414-961-7002**
E-mail: **luctay@execpc.com**

Richard Taylor enjoys collaborating with designers and architects to produce indoor and outdoor sculptural works for clients. His work ranges from quietly simple to energetic and gestural. It is composed of natural metals, painted metals or rusted and patinated metals. These sculptures and mobiles live on walls, stand in courtyards and soar in atriums.

COMMISSIONS: Rockwell International, G.E. Medical Systems, S.C. Johnson Wax Company, U.S. Robotics, Medical College of Wisconsin, Ruud Lighting, Quad/Graphics, Auto Glass Specialists, Fifield

GUILD SOURCEBOOKS: *Architect's 13*

Ted Box Limited P. 259

Theodore Box
PO Box 2325
Vineyard Haven, MA 02568
TEL **508-696-6126**
FAX **508-696-8431**
E-mail: **info@tedbox.com**
Web: **www.tedbox.com**

Ted Box's art is in private collections the world over. Each piece of furniture is designed to accommodate climactic variations without losing its precise functional properties.

For further examples of his extraordinary work — and to commission custom pieces — please contact the artist for more information.

GUILD SOURCEBOOKS: *Designer's 10, 11, 15*

Thea Schrack Photography P. 313

Thea Schrack
80 Montcalm
San Francisco, CA 94110
TEL **415-647-1174**
FAX **415-647-1182**
E-mail: **theaschrack@jps.net**

Thea Schrack's talent is best summarized as the ability to reveal the timelessness of beauty. The artist uses various cameras, techniques and film to balance the actual with the ever changing. Sepia tones and hand coloring are added to her work, creating an interpretation where reality and imagination converge. A catalog is available.

COMMISSIONS: PeopleSoft, Robert Mondavi Winery, IBM, Torani Syrup

PUBLICATIONS: *Flowers, San Francisco, Wine Country, Pacific Coast* and *Los Angeles*, panoramic book series

GUILD SOURCEBOOKS: *Designer's 15*

Elizabeth Thompson P. 121

Thompson Studios
56 Crosby Street
New York, NY 10012
TEL **212-879-8839**
E-mail: **lizabethth@aol.com**
Web: **www.elizabeththompsonstudios.com**

Elizabeth Thompson creates a wide range of work, bringing both poetry and masterful techniques to each project. Shown in this book are two pieces that highlight the variety that can be found in her work. Metropolitan Life commissioned a lyrical landscape for its boardroom that was not based on a photograph, but rather on an impression of a delta in Africa. For the other project shown, Thompson rendered an 18th-century frigate for The Delaware Water Authority's ferryboat.

With 20 years of experience, Thompson has worked for corporations, banks, hospitals, hotels and individuals. She is also a widely exhibited artist with paintings in the collections of museums, foundations and private collectors.

COMMISSIONS: New York University Hospital Oncology, Robert Wood Johnson, Wilmington Trust Company, Bank of America, Southwestern Bell Telephone, Marriott Hotel Group

Dane E. Tilghman P. 291

Dane Tilghman Artworks
PO Box 1261
107 Crump Road
Exton, PA 19341
TEL/FAX **610-524-3263**
E-mail: **Danedta@aol.com**

Dane Tilghman works in watercolor, pencil and acrylics on watercolor paper. He uses the styles of realism, cubism and tall-tale art (elongation) to achieve his objectives. Tilghman's brightly colored works often feature themes of music, landscapes, sports and imagery of Americana.

Tilghman's work graces the walls of many private and corporate collections, including an 8' x 40' mural at Turner Stadium in Atlanta, GA.

COMMISSIONS: Mural, Turner Field; poster, "One Hundred Black Men of America"; poster, Big Brothers and Big Sisters of America; poster, National Alliance of Black School Educators

COLLECTIONS: Baseball Hall of Fame; African-American Museum, Philadelphia, PA

EXHIBITIONS & AWARDS: Medal of Honor in Graphics, American Artists Professional League; Negro League exhibition, Veteran's Stadium, Philadelphia, PA

ARTIST INFORMATION

Susan Richter Todd P. 120

PO Box 145
Glenham, NY 12527
TEL 845-831-8137
FAX 845-831-0423
E-mail: richter@sunnysidegalleries.com
Web: www.sunnysidegalleries.com

Susan Richter Todd has established herself as both a two- and three-dimensional artist over the past 25 years. Her most recent work is in the form of murals. Her use of brilliant colors and fine detail expresses her understanding of the natural environment. The ability to captivate viewers and draw them into the piece is what has positioned her as a recognized muralist.

All completed work is extremely durable and environmentally friendly. Prices start at $1000.

Commissions and site-specific projects are welcomed. For additional information, visit the artist's website.

Luis Torruella PP. 226-227

1507 Ashford Avenue
Apartment 1201 Cond. Tenerife
San Juan, PR 00911
TEL/FAX 787-722-8728 (Studio)
TEL 787-268-4977 (Home)
E-mail: luistorruella@hotmail.com
Web: www.luistorruella.com

Luis Torruella, a Puerto Rican sculptor, designs in a contemporary abstract context. His Caribbean heritage is reflected in his works' color, rhythm and movement. Torruella collaborates with architects, designers and developers in public and private commissions.

RECENT PROJECTS: Installation of a 260'L horizontal sculpture, Municipality of San Juan, PR

COLLECTIONS: Museo de Arte de Puerto Rico, San Juan, PR; Mead Art Museum, MA; Performing Arts Center, San Juan, PR; Old San Juan Pier Walk, PR; Skokie Sculpture Park, IL; Innovative Systems Headquarters, SD; City View Plaza Complex, Bayamon, PR; Searle Pharmaceuticals, Caguas, PR; Citibank Main Offices, Cupey, PR; Sterling Winthrop, PA; Budweiser Caribbean, Bayamon, PR; Condado Plaza Hotel, San Juan, PR; Veterans Monument, Cayey, PR; El Convento Hotel, San Juan, PR

Luis Torruella PP. 226-227

1507 Ashford Avenue
Apartment 1201 Cond. Tenerife
San Juan, PR 00911
TEL/FAX 787-722-8728 (Studio)
TEL 787-268-4977 (Home)
E-mail: luistorruella@hotmail.com
Web: www.luistorruella.com

COLLECTIONS: La Torre de Plaza Office Building, San Juan, PR; Equifax Headquarters, Atlanta, GA; Caribe Hilton, San Juan, PR; Singer Island Hilton, FL; Swissotel, Chicago, IL; McConnell Valdes Law Firm, Hato Rey, PR; Chayote Restaurant, Miramar, PR; Caparra Classic Building, Guaynabo, PR; Stuart Enterprises Main Offices, Santurce, PR; Hyatt Dorado Beach Hotel, Dorado, PR; Embassy Suites, Isla Verde, PR; Centro Europa office building, Santurce, PR; Saint John's School, San Juan, PR; Laderas de San Juan Complex, PR

EXHIBITIONS & AWARDS: Palma de Mallorca, Spain, 2001; Galería Botello, San Juan, PR, 1997, 1994, 1992; Theatrical Institute, Moscow, 1992; Eli Marsh Gallery, Amherst, MA, 1993; numerous collective exhibitions

GUILD SOURCEBOOKS: *Architect's 14, 15*

Travis Tuck Metal Sculptor P. 109

Travis Tuck
PO Box 1832-16
7 Beach Street
Martha's Vineyard, MA 02568
TEL 888-693-3914 (Toll free)
TEL/FAX 508-693-3914
E-mail: travis@TravisTuck.com
Web: www.TravisTuck.com

Travis Tuck is world renowned for the finest in custom weathervanes. Themes can also be executed as wall or freestanding sculptures. Each heirloom-quality piece is a three-dimensional sculpture constructed in the traditional pre-1800s repoussé method from copper and 23K gold leaf. Tuck creates work that complements any architectural style or depicts any personal interest, business symbol or logo.

COMMISSIONS: U.S. Senator Frank Lautenberg; Steven Spielberg; Beverly Sills; James Taylor; Carly Simon; Dennis Conner; Gwathmey Siegel-Architects; City of Hamburg, Germany; Bloomingdale's, 59th Street, New York City

GUILD SOURCEBOOKS: *Architect's 8, 10, 11, 12, 13, 14, 15*

Angelika Traylor P. 98

100 Poinciana Drive
Indian Harbour Beach, FL 32937-4437
TEL 321-773-7640
FAX 321-779-3612
E-mail: angtraylor@earthlink.net
Web: www.angelikatraylor.com

Angelika Traylor specializes in one-of-a-kind architectural designs, autonomous panels and lamps which are easily recognized by their intricate and jewel-like compositions.

Often referred to as having painterly qualities, her works — such as the installation at Holmes Regional Medical Center shown in this book — reflect an original and intensive design process, implemented with meticulous craftsmanship and an unusually beautiful selection of glass.

She has received many awards, and her work has been featured in numerous publications.

COMMISSIONS: Holmes Regional Medical Center, Melbourne, FL, 1998; White House Christmas ornament collection, 1997, 1993; other corporate and private collections

GUILD SOURCEBOOKS: *THE GUILD 2, 3, 4, 5; Architect's 6; Designer's 7, 8, 9, 10, 11, 12, 13, 14, 15*

Tuska Inc. P. 260

Seth Tuska
147 Old Park Avenue
Lexington, KY 40502
TEL 859-255-1379
FAX 859-253-3199
Web: www.tuskastudio.com

Tuska Inc. represents the work of fine artist John R. Tuska (1931-1998). The studio offers reproductions of one of the artist's most engaging works: *Illuminates,* cutworks of the human form engaged in the motion of dance, suspended on open screens.

Each screen is assembled by hand to order in custom dimensions and materials, ranging from natural materials such as woods, steel, aluminum or bronze to contemporary polymers.

Each screen is meticulously executed and rendered in exceeding detail. True craftsman quality makes them ideal for use as window or wall hangings, room dividers, gates, shutters, landscape decorations or other custom applications.

ARTIST INFORMATION

Ellen Tykeson — P. 167

Ellen Tykeson Sculpture
1033 Sharon Way
Eugene, OR 97401
TEL 541-687-5731
E-mail: etykeson@pond.net

Timeless elegance and an emotional connection with the viewer define Ellen Tykeson's bronze figures. She brings 25 years of experience to her work, and gives a fresh contemporary look to the tradition of figurative sculpture. Tykeson enjoys the challenges involved in commission work and brings to it the strong design, mastery of form and attention to detail demonstrated in her edition sculpture.

RECENT PROJECTS: *Treasure,* over-life-sized contemporary family, Southwest Community Church, Palm Desert, CA; *Opal Whiteley,* life-sized figure of child author, Public Library, Cottage Grove, OR

GUILD SOURCEBOOKS: *Architect's 13, 15*

Karen Urbanek — P. 369

314 Blair Avenue
Piedmont, CA 94611-4004
TEL 510-654-0685
FAX 510-654-2790
E-mail: KrnUrbanek@aol.com

Karen Urbanek alternates incremental layers of hand-dyed wild silk fiber with streams of water to build wall and sculptural works that range from intimate to grand in size. Her painterly images have drama, subtlety and strength. Individual forms and multilayered pieces may encompass openwork as well as translucent, dense and highly textured areas.

These strong, crisp textiles need not be framed and may be easily cleaned.

Commissions are accepted. Visual materials and pricing available upon request.

Alice Van Leunen — P. 337

Van Leunen Studios
13631 NE Kinney Road
Newberg, OR 97132
TEL 503-538-7789
TEL 503-538-7717
FAX 503-538-7704
E-mail: avanleunen@msn.com

Alice Van Leunen specializes in mixed-media wall treatments using paper, fabric, fibers, paint, metals, metallic foil, acrylic and glass — especially dichroic glass. Works range in size from small, intimate pieces up to major architectural installations. The artist has had extensive experience collaborating with designers and architects to create site-specific works designed to meet the client's needs, and she is available to supervise installations of major works.

Van Leunen's work is represented in numerous public, corporate and private collections.

Commissions are welcome. Prices, slides and further information are available on request.

Rick Van Ness — P. 261

Sound of Light Studio
PO Box 910
Ojai, CA 93024
TEL 805-646-3616
FAX 805-646-2298
E-mail: soundoflight@ojai.net
Web: www.soundoflight.org

Rick Van Ness creates lighted sculptural assemblages made from new and found materials that are supported by structural steel interfacing. Mixed media including blown glass, handmade paper shades, brass turnings, cut stone and turned wood are merged together to create functional, lucid and elegant artwork.

Commissions and conversions of personal instruments are welcomed. Prices available upon request.

COLLECTIONS: EMI Records, Latin Department, Sherman Oaks, CA

EXHIBITIONS & AWARDS: Best of Category, La Jolla Art Festival, 2000; Best of Category, Tempe Festival of the Arts, 1998; Best of Show, Vail Arts Festival, 1995; Best of Show, Beaver Creek Fine Art Festival, 1993

Michele vandenHeuvel — PP. 156, 228

7418 Pimenton Drive NE
Albuquerque, NM 87113
TEL 505-344-9154
E-mail: imanimals@aol.com
Web: www.desertbronze.com

Michele vandenHeuvel sculpts interactive, joyful bronzes. Her pieces ask to be touched, sat next to and visited with. She strives to create works that appeal to people of every age and from all walks of life, and through her public art, brings communities together.

COMMISSIONS: Roosevelt Park, Longmont, CO, 2000; Sweetwater Park, Peoria, AZ, 2000; Old Town Transit Center, Park City, UT, 2000; Washingtonian Plaza, Gaithersburg, MD, 2000; Kimo Park, Albuquerque, NM, 1999; Bernalillo County Courthouse, Albuquerque, NM, 1999

Sheryl VanderPol — P. 123

Untapped Resource
4020 Pilgrim Lane North
Minneapolis, MN 55441
TEL 763-542-1116
FAX 763-542-1119
E-mail: sheryl@untappedresource.com
Web: www.untappedresource.com

Sheryl VanderPol is your Untapped Resource for custom artwork. Working on your choice of commercial ceramic or porcelain, inspiration and collaboration between the client and the studio results in custom handpainted masterpieces on tiles and porcelain sinks, fired to a beautiful permanency. Untapped Resource's skills expand beyond ceramic and porcelain with projects involving wall murals and trompe l'oeil.

VanderPol's work is promoted in over 25 showrooms throughout the nation, has been involved in countless award-winning commissioned works in homes and commercial properties, and is shown in scores of top publications.

Susan Venable P. 338

Venable Studio
2323 Foothill Lane
Santa Barbara, CA 93105
TEL 805-884-4963
FAX 805-884-4983
E-mail: **susan@venablestudio.com**
Web: **www.venablestudio.com**

Susan Venable's work is an exploration of surface and structure. Her reliefs are constructed of steel grids and copper wire, while the paintings are encaustic and oil. The physicality of the materials is expressed in the rich and complex surfaces.

Venable's work has been installed in public spaces, homes, corporations and museums in the United States, Europe, Asia, Mexico and Australia. These expressive and luminous pieces are low maintenance and inspire public as well as private spaces.

VitraMax Group P. 99

931 South Third Street
Louisville, KY 40203
TEL 502-589-3828
FAX 502-589-3830
E-mail: **edavbet@attglobal.net**
Web: **www.vitramax.com**

VitraMax Group's uniquely designed and fabricated architectural glass products can transform any functionality or space into an artistic statement. The company's craftspeople seamlessly blend form with function to create works for homes and offices that are stylish with a contemporary flair.

From glass sinks and vessels to shower enclosures and wall partitions, the innovative designs and quality craftsmanship which have become synonymous with VitraMax Group continue to set standards for the industry.

GUILD SOURCEBOOKS: *Architect's 14, 15*

Claudia Wagar PP. 292-293

Vine Arts Publications
301 First Street West
Sonoma, CA 95476
TEL/FAX 707-996-7054
E-mail: **claudiawagar@vom.com**
Web: **www.claudiawagar.com**

Watercolor or acrylic showcase Wagar's landscapes, still lifes and figures. Her versatility ranges from small works on paper to large mural commissions.

RECENT PROJECTS: Two 36' interior murals, Korbel Corporation

COMMISSIONS: Kaiser Medical Offices, Coocamonga, CA; Sheraton Hotel lobby, Sacramento, CA

EXHIBITIONS & AWARDS: National Endowment for the Arts grant, American Artist Achievement Award

PUBLICATIONS: *Murals of California* by Robin Dutton, *American Artist Magazine, Wine Spectator*

GUILD SOURCEBOOKS: *Architect's 8; Designer's 11, 12, 13, 14*

Wayne Williams Studio P. 314

Wayne Williams
15423 Sutton Street
Sherman Oaks, CA 91403
TEL 818-905-8097
FAX 818-995-6888
E-mail: **wwclick@earthlink.net**
Web: **home.earthlink.net/~wwclick**

"Imagine a world without pollution, trash or development. No, it's not a John Lennon ballad, but the work of Wayne Williams."
The Los Angeles Times

Wayne Williams is a photo artist who creates powerfully serene, unique images that express his love for nature. Williams works with natural light, capturing on film the singular magic moments nature provides.

Although most of his works are limited editions, Williams thrives on collaborating with clients to create commissions as well.

RECENT PROJECTS: Fine art book, *America's Vanishing Landscapes*

COMMISSIONS: The Capital Group, Kaiser, GE, Flour/Daniels

John Wehrle P. 229

Trout in Hand Productions
775 Lassen Street
Richmond, CA 94805
TEL 510-234-0645
FAX 510-234-0363
E-mail: **jwehrle@inreach.com**
Web: **www.troutinhand.com**

John Wehrle specializes in the creation of site-sensitive artworks — interior and exterior murals in paint or ceramic tile, along with more elaborate installation works combining text, paint and sculptural relief. Working with architects, contractors and communities, Wehrle produces public commissions which grace libraries, corporations and freeway walls; many have achieved landmark status.

COMMISSIONS: University of California Riverside, Los Angeles Public Library, Bakersfield Centennial Plaza, Roche Corporation, Richmond Redevelopment Agency

GUILD SOURCEBOOKS: *Architect's 9*

Doug Weigel P. 29

Steel Sculptures by Doug Weigel
PO Box 92408
Albuquerque, NM 87199
TEL 505-821-6600
FAX 505-821-9696

Doug Weigel designs and produces two- and three-dimensional sculptures and furniture in steel. Styles include Southwestern, Western and Art Deco, as well as client-commissioned ideas.

Allow four to eight weeks from design approval and contract to completion. Shipping and handling are FOB Albuquerque.

COMMISSIONS: President George Bush; Central Avenue Project, Phoenix; Petrified National Forest; Scottsdale Airport; Sandia Laboratories; Hyatt Aruba; Four Season Resort, Scottsdale; New Mexico State Collection; Balloon Federation of America

GUILD SOURCEBOOKS: *Designer's 8, 9, 10, 11, 12, 13, 14*

ARTIST INFORMATION

Shevaun Williams — P. 315

Shevaun Williams & Associates
  Commercial Photography, Inc.
221 East Main Street
Norman, OK 73069
TEL 405-329-6455
E-mail: shevaun@telepath.com
Web: www.shevaunwilliams.com

After over 20 years of experience in commercial and fine art photography, Shevaun Williams has developed a signature style. Her investigations of abstract forms yield timeless images from unique points of view. She takes familiar objects and structures and gives them dramatic new life through innovative compositions, interesting textures and light.

Work is available in a variety of sizes and subject matter, featuring locations throughout the United States and abroad. The artist accepts special assignments and commissions.

Other examples of Williams' black-and-white infrared images as well as color selections are available by contacting the artist.

GUILD SOURCEBOOKS: *Designer's 15*

Daniel Winterich — P. 100

Studio Winterich
29 Weller Court
Pleasant Hill, CA 94523
TEL 925-943-5755
FAX 925-943-5455
E-mail: dw@winterich.com
Web: www.winterich.com

Daniel Winterich is an architect specializing in the design of glass walls, ceilings and sculpture. Studio Winterich has collaborated with architects and designers on projects within the U.S., Asia and Europe. Commissioned projects are carefully conceived for each site and include design, fabrication and installation.

Solar Matrix (shown in this book) is composed of 362 Pyrex glass rods capped with dichroic glass lenses that penetrate a 15"-thick concrete wall. Water falls over each glass rod, creating a rumbling wall of white water within a field of blue and yellow light.

COMMISSIONS: Microsoft Silicon Valley Campus, Mountain View, CA, architect: Quezada Architecture; Charles Schwab, San Francisco, CA, architect: Ottolini & Booth; AvalonBay Towers, San Francisco, CA, architect: Theodore Brown and Partners; Philips Semiconductors, Sunnyvale, CA, architect: Quezada Architecture

Bruce Wolfe — PP. 168-169

Bruce Wolfe Ltd.
206 El Cerrito Avenue
Piedmont, CA 94611
TEL 510-655-7871
FAX 510-601-7200
Web: www.brucewolfe.com

Bruce Wolfe is a master of movement and emotion, a winner of awards and commissions. He has 35 years of experience in the field, and his work is collected by architects, corporations, designers, churches and individuals in the U.S. and Italy.

Wolfe's museum-quality bronze pieces range in size from tabletop to monumental. He is able to capture likeness and personality in his portraits, bringing the subject to life in bronze.

RECENT PROJECTS: Four 7.5' figures of St. Francis, St. Clair, Christ and Mary Magdalene, Santa Barbara Mission

GUILD SOURCEBOOKS: *Architect's 11, 12, 13, 14, 15*

Bruce Wolfe — PP. 168-169

Bruce Wolfe Ltd.
206 El Cerrito Avenue
Piedmont, CA 94611
TEL 510-655-7871
FAX 510-601-7200
Web: www.brucewolfe.com

COMMISSIONS: Asian Art Museum, San Francisco, CA, 2000; Fratilli Della Scuole Cristiane, Rome, Italy, 1999; Steve Silver Productions, San Francisco, CA, 1999; Hazelton Moffit Braddock School, Hazelton, ND, 1998; Foster Enterprises, Foster City, CA, 1998; San Francisco Medical Center, San Francisco, CA, 1997; Bohemian Club, San Francisco, CA, 1996; Hebrew University, Jerusalem, Israel, 1996; Hoover Institute, Stanford University, CA, 1996; St. Mary's College, Moraga, CA, 1992-2000; San Francisco Opera House, San Francisco, CA, 1967

PUBLICATIONS: *The Artists Magazine*, April 2000; *International Artist*, December/January 2000; *Sculpture Review*, Summer/Spring 2000 and Winter/Fall 1999

David Woodruff — P. 263

Woodruff Woods
192 Sonata Drive
Lewisville, NC 27023
TEL 336-945-9145
FAX 312-672-7899
E-mail: pdwoods@triad.rr.com
Web: www.pdwoods.com

David Woodruff creates one-of-a-kind hollow-formed vessels and other art objects from woods that possess great character as a result of trauma in the growing environment. This combination of genetic and environmental forces provides the raw materials for the multidimensional beauty found in Woodruff's art objects. The artist, using the wood lathe to develop the form and then finishing with a museum-quality hand-rubbed lacquer, creates art pieces that reveal the beauty of the infinite variety in nature.

COMMISSIONS: Weaver-Cooke Construction, Greensboro, NC; Novant Healthcare, Winston-Salem, NC

EXHIBITIONS & AWARDS: Top score, Krasl Art Fair, St. Joseph, MI; top score, Tennessee Association of Craft Artists Crafts Fair, Chattanooga, TN

GUILD SOURCEBOOKS: *Designer's 15*

Joy Wulke — PP. 101, 135

Joy Wulke Studio of Art & Design
26 Prospect Hill Road
Stony Creek, CT 06405
TEL 203-488-2605
FAX 203-483-8379
E-mail: wulkestudio@juno.com
Web: www.wulkestudio.com

Joy Wulke brings art and architecture together in site-specific installations of translucency and light explored through the use of glass, water, fabrics and a variety of light sources. The works reference the natural environment through images of water and land and also allude to architectural forms of geometry.

RECENT PROJECTS: Southern Connecticut State University, New Haven, CT; National Shopping Centers, Chicago, IL; American Bar Association — Commission on Women in the Profession

COMMISSIONS: Lincoln Center Film Forum, New York, NY; Bernie Brillstein with Charles Moore FAIA, Malibu, CA; Oceanside Civic Center, CA; New Orleans World's Fair; Montana State University School of Business; National Shopping Centers, Santa Barbara Corporate Center

Joy Wulke   PP. 101, 135

Joy Wulke Studio of Art & Design
26 Prospect Hill Road
Stony Creek, CT 06405
TEL   203-488-2605
FAX   203-483-8379
E-mail: wulkestudio@juno.com
Web: www.wulkestudio.com

EXHIBITIONS & AWARDS: Grounds for Sculpture, Hamilton, NJ; Urban Glass, New York, NY; Aldrich Museum, Ridgefield, CT; Bruce Museum, Greenwich, CT; Delaware Center for Contemporary Art, Wilmington, DE; Discovery Museum, Bridgeport, CT; Rockville Arts Place, Rockville, MD; Stephen Gang Gallery, New York, NY; Washington State University, Pullman, WA; Mattatuck Museum, Waterbury, CT; American Institute of Architects, Albuquerque, NM; O.K. Harris, New York, NY; Broadway Windows, New York University; Montana Arts Council; numerous Connecticut Commissions on the Arts grants; New England Foundation for the Arts; Stamford Museum & Nature Center Installation Award; first place, New Art New Materials national competition through North Carolina State University

Nancy J. Young   P. 339

802 Martingale Lane SE
Albuquerque, NM 87123
TEL   505-299-6108
FAX   505-299-2238

Young has developed a richly textural style of wall art that is both elegant and distinctive. Durable works are created in handcast paper that is then covered with a metal coating and patinated. Pieces may be framed or left unframed depending on the setting.

Young, listed in *Who's Who in American Art* since 1984, has created work for various settings including TV dramas, CD covers and U.S. embassies.

COMMISSIONS: American Express, IBM, AT&T, U.S. State Department, embassies in New Guinea and Venezuela

GUILD SOURCEBOOKS: *THE GUILD 3, 4, 5; Designer's 6, 7, 8, 9, 10, 11, 12, 13, 14, 15*

GUILD SURVEYS OF THE FINEST CONTEMPORARY CRAFT

THE BEST OF NEW CERAMIC ART

Hardbound
128 pages
9¹/₂" x 9¹/₂"
$24.99

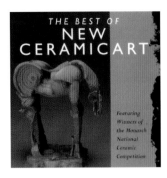

CONTEMPORARY TURNED WOOD

Hardbound
128 pages
9¹/₂" x 9¹/₂"
$27.99

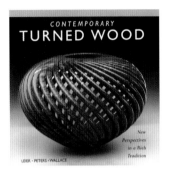

TEAPOTS TRANSFORMED
Exploration of an Object

Hardbound
128 pages
9¹/₂" x 9¹/₂"
$30.00

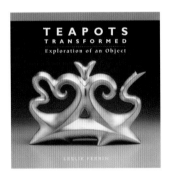

BASKETS
Tradition & Beyond

Hardbound
128 pages
9¹/₂" x 9¹/₂"
$30.00

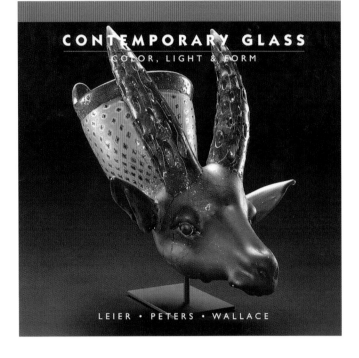

New in 2001

CONTEMPORARY GLASS
Color, Light & Form

Hardbound
128 pages
9¹/₂" x 9¹/₂"
$30.00

Showcase books from GUILD Publishing feature works of vivid originality and exceptional appeal. Each title includes 150 or more beautifully reproduced color plates; notes from the authors shine light on the artists' techniques and creative inspirations. These exhibitions-in-print belong in the library of every art lover and design professional.

GUILD Publishing

An imprint of Ashford.com. Available at bookstores, or order toll-free: 877-344-8453

From the Largest Online Collection of Original Art

BEAUTIFUL THINGS
Original Art from the Artists of GUILD.com

The objects and two-dimensional art available for sale through the online collection of the GUILD include almost 10,000 original works by 1,500 living artists. Remarkably, as evidenced in *Beautiful Things: Original Art from the Artists of GUILD.com,* the collection is distinguished by quality as much as breadth. The journey through this large and stunning volume is a trip artists, collectors — and anyone interested in all things beautiful — will want to take again and again.

Hardbound
9" x 11"
224 pages
250 color photographs
$45.00

OBJECT LESSONS
Original Art from GUILD Artists

In this second large-format showcase of art from the GUILD website, six well-known curators have selected objects and two-dimensional works pertaining to a theme of their choosing, under the encompassing rubric of "object lessons." Two hundred of their selections are showcased in this beautifully produced volume, a book which celebrates the exhilarating scope and quality of contemporary art, while reflecting on the capacity of art to move us — to possess us, while we possess it.

Hardbound
9" x 11"
224 pages
250 color photographs
$50.00
Available in October 2001

Works of Shimmering Beauty

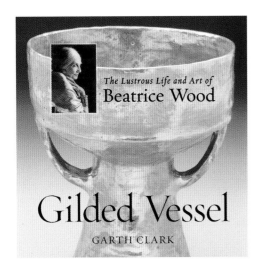

Gilded Vessel
The Lustrous Life and Art of Beatrice Wood

In 1982, when the Garth Clark Gallery opened in Los Angeles, its premiere exhibition featured the lusterware ceramics of 89-year-old Beatrice Wood. This was the first of dozens of Wood exhibitions hosted by the gallery over the next 17 years. *Gilded Vessel* is Clark's lavishly illustrated tribute to the life and art of his cherished friend.

Hardbound . 128 pages
9¹/₂" x 9¹/₂" . $35.00

Artists Explain Favorite Techniques

For Everyone Who Makes, Collects or Simply Admires Beautiful Metal, Jewelry and Ceramic Art

Color on Metal
50 Artists Share Insights and Techniques

At the dawn of the 21st century, new approaches to coloring metal have revitalized the fields of decorative metal and jewelry. *Color on Metal* features the work of 50 exceptional artists, who explain how they use enamels, patinas and applied color to enhance metal surfaces.

Hardbound . 128 pages
9¹/₂" x 9¹/₂" . $30.00

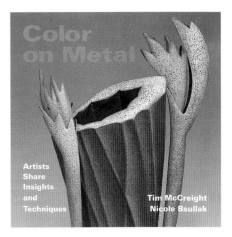

Smashing Glazes
53 Artists Share Techniques and Recipes

Contemporary ceramic artists experiment with ingredients, application and firing to create rich and varied surface treatments. In *Smashing Glazes,* 53 artists invite readers into their studios to discuss the techniques and aesthetics of their most successful surfaces.

Hardbound . 128 pages
9¹/₂" x 9¹/₂" . $30.00

GUILD Publishing

An imprint of Ashford.com. Available at bookstores, or order toll-free: 877-344-8453

AMAZING ART
AMAZING ARTISTS

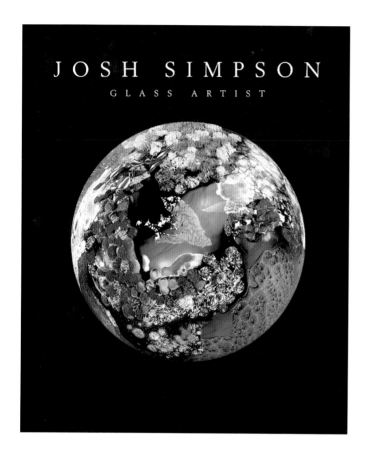

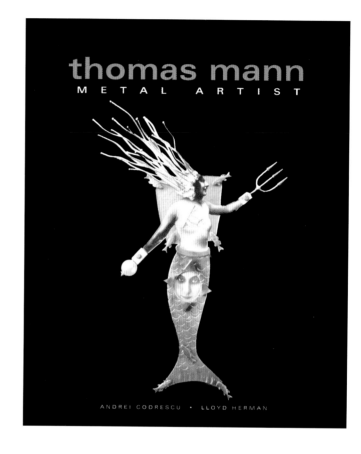

JOSH SIMPSON
Glass Artist

Josh Simpson's glass platters, vessels and sculptures are celebrated internationally for their extraordinary, complex beauty. *Josh Simpson: Glass Artist* introduces not just the artist and his work, but also the inspirations and techniques that Simpson draws upon as he creates wondrous worlds from blown glass.

Hardbound
9" x 11"
128 pages
175 color photographs
$35.00

THOMAS MANN
Metal Artist

For more than 20 years, Thomas Mann has combined high-tech materials with found elements, antique photographs and other evocative objects to create deeply appealing jewelry and sculpture. *Thomas Mann: Metal Artist* presents this extraordinary body of work in the context of Mann's development as artist and entrepreneur.

Hardbound
9" x 11"
128 pages
175 color photographs
$35.00

Available in October 2001

INDEX OF ADVERTISERS BY LOCATION

INDEX OF ARTISTS & COMPANIES